THE **COMPLETE IDIOT'S GUIDE®** TO

QuickBooks and QuickBooks Pro 99

by Gail Perry, CPA

A Division of Macmillan Computer Publishing
201 West 103rd Street, Indianapolis, Indiana 46290

The Complete Idiot's Guide to QuickBooks and QuickBooks Pro 99

International Standard Book Number: 0-7897-1966-5

Library of Congress Catalog Card Number: 98-83041

Printed in the United States of America

First Printing: May 1999

01   00   99   4   3   2   1

Trademarks

Warning and Disclaimer

Executive Editor
Angela Wethington

Acquisitions Editor
Jamie Milazzo

Development Editor
Sherry Kinkoph

Managing Editor
Lisa Wilson

Project Editor
Carol Bowers

Copy Editors
Gene Redding
Patricia Kinyon

Indexer
Greg Pearson

Proofreader
Sherri W. Emmons,
BooksCraft, Inc.

Technical Editor
Karen Boor

Interior Design
Michael Freeland

Cover Design
Nathan Clement

Illustrations
Judd Winnick

Layout Technicians
Ayanna Lacey
Heather Miller
Amy Parker

Contents at a Glance

Contents

Part 3: Special Features of QuickBooks 175

11 Special Treats for QuickBooks Pro Users 177

12 Everything You'd Rather Not Know About Depreciation 191

13 The Tax Man Cometh 201

About the Author

Gail Perry is a CPA and a graduate of Indiana University. She spent 20-some years as a public accountant, including several years at the Chicago office of Deloitte and Touche, where she specialized in providing tax services to small businesses and generally getting in everyone's hair (not necessarily in that order). Armed with a degree in journalism and a desire to work from home, Gail has spent the past several years as a tax humor columnist for the *Indianapolis Star* and has written more than 20 books, including *The Complete Idiot's Guide to Doing Your Income Taxes, Special Edition Using QuickBooks and QuickBooks Pro 99,* and *Using Quicken 5 for Windows.* She also teaches computer classes, including classes on QuickBooks, for the Indiana CPA Society.

Dedication

To Georgia and Katherine: May your lives be as filled with joy as mine is, thanks to the two of you.

Acknowledgments

When you pick up a book in the bookstore, you probably think that the author wrote the book, the printer printed the pages, and the book store manager put it on the shelf—simple, huh?

No way. An incredible number of people get involved in the book-making process, and I can only begin to thank them here. Right at the top of the list is Jamie Milazzo, who got the ball rolling on this book, hired me for the job, and kept me on schedule as we raced to get this book out in a timely fashion. I also want to thank Sherry Kinkoph, whose development of this book made sure that everything you could ever want to know about QuickBooks is nestled between these orange-and-white covers. Thanks to Karen Boor, who verified that every procedure explained in this book works the way I say it does. And finally, thanks to Rick, who reminds me there's a life beyond my crazy writing schedule.

Tell Us What You Think!

As the reader of this book, *you* are our most important critic and commentator. We value your opinion and want to know what we're doing right, what we could do better, what areas you'd like to see us publish in, and any other words of wisdom you're willing to pass our way.

You can fax, email, or write me directly to let me know what you did or didn't like about this book—as well as what we can do to make our books stronger.

Please note that I cannot help you with technical problems related to the topic of this book, and that due to the high volume of mail I receive, I might not be able to reply to every message.

When you write, please be sure to include this book's title and author as well as your name and phone or fax number. I will carefully review your comments and share them with the author and editors who worked on the book.

Fax: 317-581-4666

Email: consumer@mcp.com

Mail: Executive Editor
          Que Consumer Group
          201 West 103rd Street
          Indianapolis, IN 46290 USA

Introduction: QuickBooks to the Rescue for Small Business Accounting

There was a time when small business accounting meant big ledger books, good erasers, and the onset of terminal eyestrain. I can remember working for companies in which every number was checked and cross-checked by hand, with the use of an adding machine that featured 100 keys and a big crank handle. Invoices and purchase orders were typed on a typewriter, and for payroll tax calculations I pored over the tax tables and used a ruler to keep my eyes on the right line. And this was not all that long ago!

Thankfully, times have changed. QuickBooks, the present-day answer to dealing with small business accounting, is here to save the day.

This book covers the latest versions of QuickBooks and QuickBooks Pro. References to QuickBooks refer to both programs. References to QuickBooks Pro refer only to the Pro version.

Goodies You'll Find in Your QuickBooks Program

QuickBooks has a lot to offer the small business. This program may not be the perfect solution to every business accounting problem you encounter, but take a look at all the features QuickBooks gives you:

- ➤ Information about accounting practices among many popular industries
- ➤ The ability to compile all the information you need to prepare your tax return
- ➤ Onscreen help, including quick tips while you work and video presentations of many standard features
- ➤ All the common business forms, in standard and customizable formats
- ➤ Easy reconciliation procedures for all your bank and credit card accounts
- ➤ Reminders about tasks that need to be completed, bills that need to be paid, customer invoices that are overdue, and money that needs to be deposited
- ➤ Standard and customizable reports on all facets of your business
- ➤ Direct interaction between QuickBooks and Microsoft Excel and Word programs
- ➤ Capability to create estimates (QuickBooks Pro only) and track costs on a per-job basis
- ➤ Customer and vendor lists with storage and retrieval capacity for names, addresses, contacts, email addresses, tax information, and more

- ➤ Payroll capabilities
- ➤ Security and year-end protection

Why You Need This Book

You've got your QuickBooks program, you've got plenty of onscreen help, and you've got your QuickBooks manual. So why do you need this book on top of everything else?

The Complete Idiot's Guide to QuickBooks and QuickBooks Pro 99 gives you something none of these other help providers have thought of: a simple, plain-English take on all facets of this program. The book is written by an accountant—with a sense of humor, no less—who uses the program and who has taught QuickBooks classes for years and fielded questions from countless users of the program. Try finding that in the program manual.

This is more than another self-help book on the subject of QuickBooks. This is the book that looks through the forest of QuickBooks questions and stops to tell you about all the trees.

Specifically, *The Complete Idiot's Guide to QuickBooks and QuickBooks Pro 99* will help you:

- ➤ Get through the setup interview efficiently and quickly
- ➤ Learn when and how to protect your valuable data
- ➤ Enter back data in order to provide an historical perspective
- ➤ Keep track of everything you want to know about everyone you do business with
- ➤ Set up effective methods for ensuring that all tasks are performed on time
- ➤ Keep track of your cash flow
- ➤ Create reports that tell you all the ins and outs of your business cycle
- ➤ Get the most out of job costing and estimates
- ➤ Learn how to compute depreciation and how to circumvent the program's shortcomings in that area
- ➤ Figure out how much tax you have to pay, to whom, and how often
- ➤ Keep track of inventory and consider methods for getting around the program's shortcomings in that area
- ➤ Calculate your payroll and your payroll taxes
- ➤ Create and, more importantly, use a budget to gain control of your business

➤ Generate form letters, mailing labels, and envelopes by combining the talents of Microsoft Word with your QuickBooks data

➤ Use Microsoft Excel to create more complex reports

➤ Find all sorts of treasures on the Internet

Special Treats You'll Find in This Book

In addition to scads of useful information, you'll find the following extra special features throughout *The Complete Idiot's Guide to QuickBooks and QuickBooks Pro 99* that provide you with even more insight into the workings of your QuickBooks program.

Specific information that you need to enter appears in bold, like the following:

Type **Depreciation Expense**

Variable information that you need to enter, such as the name of a vendor or your employee's home address, appears in bold and italics like the following:

Type ***the vendor name***

In addition, you'll find little gray boxes scattered here and there along the way like roadside signs and billboards. The information in these boxes provides you with special insights into the inner workings of the program, hot tips that will make your daily life with QuickBooks a little easier, nerdy technical terms that will make you sound like a pro, and cautionary notices so that you won't drive off the main road and land in a QuickBooks ditch.

TechnoTalk

These boxes will fill your head with the language of computer nerds and accountants. Start talking like this and you'll probably get a big promotion and a corner office. You can always refer back to the information in these boxes in case someone wants to know what one of those big words actually means.

CPA Tip

These are the nuggets that you can use to keep your accounting operations on course. Shortcuts, quick tricks, and necessary accounting knowledge will help you get closer to your goals in a hurry.

Whoa!

Keep an eye out for these flashing red lights, or you might find yourself calling the QuickBooks motor club and waiting for assistance in the middle of the night.

At the end of each chapter, look for a section called "Now You've Done It!" which will give you a quick summary of everything you should have learned in the chapter. This isn't a quiz, nor is it a reprimand—if you didn't pick up a topic and want to review, you can go back at any time and read all about it.

Part 1

Meet Your QuickBooks Program

There are those who argue that nothing is more important to a business than keeping good financial records. Whether or not you agree with that philosophy, you must surely recognize that good record keeping can only benefit you and your company, or you wouldn't have purchased this book and your QuickBooks program.

Look at this first part of the book as your introduction to the world of QuickBooks and to the process of getting your company established as a QuickBooks company. If you are an old hand at QuickBooks, you might want to skip right over this section.

Chapter 1

Doing the EasyStep Tango

In This Chapter

➤ The birth of a company

➤ Beginning of the year, end of the year, points in between

➤ A great checklist to help you get organized

➤ The initial QuickBooks interview

If you've already gotten started with QuickBooks, you have your company already set up and running with this program. You can sidestep right past this chapter and head for the part of the book that will answer the specific questions you may have.

For those of you just starting with QuickBooks, this is the place to begin. The first step in using QuickBooks is the EasyStep Interview. But before you even open up your QuickBooks program, you need to make some decisions about the structure of your company.

What Type of Business Do You Want to Be when You Grow Up?

In order to be a business, you must decide what type of business you want to be. There are a few types from which to choose, and you should choose carefully, because there are important matters such as taxes, the ownership of assets, and the responsible party for liabilities at stake. Here's a quick rundown of the various sorts of businesses available, with some advantages and disadvantages of each type. This summary is presented merely to acquaint you with some general information about business entities. If you are contemplating your choices in this area, I strongly recommend you seek the advice of an attorney or accountant who specializes in business startups and who can answer questions that will be unique to your particular business.

Choosing an Entity

When choosing a business entity you should consider several factors, including any liabilities to which the business might be subject (both monetary and physical), fringe benefits that are available to some business entities but not to individuals, the rate of tax that will be assessed on the business' income, the appropriate year-end for the business, and the desired number of owners. All of these issues come into play when you are deciding which type of entity will best suit your particular business.

➤ **Sole Proprietorship**   With a sole proprietorship, you are your business. You are not a corporation. Your business doesn't exist without you. You can have employees, but you don't have partners or co-owners. You don't have to do anything to become a sole proprietorship, other than start doing your business. Legally, you are personally liable for every obligation of the business and for any damage caused by the business. If the business owes money and can't pay the bills, guess who pays—you! Income and loss of the sole proprietorship appear on the individual business owner's tax return, on Schedule C, and is taxed at the individual's tax rate.

➤ **Partnership** You can form a partnership if you want to go into business with others. Under the terms of the partnership, you can agree to share equally in the profits and losses of the business or you can agree to some split other than equal shares. Often the partnership agreement is made in writing and is legally binding. Creditors can seek satisfaction of debts from the partners of a partnership, although there is some protection offered to partners whose status is that of limited partner. However, there must be at least one general partner of a partnership, one who will ultimately be liable for debts of the business. Limited partners are liable only on business debts equal to their investment in the business plus their designated share of debts. Income and loss of the partnership are presented on tax form 1065, and then are passed through to the partners, who are taxed at their own individual rates.

➤ **Limited Liability Company** A limited liability company behaves like a partnership in which all the partners are limited partners. In a limited liability company, the creditors may seek recourse for debts owed to them only against the assets of the company. Members of a limited liability company (the business owners) are not personally liable for the business' debts. In most cases the income and loss of the limited liability company are treated like that of a partnership. There have been situations in which the IRS has required a limited liability company to be treated like a corporation for tax purposes. State rules differ in this area as well. Typically an LLC files a tax form 1065, just like a partnership. Check with a tax professional when considering the decision to set up this type of entity.

➤ **C Corporation** A C corporation is a taxable entity, one that stands alone in its responsibility to its creditors. Owners of a C corporation are shareholders who pay for the right to own a part of the company. A C corporation may have anywhere from one to an unlimited number of shareholders. Debts of the C corporation belong to the corporation, and recourse is not permitted against the shareholders unless they have specifically agreed in writing to accept responsibility for corporation debt. The corporation files its own tax return, a form 1120, and pays its own taxes. Income is passed through to the shareholders in the form of employee wages and/or dividends, both of which are taxed at the shareholders' personal tax rates.

➤ **Personal Service Corporation** This type of entity is a special type of C corporation that is subject to special rules. The PSC is a corporation that performs personal services in particular fields, including law, health, accounting, engineering, architecture, actuarial science, performing arts, and consulting. The PSC is subject to specific tax laws, including a flat rate tax at 35%, as opposed to the graduated rates that apply to the regular C corporation. The PSC reports taxable income on a form 1120.

➤ **S Corporation** An S corporation is a separate legal entity, like its sister the C corporation. The corporation is liable for its own debts, and shareholders are protected should the corporation fail. However, income is treated more like that of a partnership and is passed through to the shareholders, who are taxed on their personal tax returns and at their individual tax rates. The S corporation pays no income tax. A federal tax report is made on form 1120S, showing the income or loss for the year and the owners to whom the amounts will pass through. Among other limitations, the number of shareholders who can participate in an S corporation is 75. S corporate status is not automatically granted; the owners must file a request for such status with the IRS.

Choosing a Year-End

There are a couple of important dates to consider when setting up your company in general and when setting up your company on QuickBooks.

Internet Help for New Businesses

There are plenty of resources on the Internet that can help the new small business get off the ground and can help with all the decisions you have to make. Here is a sampling of sites that may have the answers to your questions:

The IRS offers a Small Business Corner at
`http://www.irs.ustreas.gov/prod/bus_info/sm_bus/index.html`.

Intuit presents all sorts of small business resources at
`http://www.quicken.com/small_business/`.

Learn about financing a small business and more at the Small Business Administration's Web site at `http://www.sba.gov/`.

All businesses report their income in a 12-month cycle known as a year. If the year ends on December 31, the year is a calendar year. If the year ends on any other date, the year is a fiscal year. In general, you must consider when you want your company year-end to occur. Most of us think of December 31 as the end of the year. For some businesses, however, a December 31 year-end can be difficult, unnatural, and inappropriate.

Some businesses don't have a choice of when their year will end. Sole proprietorships must use the same year-end as that of the business owner. Partnerships must prove a business purpose for choosing a year-end other than that of the general partners.

Why choose a business year different from the calendar year? There are several factors you should consider when thinking of the best time to end the year for your business:

Fiscal

A year that differs from the regular calendar year is called a *fiscal* year.

➤ **The natural business cycle**   If your business is cyclical and has a natural beginning and end on a regular, yearly basis, you will probably want to prepare your year-end financial statements and tax returns to coincide with the natural end of your business. If this natural cycle doesn't coincide with the end of the calendar year, you will want to consider ending your year to coincide with your business cycle.

➤ **Business distortions**   If your business incurs expenses during one time of the year and receives the offsetting income at another time of the year, you may want to choose your year-end so that your financial picture won't be distorted by reporting expenses without offsetting income, or vice versa.

➤ **Busy period**   If the busiest time of your year includes the end of December but carries on into January, it may be difficult to perform the accounting duties necessary to close your year on December 31. It may be more appropriate to choose a quieter time in your business cycle for closing your year.

➤ **Inventory fluctuations**   If your inventory is high at one time of the year and low at another, you may want to close your year at the time when inventory stores are low, so that your annual physical inventory count will be easier and less time consuming.

Different Cycles?

It is possible for a company's fiscal year to differ from the company's tax year. In this situation the company's financial statements reflect financial activity through the end of the fiscal year, but the tax return will be prepared for a different 12-month period known as the tax year. Speak with a tax and financial advisor if you think it is appropriate for your company to prepare its financial statements and its tax returns on two different cycles.

The decision of a company year-end will affect the presentation of financial statements and tax returns, as well as the workload of the person who keeps your accounting records up to date. If you're the one using QuickBooks, that person just might be you.

Start Date

The date on which your record keeping in QuickBooks begins is called your *start date*.

Choosing a Start Date

Separate from the choice of a year-end, you must also determine the date from which you wish to start recording your company information in QuickBooks. This start date won't affect your company in terms of tax returns or the IRS, but it will affect the first records you will keep in QuickBooks.

It is recommended that you time your QuickBooks start date to coincide with the first day of your year (either January 1 or another date if you have chosen a fiscal year different from the calendar year), the first day of a quarter or, at the very least, the first day of a month.

Ideally, if your use of QuickBooks coincides with the start of a new business, you can start QuickBooks on the very first day of your business and never have a time when your business activity isn't recorded in QuickBooks.

Keep in mind that the farther back your start date is from the day you begin using QuickBooks, the more information you will need to enter in QuickBooks. If today is March 3 and you choose January 1 for your start date, you will have slightly more than two months of information to enter. If you choose January 1 of last year for your start date, you're going to be going back and entering data for over a year's worth of activities.

On the other hand, the farther back you go with your start date, the more historical information you will have available to you in QuickBooks and the more detailed and complete your financial statements and comparative analyses will be.

Once you choose a start date, you'll want to take a look at "The Mighty Getting-Started Checklist," later in this chapter. This checklist will help you organize all the information you're going to need to bring your company records up to date in QuickBooks.

Changing Your Mind

The business decisions discussed in this chapter are significant and long lasting. They may last you for the life of your business. But what happens if your business gets going and you decide you need to make a change? Perhaps the business entity is not right for your needs, the date you chose for your year-end is not allowing you to produce financial statements that give an accurate portrayal of your company's progress, or you want to revise your QuickBooks start date so that you can enter another year of historical data.

Most of these decisions can be changed, but with varying degrees of difficulty.

Changing Your Business Entity

The change of business entity from sole proprietorship to another business form can be performed just as if you were starting a brand new business and choosing an entity. You need special permission from the IRS to choose an S corporate status; the other designations are available with no more effort than drawing up the legal papers necessary to form the entity.

Changing the type of business entity from any type other than sole proprietorship requires some legal maneuvering and, in some cases, permission from the IRS. Be sure to seek out professional advice if you plan this type of change.

Changing Your Year-End

Changing your year-end requires permission from the IRS. It doesn't matter what type of business entity your company is. You must file IRS Form 1128, "Application to Adopt, Change, or Retain a Tax Year," if you want to make any change relating to your year.

Changing Your QuickBooks Start Date

You don't need anyone's permission to change your QuickBooks start date. What a relief!

After you've begun entering your data in QuickBooks, if you decide you want to go back further and add information, you should open the Chart of Accounts List window (press **Ctrl+A**), and then double-click each asset and liability and equity account, one at a time, to open the register for that account. For each account that has an opening balance transaction, edit the transaction to change the date, and enter the correct opening balance. For accounts with no opening balance, you do not have to make an adjustment (unless there should now be an opening balance, in which case you can make an entry to show this).

If you decide you want your start date to begin at a later date than you originally chose, you may not need to make any changes at all. Your balance sheet accounts will have more information than is necessary, but that additional information won't affect your financial reports.

The Mighty Getting-Started Checklist

There are some people who might say it spoils all the fun if you're organized and know what to expect as you go through life. Many times we have no way of planning in advance for the events life throws our way, so organization in advance is a luxury we must do without. On the other hand, the more details you can nail down now, the more fun you can have later.

Here's a chance for you to gather up everything you need before you tackle the setup of your QuickBooks company records. How can you resist? Follow along with this checklist, collecting each item that is applicable to you (some items don't apply to every company). I promise you will save plenty of time when you proceed with the next step, the QuickBooks EasyStep Interview.

Getting Started Checklist

➤ Name (both legal name and dba name) and address of company

➤ Federal and state identification numbers

➤ Bank statements, cancelled checks, deposit records from the start date to the present

➤ Listing of your company's accounts, or general summary of the types of accounts you think you will need

➤ Standard information relating to all existing customers, such as name, address, phone, fax, account number, shipping address, whether or not subject to sales tax, name of contact

➤ Standard information relating to all existing vendors, such as name, address, phone, your account number, name of contact

➤ Inventory list of all items you sell, including description of items, cost, preferred vendor, standard sales price, quantity of items on hand as of the start date, quantity of items at which a reorder reminder should be issued

➤ Detailed list of all amounts you owe and to whom, as of start date

➤ Detailed list of all amounts owed to you and from whom, as of start date

➤ Sales tax information, including taxing agency, rate, and amount of sales tax you owe as of start date

➤ Any existing budget information

➤ List of employees, including names, addresses, Social Security numbers, tax withholding allowances, marital status, and year-to-date payroll information from January 1 to the start date

➤ Summary of all payroll taxes owed as of the start date

➤ Detailed list of all assets owned by the company, the original cost, date acquired, amount of depreciation claimed on previous tax returns

➤ Credit card statements you have received since the start date

➤ Detail of all transactions that have occurred since the start date, including checks written, amounts deposited, and credit card transactions

Plodding Through the Setup Interview

Now that you've collected all the information listed in the previous checklist, you should be anxious to get this company setup process underway. When you start QuickBooks you have a choice of poking around in the sample company or getting busy with your own company.

You can use the sample company as a testing ground. Experiment with the different types of reports, see what the forms look like, try your hand at customizing an invoice or a purchase order, make some entries on the forms, write a paycheck, get a feel for online banking (there is a sample online bank account!). Try out the various features without worrying about making a mistake in your own records.

Do the Interview

The EasyStep Interview is a great place to start for the first-time QuickBooks user. But what about the weathered veteran, who has used QuickBooks on previous occasions but now finds himself setting up a new company? The Interview may seem too time consuming if you already know your way around the program. Using the Interview is a choice. If you choose to bypass the Interview, you can do what many accountants do. Go right to the program and make a general journal entry (see Chapter 6, "Charting Your Accounts and General Journal Entries") that sets up the beginning balances of all of your accounts. Enter your vendors and customers as necessary (see Chapter 7, "Lots of Lists") and get right to work.

When you're ready to start entering the information for your own company, choose File, New from the QuickBooks menu. You will be welcomed to the EasyStep Interview, as seen in the following figure, and your company setup is officially underway.

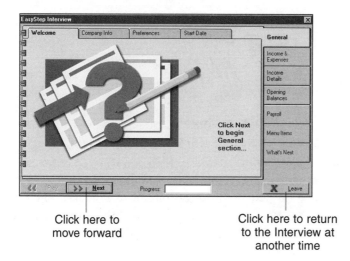

Ready, Set... Click Next *and you're ready to begin entering your company data in QuickBooks.*

Click here to
move forward

Click here to return
to the Interview at
another time

To use the EasyStep Interview, click Next each time you want to move forward one screen. It's like the game "Mother, May I?" and your computer program responds, "Yes, you may." (There may be times when QuickBooks waits for you to enter some information on the Interview screen before it will give you the "Yes, you may" to advance. If you get a Warning! box when you click Next, this is the computer saying "No, you may not!" Fill in the appropriate information and you will be able to advance to the next screen.)

At each screen either you will have a chance to read some information that the QuickBooks people think you will want to know or you will be asked to answer some questions or fill in some blanks. Keep going with the Next button and eventually you'll make your way through the entire Interview.

If you decide you want to go back and read or change a previous screen, click the Prev button and you will be taken back, usually one screen at a time. Sometimes Prev doesn't work and you don't go to the screen you just left. If you want to get back to a previous screen to change something and QuickBooks won't let you, make some notes on what you want to change and make your changes when the Interview is finished.

At any time, you can exit from the EasyStep Interview and (usually) you won't lose your place. To return to the Interview at a later date, choose File, EasyStep Interview, and you should be returned to the same screen on which you left off.

Write It Down

Here's some excellent advice for anyone using the EasyStep Interview: Keep a piece of paper by your side and write down everything you want to enter or change in QuickBooks once the EasyStep Interview is finished. You'll find there are several pieces of information that the EasyStep Interview won't let you enter. Furthermore, there can be situations where you make a mistake, but QuickBooks won't let you go back and make a correction. Just keep your own running list, and you can make all your changes in due time.

Going Back

If you leave the EasyStep Interview and return at a later time, you may find that some of the information you entered earlier has been lost. I've found the most likely information to get lost in this situation is the start date information, which is entered in the General section, near the beginning of the Interview. If necessary, you may need to click the General tab on the right side of the EasyStep Interview window, and then click the Prev button until you get back to the start date screen, where you can re-enter this information.

Who? What? Where? When?

First up in the EasyStep Interview is the General section. This is a fill-in-the-blank section that shouldn't give you any headaches at all. You're going to be asked the easy questions here, such as "What is your company's name?" "Where is your company located?" "When do you want to start recording information in QuickBooks?" "Who was that masked man?"

You will also be asked to provide a filename for your company file. You can use upper- and lowercase letters, spaces, and numerals in your filename.

Setting Up Your Income and Expense Accounts

Section two is called Income & Expenses, and the information you will be asked about here is related to the names of accounts that you will use to keep track of your income and expense transactions.

First you will be asked if you want to use the standard account names that QuickBooks has chosen for your type of business (see the following figure). Often it's easiest to let QuickBooks use its own names, and then add account names of your own to the list. If there are accounts you don't need, you can delete those account names at a later time.

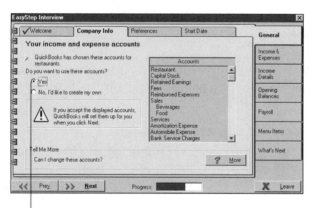

QuickBooks displays the standard accounts that it has to offer.

Click here to accept the standard accounts

You may not need to add any account names to the QuickBooks standard list, but chances are there will be specific accounts that you want to use that QuickBooks didn't think about.

For example, if you are in the restaurant business, you may want to create income accounts like Food Sales, Beverage Sales, Catering, and so on. Your expense accounts may include Perishable Food, Pantry Items, Dishware, and Laundering. Many of the account names you choose will be unique to your business.

Just What Do You Sell?

The Income Details section of the EasyStep Interview asks you for information about the types of items you sell. If your company maintains an inventory, you can enter the names of your inventory items, along with their related costs and the prices at which you normally sell them. You can also enter a reorder amount, so that QuickBooks will remind you when your supplies drop to the reorder point.

You can also enter information about services that you provide and other amounts you might charge your customers, such as delivery fees or postage.

If you miss an item in this section, you can always add to your list of the things you sell after the Interview is completed.

A Jump Start for Your Chart of Accounts

In the Opening Balances section of the EasyStep Interview, you are provided with an opportunity to enter your bank balance as of your start date and the value of all assets and liabilities in your company as of the start date.

In addition, you will enter the names of customers and vendors and the amounts associated with these companies or people as of your company's start date.

Line Up Here if You Want to Get Paid

In the Payroll section of the EasyStep Interview, you will designate the standard forms of payment your company uses (hourly, salary, and so on), the frequency of payment (weekly, biweekly, and so on), and any deductions that you apply to your employee paychecks.

The Payroll section provides you with screens where you can enter information pertaining to your employees, including name, address, phone number, regular amount of pay, deductions, marital status, number of exemptions, and so on. This is a very thorough section. The EasyStep Interview presents an excellent, step-by-step process for entering employee information.

Bits and Pieces to Wrap Up the Interview

By the time you get to the Menu Items and What's Next sections of the EasyStep Interview, you'll be long past wondering if this question and answer process will *ever* end. While it's true that the EasyStep Interview is lengthy and time consuming, it is also true, particularly for the first-time user of QuickBooks, that this Interview is thorough and provides you with an opportunity to set up nearly all the information you need to actually get started using QuickBooks.

These final sections of the Interview ask you some simple questions that relate to which choices you would prefer to see appear on the main parts of your QuickBooks menus and provide you with some general information about using the program. There's even a little sales pitch for purchasing standard forms from Intuit, and then you're finally finished!

Now You've Done It!

Now that you've finished all this getting-started stuff, you owe yourself a big pat on the back and a root beer float. Just look at all that you've learned how to do:

➤ Understand different types of business structures. See "What Type of Business Do You Want to Be when You Grow Up?"

➤ Choose a year-end for your business. See "Choosing a Year-End."

➤ Choose a start date for your relationship with QuickBooks. See "Choosing a Start Date."

➤ Collect all the right information so your company setup will be a breeze. See "The Mighty Getting-Started Checklist."

➤ Enter everything the EasyStep Interview asks for, so you can get started using QuickBooks right away. See "Plodding Through the Setup Interview."

Getting Comfy
With QuickBooks

Feel like a stranger in a foreign land? Consider this chapter your trusty tour guide. If you're new to QuickBooks or QuickBooks Pro, or to Windows programs in general, this chapter will help you sort out the various onscreen elements you'll encounter. Just so you don't feel overwhelmed, you should know that there are several different ways to perform the same tasks in QuickBooks, and this chapter will explain them all. Sample the methods presented here and choose whatever seems easiest to you.

As an experienced QuickBooks user, you may have the menus down cold and never even glance at the QuickBooks Navigator. Or perhaps you know your way around the Navigator, but you've never even turned on the Iconbar. Menus, Navigator, Iconbar—which should you use? It really doesn't matter. The commands you're accustomed to finding in one place are duplicated in the other places, so don't feel you have to know all three.

QuickBooks Basic Training

There's nothing more frustrating than opening a new program and not knowing where to begin. Thankfully, most programs work the same these days, so any experience you have with other Windows applications will come into play with QuickBooks. If you are a complete novice, this section explains the rudimentary stuff you need to know. If you're a seasoned computer user, just skip on over.

Opening and Closing QuickBooks

If you've gotten this far already, you've probably figured out how to open the program. However, to make your basic training complete, I am officially obligated to tell you how to open and close the program window.

There are two ways to start QuickBooks:

➤ Click the **Start** menu, choose **Programs**, **QuickBooks** or **QuickBooks Pro** (depending on which version of the program you bought), and then select **QuickBooks** or **QuickBooks Pro** again (a title so nice, they've placed it on the menu twice).

➤ When installing QuickBooks, you may have had the option to place a shortcut icon for the program on your Windows desktop. It's another way to start the program; just double-click the **QuickBooks** or **QuickBooks Pro** icon.

That's it. Nothing to it.

Which Version?

QuickBooks and QuickBooks Pro are so similar that you don't have to worry about learning any differences between the two when it comes to program basics. Unless I'm pointing out something unique to QuickBooks Pro (as in Chapter 11, "Special Treats for QuickBooks Pro Users"), any time QuickBooks is mentioned, you can assume I'm referring to both program versions.

What About the Interview?

The very first time you open QuickBooks, you'll be asked to jump through the EasyStep Interview. This is merely QuickBooks' way of helping you set up your business to work with QuickBooks. For more information on walking through the Interview, flip back to Chapter 1, "Doing the EasyStep Tango."

Opening Other Company Files

If you use QuickBooks for more than one company, you need to know how to get back and forth between your company files. Only one file can be open at a time. To open a different file, open the File menu and choose Open Company. QuickBooks will close the company file that you had open and give you a selection of other files. Click the name of the company file you wish to open, and then click the Open button.

When you're ready to close the program, use any of these methods:

➤ Click the Close button (X) located in the upper-right corner of the program window.

➤ Open the File menu and choose Exit.

➤ Press Alt+F4 on the keyboard.

Unlike other programs you may be used to, you don't have to save your work or give the file a name. QuickBooks takes care of all that for you as you work.

Back Up Your Data

QuickBooks doesn't bother reminding you about backing up your data from time to time. You only have to suffer through one computer meltdown to have the backup rules branded on your memory forever. Back up frequently and you'll never be sorry. See the section "Backing Up Your Data" in Chapter 3, "Security and Protection of Your Data," for complete coverage of this topic.

Who Said Anything About Updates?

Isn't this odd? You just bought the QuickBooks program and already you're getting little messages about updating! From time to time you will see a little onscreen message asking if you would like to update your program. Click Yes and QuickBooks will send you hurtling through cyberspace right to Intuit's Web site. There you can download a maintenance release if there is a change to the program that occurred since yours was published. This is a free service provided by Intuit. If you don't have access to the Internet, you can order updates on diskette from Intuit by calling 888-246-8848.

What Am I Looking At?

When you first open QuickBooks, after successfully completing or bypassing the EasyStep Interview, you're left staring at a screen similar to the one shown in the following figure. If you're new to Windows programs entirely, take a moment and familiarize yourself with the elements you see.

Here's a rundown of what you're looking at:

Title bar   This topmost area of the program window displays the name of the program (in case you forget what program you're working with), as well as the name of the company file you are using.

Menu bar   You'll find all the necessary commands for using QuickBooks scattered about in these main menus.

Minimize button   Click this button to reduce the program window to a button on the Windows taskbar.

Maximize/Restore button   Click this button to enlarge the program to fill up the entire screen or to return the window to its original size.

Close button   Click this button, the one with an X in it, to close the QuickBooks or QuickBooks Pro program entirely.

26

QuickBooks Iconbar   These buttons provide shortcuts to the main features of the program. This feature isn't turned on by default, but you will learn how to turn it on later in this chapter.

QuickBooks Navigator   Use this small-scale window and its various tabs to navigate the program's many features in a flash.

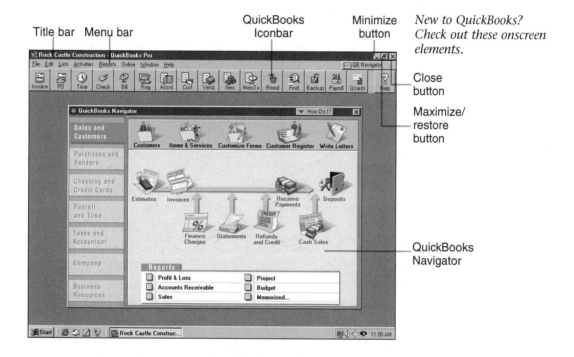

Title bar   Menu bar   QuickBooks   Minimize   *New to QuickBooks?*
                                                   Iconbar   button   *Check out these onscreen*
                                                                                    elements.

Close
button

Maximize/
restore
button

QuickBooks
Navigator

Little Window Ins and Outs

Just about every feature in QuickBooks opens a miniature window onscreen, such as a list of vendors or an invoice. The feature windows work just like the program window. They have title bars depicting the name of the window, plus minimize, maximize/restore, and close buttons in the upper-right corner. Check out the next figure to see what I mean.

Most QuickBooks features open into their own windows, such as this Purchase Order window.

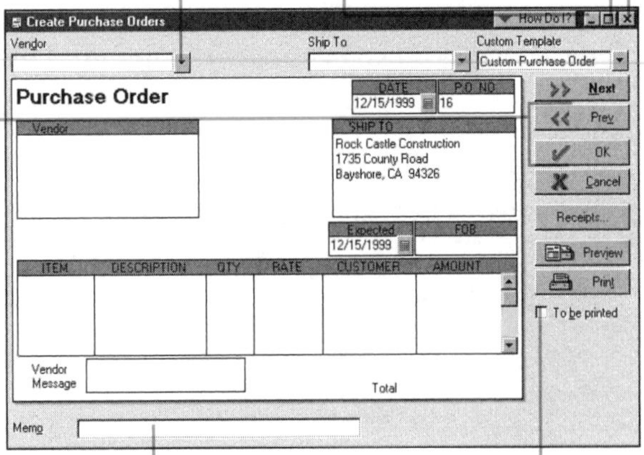

Click to display a drop-down menu list

Minimize button

Maximize/ restore button

Close button

Click buttons to open other windows or close the existing window

Click and type your data in these boxes

Click to check or uncheck the option box

Some windows aren't really windows, but dialog boxes instead. If you've used other applications, you may be familiar with dialog boxes. They, too, are miniature windows or boxes that let you choose from or fill in various options.

Regardless of the type of window you open in QuickBooks, its contents may include simple lists or detailed forms. You'll also find buttons, check boxes, text boxes to enter data, drop-down arrows that display additional menu lists, and so on. These window elements are fairly straightforward and easy to use. Basically, navigating windows is all about clicking, choosing, and sometimes typing.

To close a window without saving your changes, click the Cancel button, or press Esc on the keyboard. You can also click the close button, if the window has one. If you made any changes, QuickBooks may ask you if you want to save them or not.

Okay. Those are the basics for finding your way around the program window. The remainder of this chapter will introduce you to the primary QuickBooks tools for using the many features.

This Window Is Too Small!

Most of the windows you open in QuickBooks, such as the Chart of Accounts list or an invoice form, can be resized and relocated. To change the size of a window—make it either bigger or smaller—place your mouse pointer on any outside border of the window. The pointer will change to a double-pointed arrow. When you hold down the mouse button and drag your mouse, the window will stretch or shrink, depending on the direction you drag. To move a window to a new location on the screen, point to the blue title bar of the window and click and hold. The window will move along with your mouse and drop in place wherever you release the mouse button.

QuickBooks Provides a Clickable Navigator

Use the QuickBooks Navigator window (see the following figure) to quickly get from one place to another in a logical fashion. If QuickBooks Navigator isn't displayed, click the **QB Navigator** button in the upper-right corner of the program window.

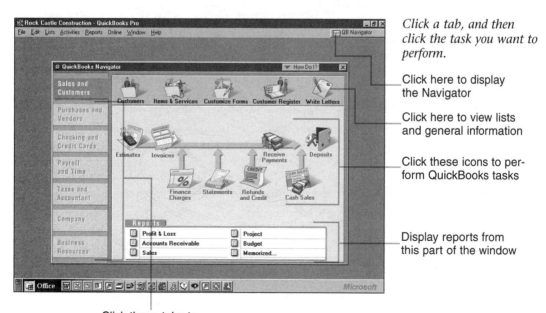

Click a tab, and then click the task you want to perform.

Click here to display the Navigator

Click here to view lists and general information

Click these icons to perform QuickBooks tasks

Display reports from this part of the window

Click these tabs to change categories

QuickBooks' features are neatly organized on the topical tabs you see on the left side of the Navigator window. Click the appropriate tab to perform these tasks and more:

Sales and Customers   Create estimates (QuickBooks Pro only), invoices, or monthly statements, record money received, view the Customer List, customize forms, write letters, view reports of profit and loss, sales, accounts receivable, budget.

Purchases and Vendors   Create purchase orders, record receipt of merchandise, enter and pay bills, view the Vendor List, view reports of inventory, profit and loss, payables.

Checking and Credit Cards   Write checks, enter credit card transactions, transfer money between accounts, reconcile bank account, view check register and transaction reports.

Payroll and Time (or Payroll and Employees) Enter time, create paychecks, process payroll tax forms, view Employee and Payroll item lists, view payroll reports.

Taxes and Accountant   Make journal entries, process sales tax, prepare accountant's review copy of your company file, view Chart of Accounts, print 1099s, view financial statements and tax reports.

Company   Adjust preferences, passwords, and company information, set up budgets, write letters, view To Do list, update QuickBooks.

Business Resources   Visit QuickBooks on the Internet, read about QuickBooks and your industry.

To close the QuickBooks Navigator, click the close button (X) in the upper-right corner of the Navigator window. You can always reopen the Navigator by clicking the **QB Navigator** button that resides in the upper-right corner of your QuickBooks screen.

How Do I?

Many of the QuickBooks windows include a little How Do I? button at the top right corner of the window. Click this button to see a drop-down list of special help topics that directly relate to the window you are viewing. See "Help Is on the Way," later in this chapter, for more information about the help that QuickBooks provides.

Ordering Your Commands Via Menus

In lieu of the Navigator, or in concert with the Navigator, you can make your task choices using the QuickBooks menu bar (see the next figure). To use a menu, click its name, which produces a drop-down menu list. To select a command from the menu, click the command.

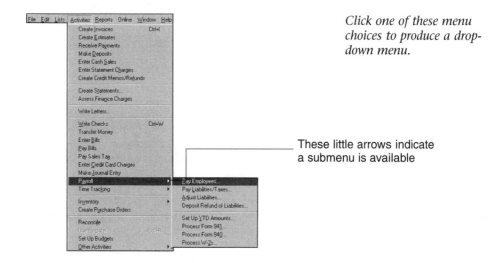

Click one of these menu choices to produce a drop-down menu.

These little arrows indicate a submenu is available

Having a bad mouse day? You can access the menus from the keyboard by pressing the **Alt** key, followed by the underlined letter of any menu title (for example Alt followed by A opens the Activities menu). When the drop-down menu appears, type the underlined letter, if there is one, for the menu command of your choice. Or, use your arrow keys to move up and down the menu until you reach the desired command, and then press the **Enter** key.

Secret Menu Choice

The first letter of each menu choice is underlined, enabling you to press **Alt**, and then type one of the underlined letters to open the associated menu. But what about the Online menu? There is no underlined letter in Online. I can't tell you why the O isn't underlined, but I have discovered that pressing **Alt** followed by the **O** (as long as you let go of the Alt first) does open the Online menu. I guess they just forgot to underline the O.

Using the Iconbar

QuickBooks' Iconbar is a collection of commonly used commands and features. You can activate one with a click of a button. However, the Iconbar doesn't automatically appear when you use QuickBooks—you have to state your desire to see the icons. Do this by opening the File menu and choosing **Preferences**. This opens the Preferences box, as shown in the next figure.

Use the Preferences box to turn on your Iconbar.

Click here to open
the Iconbar options

Click here to see both
icons and descriptive text

Click the **Iconbar** icon on the left side of the box, and then click the **Show icons and text** option. There are also options to show only icons or only text. Click **OK** to exit the box. The Iconbar now appears at the top of your screen, as shown in the following figure.

Icons make short work of finding your way around QuickBooks (buttons may vary, depending on choices made in the Interview).

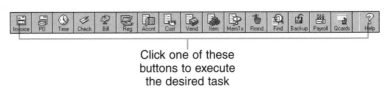

Click one of these
buttons to execute
the desired task

The icons take the place of some menu choices and Navigator choices, although there aren't as many icon buttons as there are tasks in QuickBooks. You must still rely on the menu bar or the Navigator to perform some QuickBooks tasks.

Help Is on the Way

There are so many ways in which you can get QuickBooks help—you'll never have to worry about not getting your questions answered. Just look at all these options:

➤ **Start here** You've got this book in your hands anyway—you might as well use it. Scan the Contents for major subjects, sift through the Index for specific topics. *The Complete Idiot's Guide to QuickBooks & QuickBooks Pro 99* is filled with step-by-step instructions for completing all the common tasks, as well as a little humor to brighten your day.

➤ **Click around** Your mouse will take you to lots of onscreen help sources. Turn on Qcards by opening the Help menu and choosing **Hide/Show Qcards**. These little tips will pop up in their own windows, as shown in the following figure, and give you instructions for every entry you're about to make.

Useless Icons

Do some of the icons on the Iconbar represent tasks you never use? Do you wish you could add to the Iconbar with buttons for your favorite QuickBooks features? You can try waving a magic wand over your computer screen and whispering magic words to the Iconbar. You may have more success, however, by turning to the section "Using the QuickBooks Iconbar," in Chapter 17, "This Is YOUR Program."

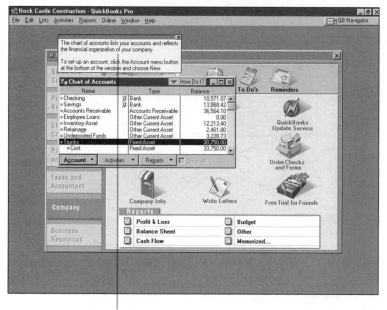

Qcard help

Qcards are little pop-up boxes that offer help with the task you're trying to perform.

➤ **How Do I?** Many windows contain a How Do I? button. Clicking this little button provides you with a drop-down menu of common questions concerning that particular window. Check out the next figure to see an example. Click any question, and you'll be transported directly to the QuickBooks Help screen that answers your question.

Use the How Do I? drop-down menu to find specific help topics related to the window you're viewing.

Click here

➤ **Using Help Index** For more detailed help, open the Help menu and choose **Help Index**. This opens the Help Topics dialog box, as seen in the next figure. Enter a topic, or scroll through the list of Help topics, and then double-click the topic for which you want more information. A Help window opens with information about the topic you selected. To close the Help window, click its Close (X) button.

Use the Help Topics window to look up a topic and open a Help window displaying information about the topic.

Enter a topic

Double-click the topic that most closely matches the topic you want to look up

A separate Help window opens for you to read more about the topic

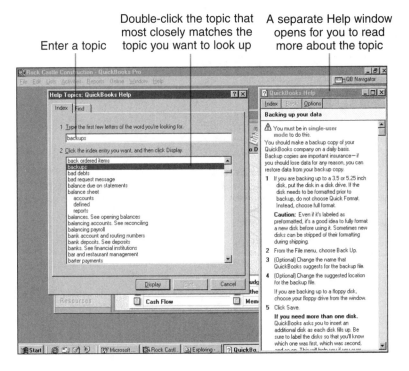

➤ **Using the Find Feature**   For even more thorough digging, open the Help menu, choose **Help Index**, and then click the **Find** tab. You can enter a word and QuickBooks will search through all of its Help screens for every occurrence of that word. Then it will display a list of related topics that contain your word. In this way, you can discover Help topics that contain references to your topic, even when yours isn't the main topic.

➤ **Head for Cyberspace**   Open the Online menu, click **Intuit Web Sites**, and then choose **QuickBooks.com Technical Support**. This logs you onto your Internet account (providing you have an account) and to the Intuit Web site. You can find answers to Frequently Asked Questions (FAQs) or visit the User-to-User Forums (click **User to User**, located at the left side of the window, as shown in the next figure), where you can register for free, and then post your own questions and get quick answers. (To learn more about using QuickBooks on the Internet, check out Chapter 20, "QuickBooks and the Internet.")

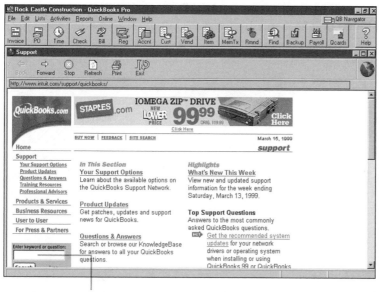

Head for the QuickBooks.com Web site and find tons of useful information about your program.

Click here and you can enter your own questions, which will be tackled by QuickBooks experts

➤ **Intuit Technical Support**   If you don't have the time to scour the Internet or flip through books, you can hire QuickBooks to do the legwork for you. Purchase technical support from Intuit (call 888-329-7276 and ask for support plan options), and you will get top-notch help from the experts.

Now You've Done It!

If you can't find your way around QuickBooks by now, go to Jail, go directly to Jail, and forget about collecting that $200.

➤ Use the Navigator for a totally logical and visual display of how QuickBooks is set up and which tasks can be performed. See "QuickBooks Provides a Clickable Navigator."

➤ You say you prefer the more traditional, menu-driven approach to finding commands? No problem. See "Ordering Your Commands Via Menus."

➤ Another quick way to give orders to QuickBooks is by clicking the Iconbar. See "Using the Iconbar."

➤ Don't spin your wheels when you have a QuickBooks question—there are myriad options for getting help in a hurry. See "Help Is on the Way."

Chapter 3

Security and Protection of Your Data

In This Chapter

➤ Setting up password protection for your files

➤ Limiting access to your files by different users

➤ Protecting prior year data

➤ What happens if you lose your password?

➤ Backing up QuickBooks data files

This chapter is intentionally placed early in the book because your company accounting data is extremely sensitive and important to you. Before you enter any information in your QuickBooks file, you need to know how to protect that information from loss, from people who aren't supposed to see the information, and from office employees who unknowingly stick cute refrigerator magnets on the side of the computer and delete your hard drive files.

By learning this information first, you can proceed with entering information in your QuickBooks file, confident that you've taken steps to ensure its safety.

Who Will See Your Files?

When thinking about security and protection for your QuickBooks file, consider which people will have access to this file. If you have your own business and you work by yourself, then many of the file protection features discussed in this chapter might not be of interest to you.

However, there are some features in this chapter that will be meaningful to anyone, in particular the section on backing up your data, which is a form of protection.

So, if it's just you and the computer, you may want to skip ahead to the section called "Backing Up Your Data" and pass over the material that covers security and password protection.

For the Administrator's Eyes Only

The first step in setting up password protection is to designate one person in your company as the *administrator*. This person will have complete access to the entire QuickBooks program and is, of course, authorized to wear an important-looking "Administrator" badge and have a song written in his honor. This is the person who will create the security restrictions for the other users of the program.

If control is an important issue among the owners of the company, and you want to ensure that no one member of the administrative staff has the right to make certain changes without the authority of others, then it may be that you'll designate an outside person rather than someone from within your company. For example, your company accountant or another trusted person could be the administrator and would oversee the controls of the company. In any case, one person must be designated as the administrator. This person will perform the security setup for the rest of the company.

Choosing an Administrator

When choosing an administrator, keep in mind the fact that the administrator is someone who really shouldn't be off the premises very often. The administrator needs to be available, in case someone has difficulty accessing certain areas of the QuickBooks program, or in case someone forgets a password. Also, remember that more than one person can have knowledge of the administrator password, so you don't necessarily have to limit these controls to only one user.

You may have already begun the security process. If you indicated during the EasyStep Interview that more than one person would have access to your QuickBooks file, you saw a message at the end of the Interview asking if you wanted to set up users at this time (see the figure below). If you passed on that option at the time, you can set up your administrator and users now.

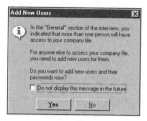

This message appears after the EasyStep Interview if you indicated that you are not the only one who will be authorized to use your QuickBooks file.

When setting up your administrator for the first time, open the File menu and choose **Set up Users and Passwords, Set up Users**. The first window that will appear is called Set Up QuickBooks Administrator. You'll use this window to establish a name and password for the administrator, who has top-level access to all of the information in your QuickBooks file.

Fill in the administrator's name. By default, QuickBooks has filled in the name Admin (see the next figure), and you can keep that name or change it to something else. Click inside the first password text box and enter a password for the administrator. Confirm the password by entering it a second time in the Confirm Password text box.

What's Allowed?

When creating a password in QuickBooks, you are limited to 15 characters. These characters can include spaces, letters, and numbers. The password is not case sensitive, so it doesn't matter if letters are uppercase or lowercase.

Enter the name and password for your company administrator.

Notice that you don't have to enter a password for the administrator; it's optional. If you leave the password areas blank and just click OK, the administrator will be set up with no passwords. This means that the administrator (or anyone else) can open the QuickBooks program and identify himself as the administrator (otherwise known as *logging in as the administrator*). In this scenario, the administrator (whoever it is) can enter the program with full administrator rights, including access to all areas of the program. This may not be a good idea if you have confidential data to protect.

However, if you set up a password for the administrator, the next time you enter the program—even if the administrator is the only user you have identified—you will be asked to enter the administrator's password prior to having access to any of the files. So enter a password or not, as you choose. Just make sure you etch it in your memory.

After you click OK and have signed up the administrator as the user of your program, the User List window appears (as shown in the figure below). The next section discusses setting up new users.

Click **Add User** *to set up a new user.*

How Many Can Play This Game?

There's no limit to the number of people to whom you can give access to your program. There is a limit in QuickBooks Pro to the number of people who can use your company file at the same time on different computers, and that limit is five; five different computers can access the company file simultaneously (see "Using QuickBooks on Multiple Computers" in Chapter 11, "Special Treats for QuickBooks Pro Users," for more information).

But you can have 25 users, 100 users—as many or as few as you want—giving all of them passwords and access to the company files, just at different times. Perhaps you have one computer on which your QuickBooks file is saved, but your business is such that you have a 24-hours-a-day phone order business, and you want different people to be able to access your file 24 hours a day. Or perhaps your business is a retail store where several sales clerks use the same computer throughout the day. In these situations, each of those staff members can be signed up as a user with his own password and can take turns using the computer.

What Your Users Need to See

You need to think seriously about what kind of information is stored in your QuickBooks file, who all of your QuickBooks users are, and what areas of the program are important for those users to see. It may be that one person enters invoices, and that's all. That person would need to have access to certain areas of the program, including the ability to enter invoices and add customers and jobs to the Customer:Job list; but that user may not have any need to access the payroll area of the program or to produce reports.

Before you start setting up users and passwords, take a few minutes to make a list of all the people in your company who will be using this program. Along with their names, include the areas of the program that each needs to be able to access. Think carefully about what information you want to make available to your employees when you're getting ready to set up users.

Setting Up Levels of Security

When you set up users in QuickBooks, you will establish a password for each user and designate which areas of the program the user has access to. In the paragraphs to come, you'll go through an example of setting up a user and see how to assign to that user the rights to use particular areas of the program.

Adding a New User

If the User List box is not visible on your screen, open the File menu and choose Set up Users and Passwords, Set up Users. The User List will appear (see the previous figure). From the User List window, click the Add User button, and the Set Up User Access and Password window will appear (see the next figure). On this screen, enter the name of a new user and a password for that user.

Note that a user other than the administrator—even one to whom you have assigned all rights—does not have permission to set up other users. Only the administrator can set up other users. However, you may want to have the new user sit down at the computer and enter his or her own password, so that the information is private.

Stuck for a Password?

It's important to choose a password that other people won't figure out. On the other hand, don't choose something so obscure that you'll forget it yourself! You may want to consider using an important date, a family nickname, the name of a childhood friend—something you're likely to remember but others may have a hard time figuring out.

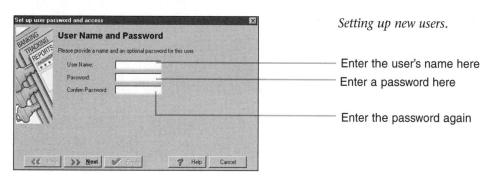

Setting up new users.

Enter the user's name here

Enter a password here

Enter the password again

After you enter a new user's name and password, click the Next button. You're then expected to decide if this user is to have access to Selected areas of QuickBooks or All areas of QuickBooks.

If you choose All areas of QuickBooks, that user will have rights similar to those of the administrator, although these rights do not include the right to set up new users or change the closing date.

If you choose Selected areas of QuickBooks, you'll be taken on a tour of several screens on which you need to mark whether the user has No Access, Full Access, or Selected Access to each area of the program.

The areas to which you will consider giving access rights are listed below. Depending on some of your company preferences, you might not see all of these options. (For example, if you indicated your company does not track inventory in QuickBooks, you won't see the Inventory option.)

➤ **Sales and Accounts Receivable** Includes entering invoices, cash sales, receiving payments, writing estimates, and preparing statements.

➤ **Purchases and Accounts Payable** Includes entering bills, paying bills, entering credit card charges, entering purchase orders, accessing the vendor list, and preparing accounts payable reports.

➤ **Checking and Credit Cards** Includes writing and printing checks, making deposits, and credit card activities.

➤ **Inventory** Includes entering purchase orders, receiving items purchased, adjusting inventory, and accessing inventory reports.

➤ **Time Tracking** Includes entering time sheets, running time reports, and importing and exporting timer files.

➤ **Payroll** Includes entering paychecks, printing paychecks, printing payroll tax forms, accessing the employee list, and accessing payroll reports.

➤ **Sensitive Accounting Activities** Includes transferring funds between accounts, reconciling bank accounts, making general journal entries, and performing online banking activities.

➤ **Sensitive Financial Reporting** Includes accessing balance sheet, income statement, and profit and loss reports.

➤ **Changing or Deleting Transactions** Includes changing or deleting transactions before the closing date.

Selected Access means that you can choose from allowing the user to

➤ Create transactions only

➤ Create and print transactions

➤ Create transactions and reports

Make your choice on each of the screens, indicating which areas of the program the user has access to. On the last screen you'll see a summary of all the choices you've made (see the next figure). Review the information on this screen, and click **Prev** to go back and correct any errors. Click **Finish** when you are satisfied that everything is correct, and you'll be returned to the User List window. Click **Close** when you are done entering and setting up access for users.

Getting Help with Security Decisions

While entering access rights for users, look carefully at the description that accompanies each screen. For more information, click the **Help** button on any of the access screens. Help gives details of exactly what is covered by each area. Making careful decisions during this setup process will save you from the aggravation of having to go back and make changes later, after the passwords are in place.

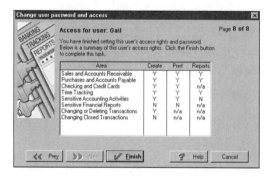

If the information on this screen is incorrect, click the Prev button to go back and change the access rights for this user.

Once you've set up passwords and different users for your company, the next time you open your company file in QuickBooks you'll be confronted with a login window (see the figure below). In this window you will be prompted to enter the name of the user who is using the program and that user's password. Type in the passwords and click **OK** to open the program with the appropriate access rights for the user.

Enter your username and password on the login screen.

Psst! I'll Tell You My Password if You'll Tell Me Yours!

If the passwords being used in your program are no longer private—for example, if someone in your company has discovered someone else's password and has gotten access to areas of the program he should not have—you can change the password in QuickBooks.

A user can change his own password at any time by opening the File menu and choosing **Set up Users and Passwords, Change Your Password**. Enter the original password, and then enter the new password. Enter the new password yet again for verification.

Someone Should Know the Passwords

It's a good idea to keep a record of every user and that user's password somewhere in your company, locked in a file cabinet or safe deposit box. Should something happen to the administrator (he has a skiing accident, for example, and is in traction for six weeks), it is important to have a place where this information is stored so that business can continue.

For extra security, you can leave this information (particularly the administrator's password) in the hands of the company attorney or some other trusted outsider.

Oh No! I Forgot My Password!

What happens if you really mess up and forget your password, and you don't have a list tucked away somewhere showing the passwords for all the users in the company? Besides having to bear the ridicule of your colleagues (although, if they call you enough silly names, you may have your memory jogged and remember your password), you run the risk of losing productive time because you can't access your QuickBooks program.

Actually, if the person who lost his password is someone other than the administrator, this is really not a big deal.

As the designated administrator, you can delete the name of the user who forgot his password from the User List, and then add the user back as a new user. Log on as the administrator, open the File menu, and choose **Set up Users and Passwords**, and then **Set up Users**. Click the user's name on the User List, and click the **Delete User** button. Confirm that **Yes** you really want to get rid of that user, and the user will be removed from the list.

Click the **Add New** button in the User List box to add the user back to your QuickBooks list of users, assign a new password, and assign the appropriate user rights to this user.

What *is* a big deal is if the administrator forgets his password. The difficulty is that if the administrator can't log on, no changes can be made to any information on the User List. If someone else forgets his password, and you want to delete that user and assign a new username, it can't be done. If there are areas of the program to which only the administrator has rights, no one will be able to access those areas.

If changes need to be made in areas of the program that are protected and restricted from the other users and the administrator can't log on, you may be faced with a very serious problem.

However, if you've forgotten the administrator's password, you can request help from the good folks at Intuit. Call QuickBooks technical support (888-320-7276). Call from your computer, and the technical support person will walk you through certain onscreen steps. Then you'll be asked to dispatch a copy of your data file to Intuit. Intuit will remove the password from the administrator. Be aware that there is a fee for this service.

Year-End Considerations

Many accounting programs include a feature that enables you to close the books as of the end of the year. The term "close the books" comes to us from the ancient Minoans (the same friendly folks who brought us the Minotaur—the beast who used to feed on young Greek women). The accountants in this culture would ceremoniously close their ledgers of account at the end of each year, devour a few young Greek women, and perform ritualistic dances to signify the end of yet another exciting accounting cycle. As you can imagine, closing the books was a pretty festive event.

Times have changed slightly since those exhilarating days. So have accountants, I might add. Anyway, back on the subject, once all of the adjustments relating to the year-end have been entered in a program, this closing of the books process is encouraged. In some accounting programs, after you indicate you're closing the books, you no longer have access to forms and transactions in the prior year. Closing the books locks in the numbers from the prior year and keeps them secure so that no one can inadvertently or intentionally make a change in the prior year company information.

Why close the books? One reason for protecting the transactions of the prior year is that, once the year has ended and financial statements have been prepared, you want people to be able to rely on those statements. If someone has the right to go back in and change the numbers from last year and then print new financial statements, the original statements lose their value.

QuickBooks doesn't exactly buy into this closing of the books process (nor does it encourage the devouring of young Greek women). Instead, there is a process by which you can prevent unauthorized people from changing prior year transactions (see "Protecting Prior Year Data," later in this chapter). They don't get eaten or anything if they try, they just get a message that last year's numbers are off limits. That's about as close to the Minotaur as QuickBooks gets.

When Is a Year-End Really a Year-End?

If yours is a calendar year company, you probably think the end of the year occurs at midnight, December 31. In a way you're right, but in another way you're wrong. No matter where your year-end falls on the calendar, there's generally work to be done in a company file after the last day of the calendar year or the fiscal year and before the financial statements for the year-end are prepared.

When you analyze the preliminary year-end reports of your company and the information that has been entered in the past year, you may find errors, omissions, or transactions that need to be changed. In addition, if your company has inventory, you will take an end-of-the-year physical inventory count, and there may be adjustments required as of that count. See Chapter 14, "Tracking Inventory (or Not...)," for more information about using QuickBooks to account for inventory.

If your company owns depreciable assets, there may be an end-of-the-year depreciation expense adjustment that needs to be made. If you have your records examined by an accountant at the end of the year, the accountant may provide you with information about changes that need to be made before you close your year in QuickBooks.

When the year is definitely over and all adjustments have been made, you'll prepare a set of year-end financial statements, such as an income statement, a balance sheet, and a cash flow report, and then you'll be ready to think about making the prior year information in your QuickBooks file inaccessible or unavailable to change.

Protecting Prior Year Data

Note that only the administrator has the right to enter a closing date. To protect your prior year information and establish a closing date, open the File menu and choose **Set up Users and Passwords**, **Set up Users**. This opens the User List (oh, that again). At the bottom of the list box, click the **Closing Date** button. You'll be asked to enter a date.

This should be the last date of the year or the time period for which you plan to make information in QuickBooks unavailable to change. Generally that will be the last day of your calendar year. When you enter a date as the closing date and click **OK**, that date becomes the official closing date.

Pre-Closing Date Reports

Entering a closing date prevents any users who have not been given rights to make changes prior to closing dates from being able to change or delete transactions prior to the chosen date. Note, however, that anyone who can access reports can still access reports from the period prior to the closing date.

What if I Really Need to Change Last Year's Information?

Once you've protected your prior year data by indicating a closing date and choosing which (if any) users of the program have rights to change transactions prior to that date, there may be situations in which you have to go back and make changes. Maybe you established the closing date restriction and then your accountant called with a last-minute change that needs to be entered in the prior year records.

If you need to make a change to your financial records after you've established a closing date (for example, on January 23rd you find out you need to make an adjustment for depreciation expense for the year ended December 31st), the administrator (or anyone who has access to information before the closing date) can do this. Just enter or change a transaction the way you normally would, dating the transaction on or before the closing date. When you click OK to complete the transaction, you will see a message reminding you that you are about to change information prior to the closing date (see accompanying figure). Click Yes to indicate that you really want to do this.

This message box appears if you try making changes that are dated prior to the closing date.

Backing Up Your Data

There's absolutely no question that you need to back up your QuickBooks information regularly and frequently. This financial information is the framework of your company, it's the bones that hold the body together. A loss of your QuickBooks accounting information could be devastating to the ongoing operation of your business. You simply can't afford to risk losing this information. Therefore, you absolutely must back up your data and keep it secure.

Your File Is Password Protected, But Is It Safe?

Putting passwords into your QuickBooks file to restrict users to certain areas offers a great amount of protection in terms of what different users can view in the program and what areas of the program they have the right to change. However, password protection does not protect your QuickBooks file from computer catastrophes.

There are many ways in which your computer information can be corrupted.

➤ Physical damage can occur to your computer and the hard drive within it.

➤ There can be a theft that results in your computer being removed from your company premises.

➤ If you use your computer to go online, a virus can be downloaded that can damage your files.

➤ Well-meaning employees can bring in giant magnets and stick them on the side of the computer.

➤ Even though your QuickBooks information is password protected within the QuickBooks program, there might not be controls in place to stop a savvy computer user in your company from accessing the file containing your company records and deleting or damaging that file.

Because there is so much risk and so much at stake, it is imperative that you back up your QuickBooks data.

Backing Up in the 21st Century

Consider backing up your QuickBooks data online, through a service offered on the QuickBooks Web site at www.quickbooks.com. The service is provided by Safeguard; they will provide remote backup and storage of your QuickBooks files—for a small fee, of course.

How, and How Often, Should I Back Up?

There are many different ways to back up your company data and keep it safe. You can consider a tape backup system, an external hard drive, a zip drive, floppy disks—all of these methods involve making a duplicate set of your QuickBooks data and then storing it somewhere outside of your computer.

In fact, it makes sense to make a backup set of your data and store it completely outside of the company, perhaps in a safe deposit box.

You'll know how often you should back up your company files when you consider how long you want to spend restoring lost data and entering information since the last backup.

If you back up your files once a month and nearly an entire month has gone by when your QuickBooks file becomes damaged, you'll have nearly an entire month of data to re-enter. If this is not viewed as a problem, then backing up once a month might be sufficient.

If you enter enough transactions on a daily basis that even re-entering an entire day of work is going to disrupt the operation of your business, then you definitely want to back up on a daily basis. The decision about the frequency of your backups should be based on several criteria, including how your backup system works and how much time you want to spend re-creating data.

How Do I Back Up in QuickBooks?

To execute a backup in QuickBooks, follow these steps:

1. Open the File menu and choose **Back Up**. You will be asked if you are interested in finding out about backing up to a remote location. Click **Yes** to link to the QuickBooks Web site and learn about this service.

2. The Back Up Company To dialog box will appear (as shown in the next figure), in which you'll be asked to give a name for the file you'll be backing up and a location where that information will be stored.

Enter the name of the backup file in the File Name text box.

3. To change which drive and folder you want to save to, click the **Save in** drop-down arrow and locate the drive or folder. If the folder you want to save to already appears in the list box, double-click it. If you are backing up to a floppy disk, click the **Save in** drop-down arrow and select the floppy disk drive (be sure to insert the disk).

4. In the File name text box, enter the name of the file to which you want to back up this information.

5. Do not change the information in the Save as type field. This information is required by QuickBooks in order to restore the file at a later date.

6. Click the **Save** button. Your QuickBooks file will be closed, and the information will be backed up in the location you indicated.

Restoring Data from Your Backup

Let's say your worst Quicken nightmare is realized—you've had a devastating computer crash in your company and none of your QuickBooks company information is accessible. Don't worry—never fear! You've backed up your file! Breathe a great sigh of relief. Mind you, you may still have to spend a few hours re-entering data that was entered after the last backup, but then you'll be back in business.

To restore the information that you backed up, follow these steps:

1. Open the File menu and choose **Restore**. The Restore From window appears.

2. Use the **Look in** drop-down arrow to locate the drive and folder where you stored your backup copy. If it's on a floppy disk, pop the disk in the drive first.

3. From the list of filenames, select the backup file you want to use, and then click the **Open** button.

4. A Restore To window will appear, as shown in the next figure (this window looks very much like the Restore From window, except the title is different). Locate your QuickBooks file (not your backup file, but your regular data file) and select it.

5. Click the **Save** button.

Enter the name and location of your regular QuickBooks data file.

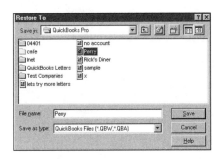

6. If there's any remnant of your original file still on your computer, you'll get a message prompt indicating that a file exists and asking if you want to replace it. You can click **Yes**.

7. Yet another message appears, asking if you want to delete the entire file and reminding you that if you restore from backup you will completely replace the file that is currently on your computer. Make sure that the backup version from which you are restoring contains more current information than the regular QuickBooks file. From the message prompt, type **yes** and click **OK**, and QuickBooks will restore the data from your backup.

Moving Data to a New Computer

You can use the Restore To option as a copy-and-replace option by backing up your data file and restoring it on another computer. If you've purchased a new computer, for example, and you plan to start using QuickBooks on the new computer, you can use the backup and restore procedure to move your data to the new machine.

File Restoration for the Major-League Crisis

What happens if the restore from backup doesn't work? If the restoration of your data fails, or if you don't have backup from which to restore, and your original data has become corrupted, and you can't access your QuickBooks data at all, don't assume that you have to re-enter all the information from your QuickBooks file.

It is quite possible that the good folks at Intuit will be able to help restore some or all of your corrupted QuickBooks data. Contact QuickBooks technical support (888-320-7276) and explain the situation. They may be able to help you, for a small fee.

Now You've Done It

I hope this chapter gave you enough warnings and information to convince you of the importance of backing up your data. You also learned the steps involved in creating levels of security protection for your precious accounting data. In particular you learned:

➤ You can set different levels of security for the users who will have access to your program. See "Who Will See Your Files?"

➤ The administrator for your QuickBooks file has the authority to set up new users and establish security privileges for those users. See "Setting Up Levels of Security."

➤ The end of the year is here, and you want to protect your QuickBooks data from alteration once you've issued your final year-end financial statements. See "Year-End Considerations."

➤ Don't even think about not backing up your QuickBooks data. See "Backing Up Your Data."

Chapter 4

What Are These Items, Anyway?

In This Chapter

➤ What is an item?

➤ Making your own items

➤ Taking advantage of items

➤ Removing items

You survived the EasyStep Interview, learned all about the basics of using the program, and assigned any needed security options. What's next? Time to talk about items.

Item is a term used by QuickBooks to describe services and products that you purchase and sell. There are special items that help with your calculations, and there is a separate group of payroll items that represent benefits you provide to your employees.

Although this chapter is primarily about the items that appear on your purchase and sales forms, the processes of creating, using, and removing items apply to all items throughout QuickBooks and QuickBooks Pro. Why cover items before covering how to create invoices, purchase orders, and other forms? Because items are basic to most of the forms you create, and you need to know all about them before placing them on QuickBooks forms.

The Way QuickBooks Sees the World

Only 10 Items?

There are only 10 *types* of items within QuickBooks. That doesn't mean you are limited to only 10 items. You can create as many items as you like within each type.

Item

Something that appears as a line in the description section of a form, such as a purchase order, a bill, or an invoice.

QuickBooks uses the term item to refer to anything that appears as a line item on a form, such as something you sell, something you purchase, sales tax, or a subtotal. There is a fixed number of types of items in QuickBooks, 10 to be exact. Although you're not going to be tested on this list, it may be helpful to see just what qualifies as an item type:

➤ **Service**   The services that you provide

➤ **Inventory Part**   A product that you keep in stock and sell

➤ **Non-inventory Part**   A product that you sell but don't keep in stock

➤ **Other Charge**   Miscellaneous amounts you charge to customers, such as shipping or packaging

➤ **Subtotal**   The total of all items that appear before this line on a form

➤ **Group**   A collection of items presented as one

➤ **Discount**   Discounts that can be applied to customers' invoices

➤ **Payment**   A payment line that can appear on the invoice to reflect payment at time of purchase

➤ **Sales Tax**   Sales tax rates that can be applied to customer purchases

➤ **Sales Tax Group**   A group of sales tax rates presented as one item

No More Items

You may think you have a need for some type of item that doesn't appear on the accompanying list. Wrong! These are the ONLY items recognized by QuickBooks. Anything you plan to sell must fit into one of these groups. Does it seem like you're shoving a square peg into a round hole? Too bad! Push a little harder, because these are all the items you're going to get.

By setting up items, you provide yourself with a list of established information that can be drawn on when creating a sales or purchase form. For example, rather than trying to remember whether the piece of yard equipment you are selling is called a hoe or a dibble, you can review your list of items and use the name that is on the list.

When you set up an item for something you are going to sell, you set up not just the item name (such as hoe), but the sales price of the item ($10), a description (Orion model, Left-handed Hoe) and the accounts that are affected when you sell the item (cost of sales expense, equipment sales income). All that detailed information is drawn into the invoice form at once without your having to enter it each time you create a form. Ah, the wonders of technology.

The remainder of this chapter will explore the very nature of QuickBooks items and how they work. Take time to learn about them now to be ready to use them in the chapters to come. Anytime you run into a snag regarding an item, refer back to this chapter for tips on adding, changing, and removing items from QuickBooks.

Typical Invoice Items

To help you better understand how items work, let's first examine items typically found on an invoice. Every time you create an invoice (see the next figure), you include a description of the parts of services or products you are selling. These items are referred to as Service, Inventory Part, and Non-inventory Part items.

Every invoice has at least one item.

Here are some items —

Consignment Items

How do you show merchandise on your invoice that is being sold on consignment—things that you are selling on behalf of others? You still need to set up items for this merchandise. Even if you stock these consignment pieces in your place of business regularly, they are not a part of your balance sheet inventory because they belong to someone else. Hence they are Non-inventory Parts.

There are other things you include on the invoice, too: delivery charges, insurance, postage, interest for late payment (which all fall into the Other Charge item type), discounts, and sales tax (each of which has its own item type).

Typical Purchase Items

Inventory and Non-inventory Part items appear on your purchase forms. Other Charge items may appear on your purchase forms, too—amounts you pay to have items shipped to you, for example. Take a look at the figure below to see an example.

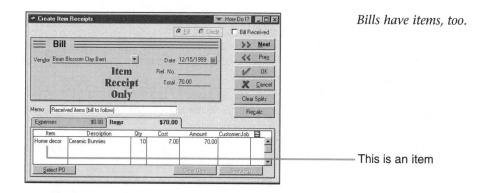

Bills have items, too.

This is an item

You might also see subtotals on your purchase forms, as well as sales tax if you pay sales tax on items. Generally, however, if you make purchases for resale to others, you won't pay sales tax yourself.

Groups of Items

You can group together certain items into one overall umbrella item called a Group. For example, if you sell a set of four-season lawn fertilizer as one package (called your 4-Season Pack) but you are also willing to sell the spring, summer, fall, and winter fertilizers individually, you would set up each season's fertilizer as a separate item but then create a Group item that includes all four. You can then sell the fertilizers one at a time or you can sell the Group without having to list all four fertilizers on the invoice. The next figure shows four items assigned to a Group called the 4-Season Pack.

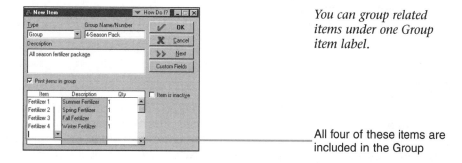

You can group related items under one Group item label.

All four of these items are included in the Group

Sales tax works in the same way. If you are required to collect sales tax for more than one municipality, rather than entering each separate sales tax on your invoice forms, you may want to refer to your county sales tax and your city sales tax simply as one item—local sales tax. You will use a Sales Tax group to combine the two taxes into one item.

Creating Your Own Items

You've seen a few examples of how items are used. Now you're ready to start recording items pertaining to your own business. Some of your items, such as types of inventory you sell or delivery charges you assess, will have been created in QuickBooks already if you took the time to go through the EasyStep Interview. During the Interview you were asked for descriptions of things that your company purchases and sells.

As you use QuickBooks over a long period of time, and as your inventory expands to include different merchandise or you begin to offer more services, your item list may grow. Each time you add an item to your business, you will also add an item to QuickBooks. For example, if you are in the business of selling ceramic bunnies, and you decide to branch out and add ceramic pigs, you will add a new ceramic pig item to your Inventory Part items. Add the item once, and you will have access to it over and over on all of your forms.

Don't Postpone Forever!

Sooner or later you must add items in QuickBooks. You can add an item when your company decides to acquire it, or you can wait until you need to refer to the item on a purchase or sales form. But that's as long as you can wait. As soon as you attempt to refer to a new item on a form, QuickBooks stops you in your tracks and insists that you go through the formal item setup procedure.

Adding an Item

There are two ways to add an item in QuickBooks, and the result is the same no matter which one you choose. If you decide to add items before you need to refer to them on forms, open the Lists menu and choose Items to open the Item List window, and then press Ctrl+N to open a New Item window. Alternatively, from the QuickBooks Navigator screen, click either the Sales and Customers tab or the Purchases and Vendors tab, click Items and Services at the top of the window, and then press Ctrl+N.

If you decide to wait, instead, until it's time to enter an item for the first time on a form, just click in the Item area of the form. A drop-down arrow appears. Click the arrow to display a list of items, as shown in the next figure. At the top of the list is the **Add New** command. Select it to open the New Item window.

Select this command

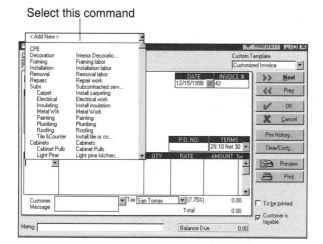

Open the item list to find the Add New command for setting up your new item.

Adding an Item on the Fly

In the Item area of your purchase or sales form, you can go ahead and try to enter the name of an item not on your item list. As soon as you finish entering the mystery item, QuickBooks will flash a message your way letting you know that it has never heard of Smoked Buffalo Chips, or whatever you've entered. At this time you should click the **Set Up** button, and you'll be transported to the New Item screen, where you can tell QuickBooks everything it wants to know about your chips.

Either way you did it, you ended up at the same place—the New Item window (see the next figure). From this window you must make several choices about your item. The choices you have to make depend in part on the type of item you select. To get things rolling, first choose your item type. (If you've forgotten about item types—and it's okay if you have, because I said you weren't going to be tested on this—there is a complete list of available items at the beginning of this chapter.) Click the **Type** drop-down arrow to display a list of items and choose the one you want.

Some of the fields in the New Item window vary, depending on the type of item you are setting up.

Click here to see the list of types

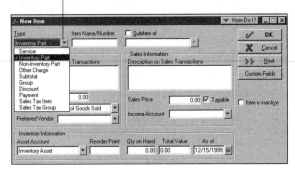

Depending on the type of item you select, you will be expected to impart some or all of the following information:

➤ Name and/or part number of the item

➤ Master item of which this is but a lowly subitem

➤ Description that should appear on purchase forms when you buy this item

➤ Amount for which you purchase this item

➤ Expense account that will be charged with the cost of your purchase of this item

➤ Name of the place from which you're most likely to buy this item

➤ Description that should appear on sales forms when you sell this item

➤ Amount for which you hope to sell this item

➤ Whether or not the sale of this item is subject to sales tax

➤ Income account that should be increased by the amount of the sale when you sell this item

➤ Account where you keep track of the value of the items you have on hand

➤ Quantity of this item that you like to keep on hand

➤ How many of this item you have on hand today

➤ List of items to be contained in a common group

➤ Amount of a discount that you offer

➤ Method of payment

➤ Agency to which you pay sales tax

When you have finished entering all of this lugubrious information about your item, click **OK** to save your changes and close the window (or click **Next** if you want to enter another item). You can take solace in the fact that you never have to enter all this stuff again.

In the process of setting up QuickBooks to contain all the data pertinent to your business, it's a good idea to sit down and enter your items all at once. This saves you from having to do it later and makes it easier when it comes time to create an invoice or purchase order. You'll learn all about creating invoices and purchase orders in Chapter 8, "The Daily Grind."

Changes Are OK

The information you enter when you set up items is not written in stone. Should you change your mind about the way you want the item description to read on your form, should the price of the item change, should you feel the need to change the inventory reorder point—it doesn't matter what needs to be changed. You can always make changes by double-clicking on an item in the item list.

Changing Information About an Item

If you read the previous tip, you'll see I already gave this section away. No matter. Let me belabor the point a moment more.

Should you, for any reason, need to change (almost) any of the information associated with an item, you can do so by opening the item list (display the Lists menu and choose Items), finding the item you want to change, and double-clicking on the item name.

A window called Edit Item will appear (see the following figure) that looks remarkably like the New Item window, with one notable exception: *The Type field is dim!* That's right—once you've created an item, you can change any little piece of information about that item that your heart desires, but you can't change the Type of the item.

This means that if you set up your new line of ceramic bunnies but mistakenly called them a Sales Tax item instead of an Inventory Part item, you are prevented from changing the bunnies over to an Inventory Part item.

What's a bunny-seller to do? Hop over to the "Getting Rid of Items" section later in this chapter, and you will learn how to make mincemeat of your unwanted Sales Tax item.

Change information
about an existing item on
the Edit Item window.

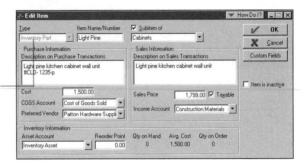

But what's this? You
can't change the Type
when editing an item

Playing Hide and Go Seek with Your Items

Sometimes items go out of fashion, or perhaps your items are seasonal and right now they're out of season. Or maybe you just have old items that you plan to retire. Whatever the reason, you can hide an item on your item list, so that you only have to look at the ones that are most current or interesting to you.

Items Can't Be Removed

Why hide an item instead of totally putting it out of its misery? If an item has been used in a transaction—even if it was only one little transaction in the entire lifetime of the item—QuickBooks won't let you do away with the item. Should you ever need to refer back to that transaction, the item must exist, or else QuickBooks will self-destruct trying to find it. (But take a look at "Getting Rid of Items" later in this chapter for additional assistance.)

To hide an item, start by opening the Item List window. Display the List menu and select **Items**. Next, click an item you would like to move out of the way. Click the **Item** button at the bottom of the list, and choose **Make Inactive** from the menu. The item appears to have disappeared from your list.

Let's have a show of hands for the inactive items.

Click here to turn on and off
the view of inactive items

But wait! Click the little **Show All** check box in the Item List window. Presto! Hidden items come floating back to life! There is a little hand next to each hidden item (see the previous figure). Click again, and the hand and the item disappear.

QuickBooks History

Here's a little QuickBooks trivia for those of you who are relatively new to the program. In earlier versions of QuickBooks, hidden list items were given a little ghost instead of a hand. The ghost was very cute and seemed much more representative of the state of partial existence that applies to hidden items. But, alas, we now have a hand.

Now you see it, now you don't.

Putting Items to Good Use

What good is an item if you can't have fun with it? I know, writing invoices and purchase forms may not be any fun for you, but the process would be a lot less fun if each time you created an invoice you had to type out the whole description of each item you wanted to sell, enter the price, figure out the total bill, and spell everything correctly.

Items are great time savers and make the entire sales process seem ever so much more professional (even if you are in the business of selling smoked buffalo chips or ceramic bunnies...). The following sections describe ways to put your item information to good use.

How Much Detail Do You Need with Your Item?

When you create your item, if you recall, you have the opportunity to enter a detailed description that will appear on your purchase forms and a different description that will appear on your sales forms.

The longer you spent entering your list of items, the shorter and less meaningful your descriptions might have become, as you yearned to complete the task. You may find, however, that there's good reason to take advantage of the Description field, especially the description that will appear on invoices. Remember—you only have to type it once (see the next figure)! Each time you place an item on an invoice, QuickBooks will go get the description that you painstakingly entered and place it *in toto* on your invoice.

Enter a thorough description of your item on the New Item window.

This description will appear on your purchase order and your bill

This description will appear on the invoice you give to your customer

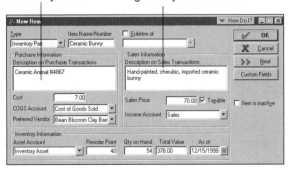

How Long Is Too Long?

You may wonder just how large a description you can enter in the Description field of an item. Frankly, I don't know. I devoted a small amount of time to entering letters in the Description area and got up to 1,500 characters before deciding enough is enough.

You can also use a narrative description to let the customer know what a thoroughly unique, high-quality, one-of-a-kind, throw-out-the-mold, hand-painted, ceramic bunny he is getting. The other stores might sell him a ceramic bunny. You're selling a masterpiece. The figure below shows what your description looks like in an invoice.

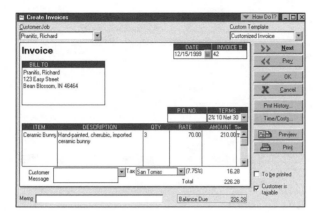

The description you entered when you set up the item flows onto the invoice.

Subtotaling with Items

Suppose you want to apply a discount to three of the four items your customer is purchasing. Or suppose there is a freight charge based on the value of two items, but not on the services you are selling at the same time. QuickBooks enables you to generate a subtotal right on the invoice (see the next figure). If you want to, you can then perform some sort of calculation based on that subtotal.

For example, let's say you are selling three ceramic bunnies and two ceramic burros, and you're charging a fee for interior decorating services. You need to apply a shipping charge to the ceramic items, which is calculated at 5% of the sales price of the items. However, you don't want the charge applied to the interior decorating services. You can subtotal the

Why a Subtotal? Why Not?

You don't need a reason for a subtotal, such as a need to apply a discount or shipping fee to some but not all of the items on an invoice. Sometimes it's just nice to see the subtotal of an invoice before the sales tax is added.

sales items in order to get a number on which to base the shipping fee (see the figure below) and leave the decorating services line out of the picture.

Use the Subtotal item to add all the items above the subtotal line.

Subtotal item

The shipping fee applies only to the subtotal amount, and then the additional fees are added after the shipping fee.

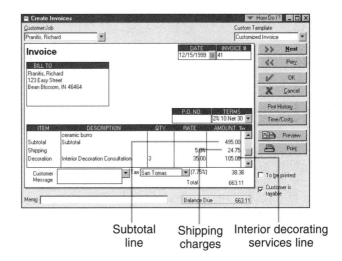

Subtotal   Shipping   Interior decorating
line   charges   services line

As shown in this example, I entered the ceramic items on my invoice form, and then entered a Subtotal item. QuickBooks adds all items above the subtotal line and places that amount on the line called Subtotal. I then added a shipping fee, which is calculated as a percentage of the line above—in this case the Subtotal. My interior decorating services are then entered as the last item on the invoice.

Order Is Everything

The order in which you enter invoice items is extremely important if you plan to use the Subtotal item. Enter the items to be subtotaled first, and then the Subtotal item. Subtotal adds everything above it, so don't enter items above the Subtotal line that aren't to be included in the subtotal.

Reports About Items

What would an item be without a report about it? QuickBooks gives you several types of item-ish reports from which you can choose. You can access these reports from the Item List window (open the Lists menu on the menu bar and choose Items). From the Item List window, click the Reports button, as shown in the next figure.

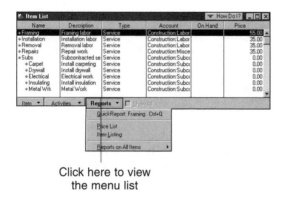

Click here to view
the menu list

Use the Reports window in any list window to view a menu of reports you can choose from.

Here are a few item reports that might interest you:

➤ The Inventory Item QuickReport displays all the purchases and sales of an item from the beginning of time, how many of the item are currently on order, and how many are on hand (see the figure below). To display the report, click an item in the Item List window, click the Reports button, and then choose QuickReport—or just press Ctrl+Q.

Use an Item QuickReport to see all the activity and the inventory status of an item.

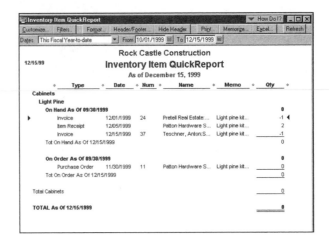

➤ The Price List report shows all your items and the price you charge for those items. To display this report, click the **Reports** button and choose **Price List**.

➤ The Item Listing report shows every item and everything you ever wanted to know about it, including description, price, quantity on hand, quantity on order, cost, whether or not it's taxable, and so on. To display this report, click the **Reports** button and choose **Item Listing**.

Then, there is Reports on All Items (found at the bottom of the Reports button menu), where you can choose from sales reports, purchase reports, inventory reports, and more—all organized by item. Poke around in these reports to get a feel for what looks interesting to you.

Getting Rid of Items

Now for the fun stuff. Remember I told you earlier that you can't delete an item? Fooled you! This section tells you how to break the rules and remove items you truly don't want to see again. Mind you, it's sneaky, but it gets the job done.

Bad Dog! No More Items for You!

Don't let those unwanted items get in your way! You too can be rid of unwanted soap scum and mildew (not to mention overpriced ceramic bunnies!) Open the Item List window (display the Lists menu and choose **Items**) and get ready to lay waste to items you no longer use.

Click an item you don't want anymore, and then click the **Item** button at the bottom of the list window and choose **Delete** (or simply press **Ctrl+D** on the keyboard). It's easy so far, right?

Okay, time for your first obstacle. You may see a message (see the accompanying figure) telling you that you have no business deleting this item because once upon a time there were some transactions involving this item and—well, we don't want to go into detail about just what those transactions might have been, but I'm sure you can imagine...

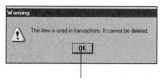

This little message stands in the way of your deleting an item.

Hmmm. It appears you have no choice but to click here...

If it happens that this item has never been involved in any transactions, QuickBooks will ask you if you're sure you want to delete the item (see the next figure), and the item will disappear when you click OK. (If QuickBooks doesn't let you delete the item, scurry to the next section to see how to get around this sticky problem.)

You're only a click away from permanently removing this item.

Merging Items

That delete trick didn't work for you? Then here's your alternative. It's a little more complicated than a simple Ctrl+D, but the end result is actually very elegant.

Let's say we have a burning desire to remove ceramic bunnies from our item list, but there have been some transactions involving ceramic bunnies, so we can't just delete the bunnies. Instead, we can choose to merge the bunnies into another item on the list—Home décor, for example. The effect is that all the baggage that goes with the bunnies gets moved over to the Home décor item and poof! The bunnies are history!

A Part for a Part

When merging items, you must merge items with other items of the same kind—no cross-breeding allowed.

Here's how the merge works:

1. Click the item you want to remove from the Item List window (such as ceramic bunnies).

2. Press **Ctrl+E** to open the Edit Item window (or click the **Item** button and choose **Edit**).

3. Change the name of the unwanted item to match exactly the name of the item into which you will merge (such as Home décor). Nothing else needs to change (see the figure below).

Change the item name to the item into which you want to merge.

Notice you can't change the type

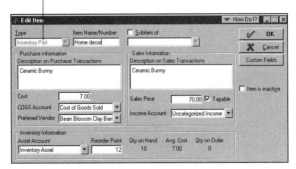

What's in a Name?

Everything, when it comes to merging. When changing the name of an item in preparation for a merge, be very careful to enter the name of the item into which you are merging *exactly* as it appears on the merge item.

4. Click **OK**. QuickBooks is going to tell you that you're trying to use a name that belongs to another item, but then it will ask you if you want to merge the two (see the next figure).

Click Yes *and your two items will become one (and live happily ever after).*

5. Click Yes! Your bunnies have left the building, and all bunny history is now part of Home décor.

Should you have occasion to pay a visit to a transaction that originally featured a ceramic bunny, you will see that the name of the item on that transaction has been transformed into Home décor.

Now You've Done It!

Now that you've mastered the material about items, you're ready for anything! Just look at all you learned in this chapter:

➤ QuickBooks classifies everything your company sells and purchases into animals called *items*. See "The Way QuickBooks Sees the World."

➤ Setting up new items is a bit time consuming, but definitely worth the effort. See "Creating Your Own Items."

➤ Use items on your forms, use them in subtotals, see reports about them—the possibilities are endless! See "Putting Items to Good Use."

➤ Remove items you no longer need or use. See "Getting Rid of Items."

Chapter 5

Time Travel, QuickBooks Style: Entering Historical Data

In This Chapter

➤ How to handle your business history

➤ The order in which to enter information into QuickBooks

➤ How to enter bills, invoices, payments, and other record-keeping items

If you are new to using QuickBooks, you have one of two choices to make right now (providing you did everything in Chapter 1, "Doing the EasyStep Tango," already). You can either begin entering your business information in QuickBooks as of the date you install the program, or you can go back to an earlier date and play catchup. Either way, this chapter is the place to be if you want to know how to enter your business history. Hurry up and get started—your historical clock is ticking!

Getting Historical

When it comes to entering business data in QuickBooks, the farther back you go in terms of dates, the more historical information about your company you will have stored in QuickBooks. Historical information is everything financial that happened to your company from your start date to today. (Of course, if your start date is today, you've got nothing to worry about.) What's the difference whether you start recording information today or go back to pick up data from months or even years gone by? Allow me to explain.

If you start using QuickBooks today without entering any financial history, you'll save scads of hours that would have been spent poring over old invoices and deposit slips and entering tedious information about events that occurred sometime in the past. If you go back and enter everything that has transpired in your company since last January 1 or since the first day you started doing business (or some other date that is meaningful to you), you will have complete financial records that give you a thorough picture of how your company is doing. You will also have the ability to produce financial statements that cover a greater period of time and that compare current company activity to prior time periods.

If you choose to skip entering your financial history now, you can always go back to some point in your company's past and enter historical information at a later time. Regardless of whether you get historic now or later, the remainder of this chapter will tell you everything you need to know to get the job done.

The Order of Business

As with most of life's little tasks, there's a right way and a wrong way to enter historical information in QuickBooks. Entering financial records properly is sometimes best left to those compulsive types who like to keep their sock drawers color coordinated. Follow the rules and you won't get hurt. Step out of line and you may find you have some extra cleaning up to do in your QuickBooks file (not to mention that you may be wearing socks that don't match).

The following six sections present the proper order for entering historical information in QuickBooks.

Entering Your Bills

First things first. The first type of information you need to enter in QuickBooks is the bills that have come into your company from the start date to today. You'll enter those amounts first because all of your other business (the payments you make and the amounts you receive for items or services you sell) stems from the purchases you make.

You can find a lot of detailed information about entering bills in the "Paying Your Bills" section of Chapter 8, "The Daily Grind," but basically here's what you want to do:

➤ First, find all of your bills. For some of you, this may be the hardest part of this chapter (particularly if you store your bills in unmarked shoeboxes under the desk or in a closet).

➤ Next, put all the bills in some logical order. The easiest way to organize your bills is probably in order of the date that appears on the bills. A better way might be to put them in order of the dates on which you received the bills, but you can do that only if you date-stamped the bills when they arrived.

➤ Finally, open the Enter Bills screen in QuickBooks, shown in the next figure. Display the **Activities** menu and select **Enter Bills**. If you prefer using QuickBooks Navigator, click the **Purchases and Vendors** tab and then click the **Enter Bills** icon.

What Happened to the Menu Choice?

From time to time you may find yourself searching in vain for a menu selection you thought was on either the Activities or the Lists menu. Both of these menus have some movable choices, which will appear either on the main menu or on the Other option on the menu. This happens based on decisions that are made elsewhere in the program. To locate missing menu choices, check under the Other Lists and Other Activities menu options. You'll probably find the menu choice hiding in the submenu.

Enter name of vendor
in this area

*Enter bills in QuickBooks
using the Enter Bills form.*

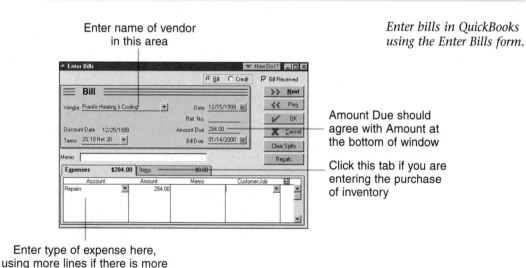

Amount Due should
agree with Amount at
the bottom of window

Click this tab if you are
entering the purchase
of inventory

Enter type of expense here,
using more lines if there is more
than one type of expense

➤ Go ahead and enter all the information from each bill, from the earliest to the most recent. Click **Next** to advance each time. Click **OK** if you're finished entering bills.

Note that when entering your old bills, you are just entering the information on the bills—not when you paid them or how much you paid. That step comes later.

Entering Your Invoices

The next step in getting your historical information into QuickBooks is to enter all the invoices you issued from the start date to the present. You'll find more detailed information for entering invoices in the "Selling Merchandise and Services" section of Chapter 8, but here is essentially what you need to know:

Using QuickBooks Navigator?

To open the Create Invoices window from QuickBooks Navigator, click the **Sales and Customers** tab, then click the **Invoices** icon.

➤ Collect all the invoices you can find from your start date up to today. Even if you voided an invoice, include that in the stack so that the numbers will follow in the proper order.

➤ Speaking of numbers, it's a good idea to put your invoices in numerical order, starting with the oldest on top and the most recent invoice at the bottom of the pile.

➤ Open the Create Invoices window by displaying the **Activities** menu and choosing **Create Invoices** (or just press **Ctrl+I** if you don't feel like using your mouse). The following figure shows what the Create Invoices window looks like.

Use the Create Invoices window to record each invoice you have stockpiled.

Customer name and job (if applicable) go here

Click here to proceed to the next invoice

Click here if you're finished entering invoices

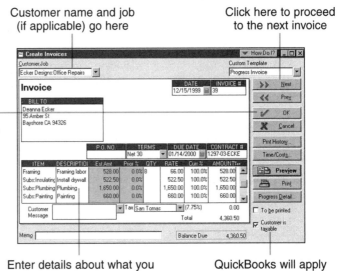

Enter details about what you are selling to this customer

QuickBooks will apply sales tax if this is a taxable sale

➤ Proceed to enter all the information from each invoice in order of invoice numbers. Click **Next** to move to the next invoice. When you're finished, click **OK** or press the **Enter** key.

Keeping Track of Cash Sales

If yours is a cash business, such as a retail store or a restaurant, you may have some form of daily or weekly cash summaries instead of invoices to enter. See "Entering Cash Sales," below, and "The Cash Business" in Chapter 8 for more information about entering your cash sales in QuickBooks.

By the way, if you already entered some invoices that were outstanding when you went through the EasyStep Interview, you can skip those invoices now.

Entering All That Money You Collected

However you receive your money—whether in the form of checks, stacks of bills, rolls of coins, credit card charges, traveler's checks, or wire cash transfers—you're going to need to record all that revenue in QuickBooks. Since you've already entered all of your invoices, you may find that recording cash is simply a matter of checking off those amounts on a screen QuickBooks provides for just that purpose. Here are the basic steps:

➤ Gather all the receipts and records you have of money you received since the start date. This information might be in the form of a receipt book, paper vouchers, or lists that accompany your bank deposits.

➤ Order this information so that the earliest amounts are first.

➤ Open the **Activities** menu and choose **Receive Payments**. This opens the Receive Payments window, as shown in the next figure. To open the window from QuickBooks Navigator, click the **Sales and Customers** tab, then click the **Receive Payments** icon.

Entering bills in QuickBooks happens through the Receive Payments window.

Use this drop-down arrow to select the customer

Enter the amount received here

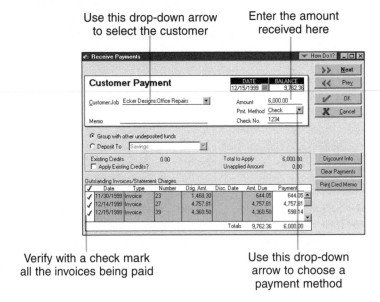

Verify with a check mark all the invoices being paid

Use this drop-down arrow to choose a payment method

➤ Choose the customer for whom you wish to enter money that you received. All invoices you entered for this customer will be listed at the bottom of the window.

➤ Make sure the amount at the top of the window matches the amount at the bottom, then click the **Pmt. Method** drop-down list to indicate the payment method.

➤ At the bottom of the window, place a check mark next to any invoice for which you want to record payment. Adjust the total in the Payment column if necessary.

➤ Click **Next** to proceed to the next Receive Payments window, or click **OK** to record your transaction and close the window.

Learn more about entering cash, checks, and charges in the "Getting Paid" section of Chapter 8.

Credits and Discounts

If you issued credits to any of your customers since the start date, you need to enter that information next. For example, a customer might have received some defective merchandise, for which you gave him a credit to offset the amount you previously invoiced.

It may also be the case that you give your customers discounts if they make payment early or if they bring you new business. Here's how to handle both scenarios:

➤ Assemble the records of credits and discounts issued since the start date.

➤ To enter discount information, first return to the Receive Payments window (open the **Activities** menu and select **Receive Payments**, or click the **Receive Payments** icon on the **Sales and Customers** tab in QuickBooks Navigator). The figure below shows the Payment window.

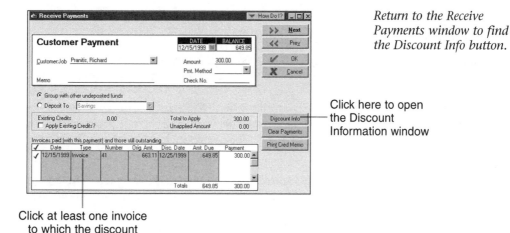

Return to the Receive Payments window to find the Discount Info button.

Click here to open the Discount Information window

Click at least one invoice to which the discount should apply

➤ Select the appropriate Customer:Job name (if applicable), select at least one invoice from those that appear at the bottom of the screen, then click the **Discount Info** button. This opens the Discount Information window (see the next figure).

Give the customer a break by filling out the Discount Information box.

Verify the discount amount here

➤ Enter a discount amount, then click **OK**. You're returned to the Receive Payments window. Click **Next** to enter additional discounts to other customers or **OK** to close the window.

➤ Entering credits is another story. To enter credits, open the **Activities** menu and choose **Create Credit Memos/Refunds**.

➤ Choose the customer and job, then enter credits in the bottom part of the window, just as you would enter sales. Click **Next** to keep entering credits or click **OK** to close the window.

Entering Cash Sales

You may receive real cash in your business (you know the stuff: green bills with funny faces on them—those new bills with the great big faces are especially funny). Cash can also be in the form of checks or credit cards. Basically, by cash sales I mean sales for which you did not previously issue an invoice. This cash may relate to a specific customer and job, or you may make cash sales to people you greet over the counter and never get to know their names. Either way, you will enter the cash on the Enter Cash Sales form. Here's what to do:

➤ Gather the information you have that supports your cash sales since your start date. This may be a cash journal, a pile of cash vouchers, daily or weekly summary sheets listing your cash sales, or the information from your daily deposit slips.

➤ Place this information in order so that the earliest cash sales (the sales closest to your start date) are available first.

➤ Open the **Activities** menu and choose **Enter Cash Sales**. The Enter Cash Sales window will appear (see the figure below). If you're using the QuickBooks Navigator tool, click the **Sales and Customers** tab and then click the **Cash Sales** icon.

Use the Enter Cash Sales window if you haven't previously invoiced the customer for this sale.

Make sure the date agrees with the date on which the sale took place

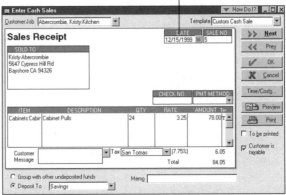

80

➤ Enter all information relating to cash sales in order, from the start date to the present. Click Next to proceed from one form to the next. When you're all done, click OK.

Entering Payments You Made

If you completed all the previous sections, all of your bills have been entered in the system, and all of the money you received is there, too. This is a good time to show where the money went. Get out your check register so that you can enter all the payments you have made since your start date. Start entering.

➤ Open the **Activities** menu and choose **Pay Bills.** (QuickBooks Navigator users can click the **Purchases and Vendors** tab, then click the **Pay Bills** icon.) The Pay Bills window appears, as shown in the next figure.

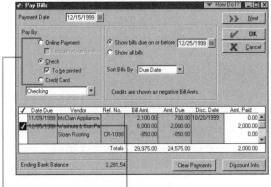

All bills currently due are listed in the Pay Bills window.

Check off the bills you want to record as being paid

Indicate the account to which the payment is to be charged

➤ In the Pay Bills window, make sure the date is right and the account designation is correct, then check off the bills that were paid with each payment.

➤ Click Next to progress from one payment to the next. Click OK when you have entered all bill payments.

For more detailed information about paying bills, see "Paying Your Bills" in Chapter 8.

Entering Your Bank Deposits

The next step to getting all your historical information into QuickBooks is to enter the actual bank deposits you have made. The previous section involved entering the money you received, so this part should follow naturally. Ready? Let's go.

➤ Get out your bank deposit slips or summary sheets that accompanied your deposits, and organize this information in order, from your start date to the present.

➤ Open the **Activities** menu and choose **Make Deposits**, and the Payments to Deposit window will appear, as shown in the following figure. If you're using QuickBooks Navigator to navigate the program, you can click the **Checking and Credit Cards** tab, then click the **Deposits** icon.

When entering historical information, this Payments to Deposit list can be quite large. Check off all the items that constitute one deposit.

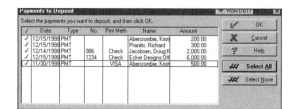

➤ Check off the deposits you want to enter for this transaction, then click **OK**.

➤ The Make Deposits window makes its appearance next. Verify that the date and bank account information are correct. Click **Next** to record the transaction and move on to the next.

Verify the date and total amount of the deposit you are recording, as well as the account to which the money is to be deposited.

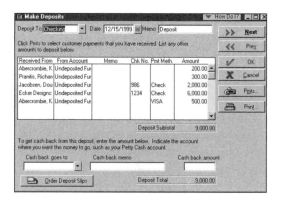

➤ When you are finished entering all your deposits, click **OK** to close the window.

For more detailed instructions about entering amounts you deposit, see "Putting Money into the Bank" in Chapter 9, "Quick Guide to Banking with QuickBooks."

Entering Your Payroll

Entering payroll is a little more involved than entering all the other historical stuff. You need to enter each paycheck than has been issued since the start date. Furthermore, if your start date is sometime after January 1, you really need to go back to the start of the year and enter year-to-date payroll information for all of your employees, or else you won't be able to produce accurate year-end forms, such as W-2 forms and the federal 940 form.

When you're ready, follow along with this list:

➤ Start this process by collecting all paychecks written since the first day of the year, or since your start date if that is later.

➤ Also collect all information about payroll tax payments you have made since the first of the year.

➤ QuickBooks will walk you through the procedure for entering the information. To get started, open the **Activities** menu and choose **Payroll**, **Set Up YTD Amounts**. Begin by entering your start date, as shown in the figure below (you may need to click **Next** to get to this screen). The start date is the date on which the payroll information should be reflected in your QuickBooks accounts and the date on which you will actually start using QuickBooks to write paychecks. Click **Next** to move to the next screen.

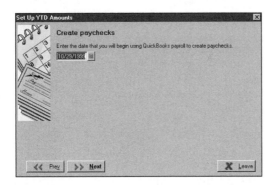

Make sure the dates agree with your plans for entering payroll in QuickBooks.

➤ Next you will enter the year-to-date payroll information for each of your employees. This may involve several screens; just click **Next** to move from one to the next.

➤ After entering individual employee information, click the **Create** button that appears. This opens a window where you can enter the payments you've already made during the year for payroll taxes.

Enter Your Employees First!

Note that you must have all of your employees already set up in QuickBooks before you can begin entering year-to-date information for them. If you need to set up additional employees, open the **Lists** menu and choose **Employees**, and then press **Ctrl+N** to open the New Employee window. You can read up on setting up employees in Chapter 16, "Figuring Out Your Payroll."

Show the payment date and the amounts paid for payroll taxes.

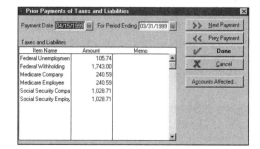

➤ Click **OK** when all payroll taxes are entered, then click the **Done** button, then click **Finish** to end the procedure.

And So On...

At this point you're probably ready for a nice QuickBooks break. (I know I am.) Before you leave, take a look at one more area of your financial records. If you have written any checks since the start date that haven't yet been recorded, now is the time to record them. This would be checks that were written that didn't go toward bills or payroll.

What kind of checks? Maybe you write a check to your landlord each month for rent, or perhaps you made some purchases without a related bill. In any case, all payments that haven't been included in your QuickBooks records must now be entered.

➤ Open the **Activities** menu and choose **Write Checks**, or click the **Checking and Credit Cards** tab in QuickBooks Navigator, then click **Checks**. A window opens that displays an actual check form.

➤ Enter the appropriate information on this form for each payment you want to record, from the start date to the present, clicking Next to continue adding payments. When you're finished, click OK to exit the window.

For more details on writing checks in QuickBooks, see "Writing Checks" in Chapter 9.

Now You've Done It!

This chapter is chock full of information about how you can get started in QuickBooks if you need to go back to an earlier date to catch up your records. In particular, you learned

➤ The order of events for entering historical information, so that you can proceed in an efficient manner when entering records for past activity. See "The Order of Business."

➤ Techniques for entering all the transactions that occurred in your company from the start date to the present. See "Entering Your Bills" and other "Entering..." sections.

Chapter 6

Charting Your Accounts and General Journal Entries

In This Chapter

➤ How to use the Chart of Accounts

➤ How to delete and hide old accounts

➤ More than you'll ever need to know about journal entries

Having fun yet? It won't stop with this chapter. To keep your business data organized, you can't beat QuickBooks' Chart of Accounts. It's home base for checking everything you've kept track of. And when it comes time to adjust amounts in your accounts, use QuickBooks General Journal Entry feature. This chapter covers both of these highly anticipated topics. What are you waiting for? Let the good times begin!

Boring Accounting Stuff: The Chart of Accounts

Yes, I did try to make QuickBooks' Chart of Accounts sound more exciting than it necessarily is in the chapter introduction, but it's not really as boring as you might think, either. The *Chart of Accounts* is a listing of all the accounts that you use to keep track of your financial comings and goings. *Accounts* is the name given to the categories that describe the types of financial activity that exist in your business.

Chart of Accounts

A group of categories into which you will categorize your company's income, expenses, debts, and assets so that you can make sense of all your business transactions in the form of professional-looking financial statements.

For example, if you are in the pet boarding business, you might have accounts to keep track of expenses such as pet food, waste disposal, and tetanus shots for your employees (just kidding… or maybe not). If you are in the catering business, you might want to monitor your costs for serving dishes, food, cookbooks, and that sort of thing. You get the picture, right?

Why Do We Need Accounts, Anyway?

Using accounts as a method of keeping track of your finances gives you the opportunity to see exactly where your income comes from and what your money is being used for. By providing detailed information, accounts enable you to analyze how your business operates and make informed decisions.

The alternative is to take all your money, put it in your bank account, and then spend it without having a clue as to how much you have earned and where it all goes. In this situation, the only useful information you would have would be the balance on your bank statement.

If your business is doing well, you shouldn't be happy merely to have cash in the bank. You should want to know why the business is succeeding, where your profit areas are, which expenses are being kept under control, what types of customers are providing you with business, and so on.

On the other hand, if your business is not performing up to expectations, you will want to determine where the shortfall is and what can be done to improve your business. You can gain knowledge about the performance of your business by comparing your financial statements, which list your various accounts, to prior year financial statements of your own and to statements of other companies in the same industry. One of the best ways to make this type of analysis is with the use of a budget, which is discussed in Chapter 18, "Making and Saving (and Actually Using) Budgets."

Creating a Useful Chart of Accounts

All right, so you've decided that a Chart of Accounts would be helpful. How do you begin? Actually, QuickBooks takes the pain out of this process by giving you a head start on your Chart of Accounts. Unless you're completely ahead of the game and already have a Chart of Accounts, you can use the standard QuickBooks Chart of Accounts for your industry. This standard Chart of Accounts is offered to you when you go through the rigors of the EasyStep Interview (see "A Jump Start for Your Chart of Accounts" in Chapter 1, "Doing the EasyStep Tango").

If you chose the standard Chart of Accounts when setting up your company, there are several accounts already in place, and you can see a list of them by pressing **Ctrl+A** at any time. Even if you don't have any accounts set up, you can view the empty account list by pressing **Ctrl+A** (see the following figure).

Other Routes to Your Accounts

Another way to open the Chart of Accounts is to display the Lists menu and choose **Chart of Accounts**, or click the **Company** tab in QuickBooks Navigator, and then click **Chart of Accounts**.

A bare Chart of Accounts window.

Click here and choose
New when you're ready to
set up a new account

Whether you start with the accounts QuickBooks offers or use your own accounts, you should consider what types of accounts will best describe your business and tell you what you need to know about how your business is operating. No one knows your business better than you do, but there are advisors in the accounting profession and experienced people in your own profession who can help you determine which items should be tracked in their own accounts.

There are five basic types of accounts: assets, liabilities, equity, income, and expenses. Each type of account is described briefly in the accompanying table and in more detail in the following sections. The specific accounts within these types that you choose to use in your business will be determined by the type of business you do and the financial items that are important to you.

Types of Accounts

Account Type	Description
Asset	Significant stuff that your company owns that you expect will have some lasting value, like buildings and cars and computers (even though those don't seem to last that long).
Liability	Amounts you owe to others. This includes ongoing amounts like the electric bill and magazine subscriptions, and also the big loans like mortgages and equipment loans.
Equity	A somewhat esoteric concept in accounting—the equity accounts represent the value of your business in terms of net profit over the years.
Income	Income is the money your company earns You want to have lots of income.
Expense	An expense is the cost of doing business— money spent in order to help you earn more income.

Liquid (as Opposed to Solid?) Assets

The term *liquid assets* is applied to cash and other assets that are expected to be used up (spent) within one year or within the current operating cycle. What's an operating cycle? It is the amount of time it takes to acquire (or create) and sell your product.

Asset Accounts

Assets are the items that your company owns. This might include company vehicles, cash, investments, equipment, buildings, amounts you have invoiced but haven't been paid (accounts receivable), or employee advances.

Asset accounts are the account names that you choose to help keep track of your assets. Usually the amount in an asset account reflects the cost of the asset.

Sometimes asset accounts are offset by amounts that reflect the change in value of the asset over time. For example, as equipment wears out, it may no longer be worth its original cost. Depreciation expense is used to offset the equipment asset account so that the amount that appears on your financial statement more closely represents the true value of the equipment. (Depreciation is explained in greater detail in Chapter 12, "Everything You'd Rather Not Know About Depreciation.")

Liability Accounts

Liabilities are amounts you owe to others. Liabilities can include loans from a bank or a person, bills you haven't paid (accounts payable), and other debts.

Liability accounts are the account names that you use to describe these amounts. The amount in a liability account represents the exact amount you owe. If you owe money on a loan, for example, you will reduce the loan liability account each time you make a payment on the loan.

Short-Term and Long-Term Liabilities

Your balance sheet should reflect both short-term (due within one year) and long-term (due in more than a year) liabilities.

Equity Accounts

Simply described, *equity* is the difference between your assets and your liabilities. Equity accounts include capital stock accounts, owners' draw accounts, and accumulated earnings (often called *retained earnings*) of the company.

At the end of each year, you will determine your company's net income or loss by deducting your total expenses from your income accounts (described next). The amount you get from this calculation will be used to increase (if you had net income) or decrease (if you had a net loss) your retained earnings account.

Income Accounts

The revenue that your company earns is called *income* and is described on your financial statements in various accounts that represent the types of income you receive. If your company sells merchandise, your income may be described as *Sales Income*. If you provide legal services, your income may be described as *Legal Fees*. If you earn interest on investments, you will probably have an *Interest Income* account.

Security Deposits—Are They Income or Assets?

If you're in the business of renting real estate or equipment and you take a security deposit, is it income? The rule is this: If you treat the deposit as if it is rent for the last month of the lease, the deposit is income. If you intend to return the deposit when all obligations under the lease are met, the deposit is an asset.

Expense Accounts

The costs of running your business are called *expenses*. The descriptions you use for your expense accounts will be derived from the types of expenditures you make. In addition to expenses such as rent, payroll, utilities, and office supplies—expenses shared by most businesses—you may have expenses unique to your own business, such as laundry expense, computer services, paint supplies, or pest removal.

There is generally more variety on financial statements in the area of expenses than any other type of account. You will need to analyze your company's spending habits (or anticipated spending habits, if yours is a new company) to determine the types of expense accounts that will do the best job of describing your spending activities.

Setting Up a New Account

You've read all about these accounts. Here's a chance to see what they look like on a sample account list. Take a look at the next figure.

Here's what your list of accounts might look like.

Rick's Diner
Account Listing
March 4, 1999

Account	Type
Checking	Bank
Accounts Receivable	Accounts Receivable
Inventory	Other Current Asset
Inventory:Beverages	Other Current Asset
Inventory:Food	Other Current Asset
Inventory:Supplies	Other Current Asset
Inventory Asset	Other Current Asset
China, silver glass and linen	Fixed Asset
Furniture	Fixed Asset
Truck	Fixed Asset
Accounts Payable	Accounts Payable
Bank Line of Credit	Credit Card
Gift certificates	Other Current Liability
Payroll Liabilities	Other Current Liability
Sales Tax Payable	Other Current Liability
Equipment Loan	Long Term Liability
Capital Stock	Equity
Retained Earnings	Equity
Catering	Income
Fees	Income
Promotional Sales	Income
Sales	Income
Sales:Beverages	Income
Sales:Food	Income
Services	Income
Cost of Goods Sold	Cost of Goods Sold
Automobile Expense	Expense
Bank Service Charges	Expense
Cost of sales	Expense
Cost of sales:Beverage	Expense

When you're ready to create a new account in QuickBooks, follow these steps:

1. Press **Ctrl+A** or display the Lists menu and choose **Chart of Accounts** to open the Chart of Accounts window. If you're using QuickBooks Navigator, click the **Company** tab, and then click **Chart of Accounts** at the top of the window.

2. Press **Ctrl+N** or click the **Account** button at the bottom of the window and select **New**. The New Account window will appear, as shown in the next figure.

Click here to choose from a list of account types

New accounts get their start here.

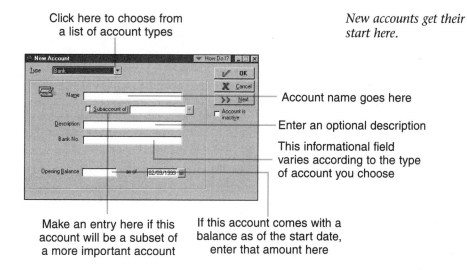

Account name goes here

Enter an optional description

This informational field varies according to the type of account you choose

Make an entry here if this account will be a subset of a more important account

If this account comes with a balance as of the start date, enter that amount here

3. Click the **Types** drop-down arrow to display a list of account types, and then pick one that will best describe the account you plan to create.

4. Fill in the name and other information that applies to this account.

5. Click **Next** if you want to enter another new account, or click **OK** to save this account and close the window.

Say Sayonara to This Account

You can remove an account from QuickBooks, if you play the game right. An account that has a zero balance (see the Chart of Accounts window in the figure below) and has had no activity can be removed by clicking on the account name and pressing **Ctrl+D** (or clicking the **Account** button and choosing **Delete**). QuickBooks will ask you if you are sure you want to delete the account. Click **OK**, and the account is gone for good.

*Remove an active
account by deleting it or
merging it into another
account.*

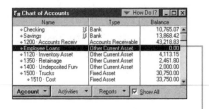

Even though an account balance
may be zero, there might have
been transactions in the account
that prevent you from deleting it

The process of removing an account is a little trickier if there is a balance in the
account, or if there have been some transactions going through this account in the
past. You don't exactly delete an account like this. Instead, you slyly *merge* the
account you no longer want into an existing account. All the past transactions associated with the account get transferred to the account into which you are merging, and
then the original account is removed from the Chart of Accounts.

To merge an account (which I'll call the *old* account) into another account (the *new*
account), click the old account name, and then press **Ctrl+E** (or click the **Account**
button and select **Edit**). The Edit Account window appears; in this window you will
change the name of the old account to match the name of the new account. Make
sure the spelling is exactly like that of the new account. Click **OK** and you'll be asked
if you want to merge the old account into the new account. Click **Yes** and you're in
business.

Hiding an Account

An alternative to getting rid of an account altogether is to simply hide the account so
that it no longer appears on your Chart of Accounts. This process is simple and easily
reversible if you decide you want to have the account back.

From the Chart of Accounts window, click the name of the account you want to hide.
Click the **Account** button and select **Make Inactive**. The account name seems to
disappear from your Chart of Accounts. But wait! Click the **Show All** check box in
the Chart of Accounts window. The account you made inactive reappears with a little
hand next to its name (see the following figure).

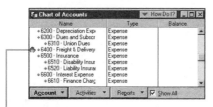

Click Show All to display hidden accounts.

This little hand indicates
the account can be hidden
again by unchecking the
Show All box

Turning On (or Off) Account Numbers

QuickBooks provides you with the ability to number your accounts. You can either use a standard numbering scheme provided by QuickBooks or create your own numbering scheme based on whatever method seems reasonable to you.

In either case, you must turn on the account numbering feature in the Preferences window. Follow these steps to learn how:

1. Display the File menu and choose **Preferences** to open the Preferences window.
2. Click the **Accounting** icon at the left.
3. Click the **Company Preferences** tab at the top of the window.
4. Click the **Use account numbers** check box.
5. Click **OK** to exit the window and implement the change.

How to Use Account Numbers

When you use account numbers in QuickBooks, the account number becomes part of the account name. Since many reports are organized by account name, you can use account numbers to control the order in which accounts appear on your reports. Instead of alphabetically, your accounts will be ordered numerically.

If you look at the Chart of Accounts window now (press **Ctrl+A**), you will see account numbers listed at the left of each account name (see the next figure).

Account numbers appear at the left of each account name.

To enter or change an account number, click an account name, and then press **Ctrl+E** to edit the account (you can also click the **Account** button and choose **Edit** from the menu). There is a field at the top of the Edit Account window for **Number** (see the following figure). Make any necessary changes to this number, and then press **OK** to close the window.

The Number field appears only when account numbers have been turned on.

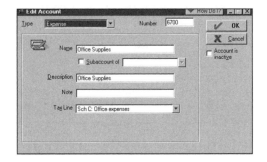

After setting up account numbers, you may find you no longer want to use them. Go back to the Preferences window (**File, Preferences**) and uncheck the **Use account numbers** box that you checked previously. At some point in the future, if you decide to turn on account numbers again, you will be pleased to find that all the account numbers you assigned previously are still saved.

More Boring Accounting Stuff: General Journal Entries

You may never need to use general journal entries. A general journal entry is a method of adjusting the amounts in two or more accounts. Most companies use general journal entries from time to time, but many people have their accountants take care of this for them.

General Journal Entry

In a traditional accounting system (traditional meaning "written by hand with lots of eraser bits getting in the way"), changes in the value of accounts were recorded in a journal, and then the amounts from the journal were transferred to the proper account. The transactions entered in the General Journal (so called because it contained transactions of many different sorts) are called *general journal entries.*

General journal entries aren't difficult though. You can make a general journal entry whenever you need to make an adjustment that doesn't lend itself to one of the standard accounting forms (such as an invoice, purchase order, or bill).

When Will I Use a General Journal Entry?

A common reason to make a general journal entry at the end of the year (or more frequently, depending on when your company needs financial statements) is to reflect depreciation expense (you'll find more about depreciation expense in Chapter 12). Here's how a simple general journal entry works:

1. Open the Activities menu and choose **Make Journal Entry**. If you're using QuickBooks Navigator, click the **Taxes and Accountant** tab and click **Make Journal Entry**. The General Journal Entry window will appear, as shown in the next figure.

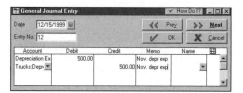

Use the General Journal Entry window to add a general journal entry to an account.

2. Verify the date and enter an optional number for your entry.
3. In the Account area, click the drop-down arrow and choose an account (Depreciation Expense, for example).
4. Enter the amount of the entry in either the Debit or Credit column, whichever is appropriate.

5. Enter an offsetting amount on the next line by clicking in the **Account** column again and choosing another account (Accumulated Depreciation, for example), and then entering the appropriate amount in the Debit or Credit column.

6. Click **OK** to close the General Journal Entry window or **Next** to continue to another entry.

In the land of journal entries (and for that matter, in accounting in general), all debits and all credits must equal each other in the end. A journal entry may have several debits and several credits, there may be only one debit or one credit, or maybe you'll have one debit and several credits. The mix of debits and credits doesn't matter, as long as all the debits add up to the same amount as all the credits. QuickBooks will let you know if your journal entry is out of balance and won't let you proceed until you have made the two sides of the entry equal.

Or Use an Opening Balances Journal Entry

An alternative to using the EasyStep Interview when setting up a new company in QuickBooks is to skip the Interview, set up your Chart of Accounts (as described earlier in this chapter), and then make a journal entry to adjust the balance of all accounts to the balance as of your start date.

Your accountant can provide you with year-end adjustments that need to be entered as journal entries. Another common situation that calls for a general journal entry has to do with the Opening Balance Equity account. This is an account created by QuickBooks to offset any opening balances assigned to balance sheet accounts. Information you enter during the EasyStep Interview, such as the value of fixed assets or the amount of accounts payable, is offset in the Opening Balance Equity account.

This Opening Balance Equity account should not appear on your company financial statements. It should be zeroed out by using a general journal entry to remove the total in the Opening Balance Equity account and offset the amount in your Retained Earnings account.

General Journal Entries Pitfalls

General journal entries are pretty straightforward, but there are a couple of things you should watch out for when working with these animals. Here's a rundown:

➤ First, QuickBooks will not automatically number general journal entries for you. That doesn't mean you shouldn't assign some numbering scheme to your journal entries. Choose a starting number that makes sense to you. You can start with 1 or 100 or use 9901 to reflect the year and the entry number, or 990201 to reflect the year (99), the quarter (02), and the entry number. Then, as you create more journal entries, enter progressive numbers.

➤ Even when you assign a journal entry number, QuickBooks won't carry that number forward to your next journal entry. (Bummer.) When you open the General Journal Entry window, you can click the Prev button to view the previous journal entry and see where you left off on numbering. Then click Next to go back to the new entry.

➤ Another problem I've had with journal entries is that, once I enter a description in the Memo column of the entry, I want to repeat that description on the other lines of the entry. This can be accomplished easily with a copy and paste method. To repeat a memo description, highlight the description that you've entered on the first line of the entry. Open the Edit menu and select Copy from the menu (or press Ctrl+C). When you are ready to enter a memo on subsequent lines of your journal entry, open the Edit menu and select Paste (or press Ctrl+V) each time you want to repeat the memo.

Take a Look at Your Journal Entries

It's important to know what adjustments you have made to your financial records. You can always double-click a number that appears on a report and view the original form or journal entry from which that number originates. I recommend going a step further and keeping hard copies of reports that list your journal entries, so that at any time you can view the changes you have made.

Prepare a journal entry report by following these steps:

1. Open the Reports menu and choose Transaction Detail Reports, By Date.
2. The report that appears shows all transactions for a designated time period, and you will need to extract just the journal entry transactions from this report. To perform this extraction, known as a *filter*, click the Filters button at the top of the report.
3. In the Filter list that appears, choose Transaction Type.
4. From the Transaction Type list, choose Journal.
5. Click OK to produce a report of only your journal entry transactions.

Find out more about creating reports in QuickBooks in Chapter 10, "Getting Useful Information Out of QuickBooks."

Now You've Done It!

You successfully skimmed the surface of the way accounting works and how various accounting rules affect your record-keeping process. Here's what you learned:

➤ Basic crash course information about the Chart of Accounts. See "Boring Accounting Stuff: The Chart of Accounts."

➤ How to make a general journal entry. See "When Will I Use a General Journal Entry?"

➤ How to produce a journal entry report. See "Take a Look at Your Journal Entries."

Chapter 7

Lots of Lists

In This Chapter

➤ Keeping track of customers, vendors, accounts, and more

➤ Adding entries to your lists

➤ Editing the information on your lists

➤ Removing information from your lists

You use lists to keep yourself organized, and QuickBooks does too. Right at this minute you probably have several lists going: a grocery list, a list of things you need to do in the near future, a list of things you didn't get finished in the near past, a wish list of books you want to read or movies you want to see. Mind you, not all lists are written down, but mental lists still count as lists.

QuickBooks keeps lists, too. All the bits and pieces of information about your company are stored in the form of lists. A list is like a database or a collection of information. In this chapter we'll cover a variety of different kinds of QuickBooks lists, what you need to know about them, and how they're used in this program.

Lists of Accounts, Suppliers, Customers, Chores, and More

The following is a description of the main types of lists you will find in QuickBooks. In addition to these big-league lists, there are a number of minor-league lists, such as shipping terms, job status, classes, and friendly messages you can send to your customers. We'll cover these other lists as they come up in the course of working with QuickBooks. Here are descriptions of the big guys:

➤ **Lists of Customers and Jobs**   The Customer:Job List includes the names of all the people or companies with whom you do business. These are the people/businesses who purchase your services or goods. You'll refer to members of this list every time you create or work with a form in QuickBooks where you are asked for the name of the person or company with whom you're doing business. At the top of the invoice form, for example, the very first field is Customer:Job. When you enter a customer name (and, if applicable, a job name), you're drawing from the information that's on this Customer:Job List.

➤ **Accounts**   Your Chart of Accounts forms a list in QuickBooks. Whenever you're asked to indicate the account to which an income or expense item relates, the list from which you draw is the Chart of Accounts. Income accounts such as sales revenue, legal fees collected, catering income, or interest income are included on the Chart of Accounts. Expense accounts like rent and repairs and the cost of reference books (such as this one!) are included on your Chart of Accounts. So are assets, such as your cash accounts or the company car, as well as liabilities, such as that loan you took out to pay for the company car. If you're paying the electric bill and you are asked to identify the name of the account to which the expense should be charged, it is to the Chart of Accounts List that you look for an account name.

➤ **Vendors**   All of the companies and the people from whom you purchase inventory, supplies, and services are considered to be vendors. When you're asked for the name of the company or person who sent you a bill for the cost of shelving for your display cases or the inventory items you plan to place in those cases, you will choose a vendor from the Vendor List. To add new vendors to your list, see the section "A New Member of the Family," later in this chapter.

➤ **Items**   Items is a term used by QuickBooks to describe everything that you sell—whether it is merchandise or services—and everything that appears on an individual line on your invoice or purchase order forms. Each thing that you sell is an item, including time for services rendered. Also included in items are delivery expense, copying and postage, and the sales tax you may charge. Items also include subtotals as items, because a subtotal is something that might be listed on your invoice forms. (To add new items to your lists, see the section "A New Member of the Family," coming up later in this chapter.)

➤ **Chores**   QuickBooks lets you create a To Do List where you can keep track of any type of information about which you want to remind yourself. As you enter information on your To Do List about phone calls you have to return, the date of your best friend's birthday, a reminder to pick up the dry cleaning on the way home from work—anything about which you need to be reminded, be it business or personal—QuickBooks will check the date on which the chore or the task needs to be accomplished, then that chore will be added to your reminders list that is displayed when you start your program. (To add new items to your To Do List, see the section "A New Member of the Family," found later in this chapter.)

Typical List Information

Each type of list requires different information when you set it up. However, the process of setting up information that goes in your list is the same, regardless of which list type you are setting up.

To look at a list, open the Lists menu and then click the name of the list you want to see. (You can find all of your lists on the Lists menu and scattered throughout the QuickBooks Navigator tabs.) A sample list, the Vendor List, is displayed in the next figure.

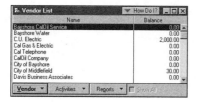

The Vendor List shows the name and current balance owed to each vendor.

Generally, there will be three buttons at the bottom of the list window. The leftmost button is named after the list itself (on the Vendor List, the left button is called **Vendor**). Clicking this button drops down a menu that includes commands to add a new member to the list, edit a member, delete a member, make a member inactive, and print a list. Specific instructions for doing these things are explained throughout the remainder of this chapter.

The center button is the **Activities** button. The activities, which can be seen in a drop-down menu when you click this button, vary from one list to the next. Basically the activities presented on the drop-down menu include using forms to which the current list might apply. For example, in the Vendor List, the activities include entering bills from vendors and issuing purchase orders to vendors.

Closing List Windows

To quickly close any list window displayed, click the window's close button (X), located in the upper-left corner of the window. If you need help with a list, click the **How Do I?** button to display a drop-down menu of topics.

The right button is a **Reports** button. Click this button to choose from several QuickBooks reports related directly to the list. For example, by clicking **Reports** in the Vendor List window, you can choose to display a phone list of all of your vendors. You can open a similar report from the Customer List.

Creating Notes

You have an opportunity in QuickBooks to create notes that relate to the information on your lists. Instead of using paper "sticky" notes throughout your day, jot down notes inside QuickBooks. Write yourself notes about the items you order from vendors. Record important dates about the work you do for a customer. Or use the To Do Notes List to remind yourself to do something specific.

The figure below shows an example of the Notepad window. Each note is date stamped with the date the note was recorded.

Enter information about this customer in the Notepad window.

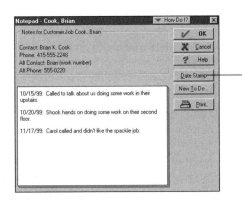

Click this button to place today's date next to your note

When you get ready to create a note, the "how-to" will depend on which list is displayed. The following is the process for adding notes to the different lists.

➤ When the Customer:Job List is opened, it displays a Notes column. Move the mouse inside this column to see the cursor change to a little notepad icon. Double-click in the Notes column for the customer to whom you are adding a note. This displays the Notepad window. Type your note, then click **OK**. A notepad icon appears in the Notes column for that customer.

➤ When the Vendor List is opened, it does not display a Notes column. Notes are added by double-clicking the vendor's name, then clicking the **Notes** button. Type your note, then click **OK**. Nothing appears in the Vendor List to indicate a note is attached to a vendor.

➤ The To Do Notes List (displayed by opening the Lists menu and selecting **To Do Notes**) displays items that you've asked QuickBooks to remind you to do. To add a note to this list, click the **To Do** button in the lower-left corner (or press **Ctrl+N**). In the To Do window, type your note. You can also set a reminder for this item to appear in your Reminders List. When your note is complete, click **OK**. The item appears in the list, along with the date QuickBooks is to display a reminder.

Editing an existing note also depends on which list is displayed. Edit customer notes by double-clicking the **Note** icon in the Customer:Job List. Edit vendor notes by double-clicking the vendor and then clicking the **Notes** button. To Do items are changed by double-clicking the item in the To Do List.

Making a To Do List

A To Do List can come in handy with all kinds of QuickBooks projects. To make such a list, click the **Company** tab on the QuickBooks Navigator, then click **To Do's**. You can also open the Lists menu and choose **To Do Notes**. The To Do List window looks like all the other QuickBooks list windows you've been learning about. To add an item to the list, click the **To Do** button and choose **New** (or press **Ctrl+N**). Fill out your note details and click **OK**. The item is now added to the list window. To mark items completed on the list, select the item, click the **To Do** button, and choose **Mark as Done**, **Make Inactive**, or **Delete**. You can even print the list (select **Print List** from the drop-down menu). Click the window's close button (**X**) to exit the window.

Creating Reports Based on Your Lists

Once you've created a list of all your inventory items, customers, vendors, and so on, what next? You can print a report showing all of the entries on your list by opening the list window, clicking the left button at the bottom of the list window, and choosing **Print List** (or just press **Ctrl+P**). A printed command will be issued to print a hard copy of all members of this list (see the following figure).

The Print List command sends a report directly to your printer that includes all available information about the entries on your list.

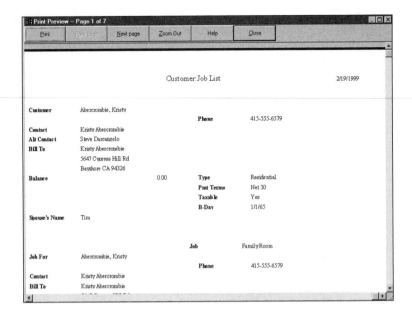

In addition, there are particular reports associated with each list. Click the **Reports** button in any list window to see the reports associated with that list. For example, with the Customer and Vendor Lists you can choose reports listing the names of all the entries on the list with phone numbers. For any list, you can click an entry on the list, click **Reports**, and choose **Quick Report** to show detailed information about transactions involving that entry. Click the **Print** button at the top of any report window to print a hard copy of that report.

Adding to Lists

You can add a new entry to any of your lists by displaying the list and then pressing **Ctrl+N** (or just click the leftmost button in the bottom of the list window and choose **New**). The window that appears will provide you with fill-in-the-blanks for each piece of information relating to the type of list. No matter which type of list you are adding to, you will be asked for the name of the entry and other pertinent information regarding the entry.

Each list requires different information as you set up new entries for these lists. For example, if you are entering a new member to your Customer List, you will be asked for the name and address of the customer, the customer's account number, and whether or not the customer is taxable.

If you are entering a new vendor, you'll be asked if this vendor is required to receive a tax form 1099. If you're entering a new account, you'll be asked for the beginning balance of the account.

A New Member of the Family

The process of adding new entries to lists is quite similar, no matter which type of list you are expanding. For this example, we'll add a new vendor to the Vendor List.

1. Open the Vendor List by displaying the Lists menu and choosing **Vendors**. The Vendor List window will appear.

2. Press **Ctrn+N** or click the **Vendor** button in the lower-left corner of the list window and select **New**. The New Vendor window will appear, pristine, with all its blanks waiting to be filled in.

3. Start by entering the vendor name (see the next figure). The way you enter the name here is the way in which the name will appear on your purchase orders, bills, and checks that you write to this vendor. It's always good to type carefully and spell the name correctly. If you spell the name correctly here, the name will appear spelled correctly on your forms from this time forward.

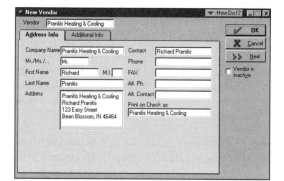

Enter all the goods on this new vendor.

So Picky!

When you add new entries to your lists, you may find that there is some information that is required and some that is optional. QuickBooks doesn't want to let you know what is required until you try to close the window in which you are adding new information. If you have left off some necessary piece of information, you'll get a nasty onscreen message from QuickBooks, letting you know what you forgot.

Need Customized Info?

If there's information that you'd like to track, such as email addresses or birth dates, and there's no space for that information in your current list, you can create a custom field for the information. See "Setting Up Custom Lists," later in this chapter.

4. Fill in the remaining blanks in the window by clicking in each field or pressing Tab to advance from one field to the next, entering all the information you have about this vendor.

5. Once you've entered all the information for this new vendor, click Next if you want to enter information for another new vendor, or click OK to close this window. Your vendor will appear alphabetically on the list.

Adding to Lists "On-the-Fly"

Rather than opening up the list window and entering a new vendor, you can wait until you need to refer to that vendor and add the vendor as you work on a form.

For example, I have just purchased some James Dean memorabilia to adorn the walls of my customer waiting room, and I need to record the bill for this purchase. I went to the James Dean Gallery in Fairmount, Indiana, to acquire these movie posters and other artifacts, and I realize when I'm entering the bill for this purchase that the James Dean Gallery is not on my Vendor List.

Instead of opening the list window and entering a new vendor, then returning to my bill form, I can go ahead and enter the James Dean Gallery right on my bill form. When I type in the name of the vendor and try to move to another field, I get a message from QuickBooks, shown in the figure below, saying that this vendor is not on the Vendor List.

QuickBooks sends a message when a new vendor is not yet on the Vendor List.

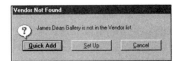

The message prompt box gives me (and you too, when you run across it) three options for proceeding:

➤ **Quick Add**   Choosing this option places the vendor name only on your Vendor List. This is the same method of entry that you used in the EasyStep Interview—simply entering the name and no additional information. If this is a one-time purchase and you don't expect to do business with this vendor in the future, it could be that entering the name is completely sufficient.

➤ **Set Up** Click here and the New Vendor window appears, just as if you had pressed **Ctrl+N** from the Vendor List window. Enter all pertinent information about this vendor. (For help in completing these fields, turn back to the previous section "A New Member of the Family.") Click **OK** when the form is completed to return to your bill form.

➤ **Cancel** If you select this option, then you won't get to fill out the bill with the name of this vendor, so this really isn't a helpful option at all. QuickBooks won't let you enter the name of a vendor without adding that vendor name to your list.

Setting Up Custom Lists

When you set up vendors, customers, or employees (see "Setting Up Employees" in Chapter 16 for more information about this), there are numerous fields for you to fill in. Sometimes, however, the field selection is not comprehensive enough. There may be information that you need for which there are no fields.

For example, you may want to enter the email address for each of your vendors. You can create your own fields that will appear on each New Vendor (or Customer or Employee) form, to enable you to keep track of additional information.

The process for creating a customized field is the same for each list type. Our example works with a Customer List:

1. Double-click any customer in your Customer:Job List.
2. Create a new field by clicking the **Additional Info** tab, then clicking the **Define Fields** button. The Define Fields window will appear (see the next figure), and you can create up to 15 new fields.

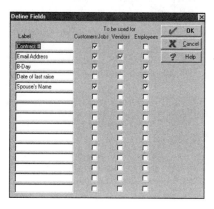

Enter a new field name on this screen, then check off some or all of the types of lists that will use this field.

3. Type a field name for each custom field and click the **Customer:Job**, **Vendor**, and **Employee** check boxes to indicate on which of these lists the new fields should be made available.

4. When each custom field has been defined, click **OK**.

Changing the Stuff on Your Lists

Sometimes the information that you entered on your lists needs to be changed. Maybe you typed Westar Oil Company instead of Western Oil Company as the name of a customer. It would be embarrassing to have the customer name spelled incorrectly on your invoices, so you will want to correct the spelling of the customer name. Or, maybe a customer has moved and has sent you a new address. You'll want to enter the new address on your Customer:Job List so that, if you prepare an invoice for this customer, it will get mailed to the correct address and not get buried in the dead letter box.

Editing an Existing List Entry

To edit an entry from a list, open the list that contains the entry you want to change, click the name of the entry that will change, then press **Ctrl+E** (or just double-click the entry).

The edit window will appear for that particular entry, and all of the original information you entered for that customer or vendor will appear. From here, you can change any information that is incorrect. The next figure displays an Edit window for a vendor.

Double-click a vendor name to open the Edit Vendor window, in which you can change or enter additional information about this vendor.

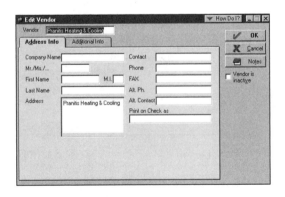

Once you've finished editing this entry, click **OK** and your changes will be put into place.

Performing Massive Editing Jobs

If you went through the EasyStep Interview setup process, a lot of your list information may have been entered at that time, such as vendors. However, in the setup you entered the names of vendors, customers, and items, but you didn't get a chance to enter all the picky details, like the address, the contact name, her favorite cologne, and so on. You may want to go back to the lists and fill in additional information.

Changes All Over

If you make changes to a member of one of your lists, all forms containing the changed information will be immediately updated. For example, if you change the address of one of your vendors, any purchase orders, bills, or checks for this vendor will be updated to the new address.

Open the list for which you want to enter additional information. Start at the top of the list and double-click each entry on the list. As you double-click an entry, the edit window will appear, as shown in the previous figure. Make your changes, click OK, and go on to the next entry on the list.

Getting Rid of Unwanted Listed Information

Are you no longer doing business with a vendor? Did a customer move out of state? Have you stopped selling a particular inventory item? Or did you enter a vendor on your list twice, with two different spellings of the name (Cal Gas & Electric and California Gas & Electric)?

For whatever reason, you may need to remove an entry from one of your lists.

Are You SURE You're Never Going to See This Customer Again?

You can permanently remove an entry from one of your lists only if there has been no activity relating to that entry. If you've made a purchase from a vendor or if you've made a sale to a customer, even if the current account balance for that vendor or customer is zero, QuickBooks won't let you delete that entry from your list. Try it and you get one of QuickBooks' little warnings (see the next figure) that are the equivalent of saying "Not so fast, pardner!"

QuickBooks won't let you get away with removing an entry from a list if you have entered a transaction in the past involving that person or company.

Whenever there have been transactions involving an entry from a list, there is historical information associated with that entry in your file. By removing the entry from the list, you would be removing the link to that information. In other words, if you went back to open an invoice from six months ago that involved a particular customer, and that customer is no longer on your Customer List, QuickBooks will self-destruct when you try to open the invoice and there is no information relating to the name and address of that customer. Trust me, this is not a pretty sight.

This is not to say that you can't delete some of the entries on your lists. If you want to get rid of a vendor you no longer need, go ahead and try deleting it. Click the name of the vendor you want to remove, then press **Ctrl+D**. If there have been no forms issued involving this vendor, you're home free. QuickBooks will ask if you're sure you want to go through with this (see the figure below). Click **OK**, and poof! The vendor is history. If QuickBooks won't allow an entry to be deleted, see the following section on "Hiding Entries" to make it go away.

*One press of the **Ctrl+D** key combination and this vendor is a goner.*

Hiding Entries

The next-best thing to removing an entry from a list is to hide the name. To hide an entry, click the entry that you want to hide, click the left button at the bottom of the list window (**Account**, **Customer:Job**, **Vendor**, whatever), and choose **Make Inactive**.

The entry is out of sight and out of mind. Almost. If you decide you want to take a look at members of the list that you've hidden, click the little **Show All** check box at the bottom of the list window. All the hidden entries suddenly come back to life, and a little hand icon appears to the left of each formerly hidden entry (see the following figure). In earlier versions of QuickBooks, this icon symbol was a ghost, which seems much more appropriate to me than the hand, but nobody asked my advice.

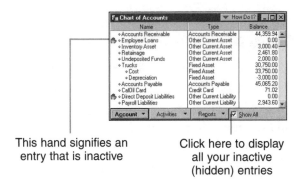

This hand signifies an
entry that is inactive

Click here to display
all your inactive
(hidden) entries

*Hidden list entries don't
have to stay hidden.*

Merging Entries on Your Lists

If QuickBooks won't let you delete an unwanted entry on your list and you prefer not to hide the entry, your third option is to incorporate this member of your list into another member of your list. For example, if you entered the same company name on your Vendor List twice, but with different spellings (Cal Gas & Electric, California Gas & Electric), you can merge one name into the other so that you are left with only one of the names on your list.

All of the activity relating to the company you merge *from* (Cal Gas & Electric) transfers to the company you merge *to* (California Gas & Electric), so that if you decide to go back to a form that was issued in the name of Cal Gas & Electric, it will now come up with California Gas & Electric on the form. Any reports you prepare for California Gas & Electric will include information from both companies. What a relief, eh?

To accomplish this merging process, click the bad name, the one you want to remove. Press **Ctrl+E** (or double-click the entry) to open the edit window. Change the name of the entry to *exactly* the same name as the entry into which you want to merge. It is extremely important that you spell the name exactly the way it appears on the list. Make no other changes in the edit window, click the OK button, and you will see a message from QuickBooks asking if you want to merge the two vendors (see the next figure). Click Yes, and the vendor (Cal Gas & Electric in my example) no longer exists, and all of its historical information has been transferred to the new name (California Gas & Electric).

*Click Yes to merge two
list items into one.*

113

Now You've Done It!

You've learned everything you should need to know about working with lists in QuickBooks. Here's what you picked up:

➤ QuickBooks stores all sorts of useful information about your vendors, suppliers, accounts, inventory items, and so on in database lists. See "Lists of Accounts, Suppliers, Customers, Chores, and More."

➤ You learned how to access reports showing all the entries on your lists. See "Creating Reports Based on Your Lists."

➤ You can add new information to any of your lists on-the-fly from any of your QuickBooks forms. See "Adding to Lists 'On-the-Fly'."

➤ You can edit the information in your lists to correct spelling or add new facts. See "Changing the Stuff on Your Lists."

➤ Tired of dealing with a customer? Scratch him off the list! See "Getting Rid of Unwanted Listed Information."

Part 2

Using QuickBooks for Everyday Business

One nice thing about QuickBooks is that you don't have to be a slave to your computer program, working with it from sunup to sundown. Follow the pointers in this part of the book and you'll see how easy it is to get yourself on a regular schedule, entering your company information in QuickBooks when it is convenient for you.

Learn how easy it is to set up a comfortable schedule, entering your information in QuickBooks on a regular basis, without letting piles of data entry forms accumulate until you can't see over the top of the stack.

Chapter 8

The Daily Grind

In This Chapter

➤ Make your own purchase orders

➤ How to record sales

➤ How to handle returns and discounts

➤ Oodles of details about paying bills

➤ Learn about special considerations for cash businesses

You are in the business of making money. It doesn't matter to me what you do to make your money—whether you've got a lemonade stand in front of your house or you're raising pet hamsters in the backyard. My job is to show you how to record your money-making endeavors in QuickBooks. Part of making money is spending money—you've got bills to pay, and there may be items you purchase then turn around and sell to your customers at a profit. These operations represent the daily routine of your business—a revolving door of merchandise in, merchandise out, services provided, invoices sent, money in, bills received, bills paid, money out. This chapter focuses on the routine reporting techniques you will use to record your business cycle.

Purchasing and Receiving Merchandise to Sell

My kids used to play "store" with me when they were young. They would raid the kitchen for utensils and ingredients they knew I used often, then set up a counter display and try to get me to purchase the items from them for pennies. Not only would I have to pay to reclaim my precious kitchen tools, but I got the job of putting them away again. For reasons I'm not sure I fully understand, I would encourage this activity, thinking the kids were getting their first lessons in commerce.

Your business probably runs on a slightly more sophisticated level than the kitchen store at our house, but the rules are similar. You have to provide something to sell—be it merchandise (preferably not plundered from your mother's kitchen cupboards) or services. You need a display, some advertising, or some way in which to get the word out to potential customers. And you need to collect money when customers buy your wares. Once you get your money, you can buy the things you need to make your business keep running, and the whole cycle begins anew. This section contains the nitty gritty details about how to go about doing all that with QuickBooks at your side.

I'll Take 3 of These, 200 of Those

When you purchase items for use in your company—whether you are purchasing these items for resale to your customers, for use in a manufacturing or preparation process, or for your own consumption—you have an option of issuing a purchase order form. The purchase order serves two purposes.

No Vendor?

When creating a purchase order, if the vendor name doesn't appear on the list provided, choose **Add New** at the top of the list and enter appropriate information for the vendor. There's more info about adding vendors in Chapter 7, "Lots of Lists." See the section titled "A New Member of the Family."

First, the purchase order provides a paper document that you can give to your supplier as evidence of the order you want to make. Your copy of this document can be used to check off items as they are received.

In addition, by issuing a purchase order in QuickBooks, you establish the existence of the order in your record-keeping system. The purchase order also provides a cross-reference that can be used when you are ready to enter the related bill into your system. With a purchase order on file, you simply enter the vendor name on your bill and check off the related purchase order. QuickBooks prepares the bill for you.

The use of purchase orders is optional, but if you choose to use this feature, here's how you do it:

1. Open the Activities menu and choose **Create-Purchase Orders**, or click the **Purchase Orders** icon on the **Purchases and Vendors** tab of QuickBooks Navigator.

2. When the Create Purchase Orders window appears (see the following figure), enter the name of the vendor or supplier from whom you want to place an order. Click the **Vendor** drop-down arrow to make a selection from your Vendor List. The vendor address will be filled in automatically, based on your selection.

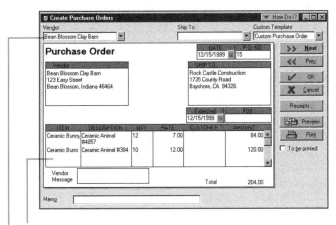

You can use the purchase order form to record your orders in QuickBooks, and you can give this form to your suppliers.

Enter items you want to order here

Enter name of supplier (vendor) here

3. Verify the date and make any necessary changes. To change the date, click inside the **Date** field and type one in, or click the **Date** icon at the end of the field and choose a date from the pop-up calendar.

4. Fill in the information at the bottom of the screen, such as the item(s) ordered, the quantity, and the anticipated price. Click on the first line, and the Item column displays a drop-down list of inventory items or services (click the drop-down arrow to see the list). You can select from the list or enter a new item (but then you'll have to record information about the new item before continuing). Continue entering information for each appropriate column on the order form. Notice that QuickBooks keeps a running tally of the total at the bottom of the form.

A Word About the Calendar

Many of the forms you work with in QuickBooks have Date fields. One way to quickly fill them in is to use the Date icon at the end of the field. A click on the icon displays a pop-up calendar for the current month. To change the month displayed, click an arrow at the top of the calendar. The left arrow moves back month by month and the right arrow moves forward. To choose a date from the calendar, simply click on the date. This immediately inserts it into the Date field on the form. Pretty cool, huh?

Need Help with Items?

The world of purchase orders revolves around items, whether it's inventory items you sell or services you sell. For more information on creating inventory list items, check out Chapter 7.

5. Click **Print** if you want to print this purchase order right away. The Print dialog box appears, and you can change any print options before actually printing (or just click **Print** to start printing). If you choose not to print, QuickBooks will store the purchase order for later printing.

6. Click **Next** to move on to another purchase order form, or click **OK** if this is the last purchase order you're going to work on right now.

If you chose to print later, the Reminders dialog box may appear, as shown in the next figure, after you exit the Create Purchase Orders window. Notice that the purchase order (or orders, if you made more than one) is listed in the things you need to do. To print the purchase order at a later time, just open the Purchase Orders list (display the Lists menu and choose **Purchase Orders**). From the Purchase Orders List window, double-click the order you want to print, then click the **Print** button. The Print dialog box appears, and you can start printing the form (click the **Print** button). Click **OK** to exit the Purchase Orders window.

120

Here's a reminder about my purchase orders

The Reminders dialog box will let you know you have purchase orders to be printed.

Your Order Is In!

You know how much fun it is to receive packages at home—especially if it's your birthday. Just think—some businesses receive packages every day! When you receive a package in your business (you might call it a shipment or a delivery—it still seems like a present to me), you should record the event in QuickBooks.

If the items you receive include inventory items that need to be recorded in QuickBooks, you will want to record their arrival as soon as possible so that your records show the correct quantities of inventory you have in stock and available for sale.

If a bill is received with the shipment, you will record the bill at the same time. No bill? Then just record the fact that you received the goods and enter the bill when it arrives.

Here's how to record the delivery when you get the bill at the same time:

1. Open the Activities menu and choose **Inventory, Receive Items and Enter Bills**. Or from the **Purchases and Vendors** tab of the QuickBooks Navigator screen, click **Receive Items with Bill**. This opens the Enter Bills window, as shown in the next figure.

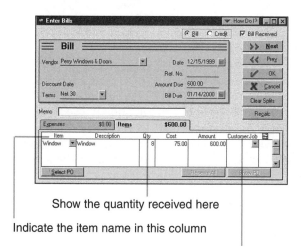

Enter items received on this form.

Show the quantity received here

Indicate the item name in this column

If this purchase is directly related to a specific customer, you can enter the customer name here

121

2. Now you can set about copying information from the actual bill. Enter the vendor name, the date of receipt, the date due, and the amount due on the bill. This form works just like the purchase order form you learned about in the previous section. Click the **Vendor** drop-down arrow to select a vendor, use the **Date** icon to select dates, and type an amount in the Amount Due field.

3. In the lower section of the Enter Bills form, on the **Items** tab (see the previous figure), enter any inventory items received—the item name, quantity, and any other information that doesn't fill in automatically.

4. If your bill is for expenses not related to inventory, click the **Expenses** tab and enter the account to which the expense is related, the amount, and any descriptive information.

5. Click **Next** if you're ready to enter another bill, or click **OK** to save your information and close the window.

If you received the items but no bill, there's another route you can take to record the items you received. Start by opening the Activities menu and choosing **Inventory, Receive Items**. If you prefer using QuickBooks Navigator, click the **Receive Items** icon in the **Purchases and Vendors** tab. The Create Item Receipts window opens, as shown in the next figure. Here you can enter the information just as you would if the bill was received at the same time.

Use the Create Item Receipts window to enter items received without a bill.

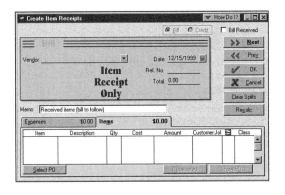

When the bill eventually arrives, open the Activities menu and choose **Inventory, Enter Bill for Rec'd Item**, or click the **Receive Bill** icon in QuickBooks Navigator. Use the Vendor drop-down list to select the vendor name. Check off the items for which you are being billed as they appear in the bottom of the form (see the following figure). When finished, click **OK** to close the window.

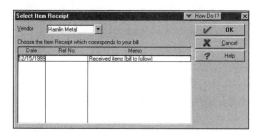

Click the listing that refers to the bill you received.

Selling Merchandise and Services

It is extremely important to account for everything you sell in your QuickBooks file. You need to know how well your business is doing, and knowing the amount of income you earn is a big part of tracking your progress. Whether you sell merchandise or perform services for revenue, you need a way of monitoring the amounts you have earned and preparing the documents that will tell your customers how much they owe you. The following sections cover how to track things you sell.

Are You Shipping Your Items?

If you send your items to your customers, rather than having customers come to you to pick them up, it may be useful to you to prepare a shipping ticket. The shipping ticket will provide a record of the quantity of items shipped, gives your packing department a list to follow when they are preparing the shipment, and supplies your customers with a written record of the items that are supposed to be in the package.

Unfortunately, QuickBooks doesn't provide you with a shipping form. Or so it would seem. With a little creative form construction, you can design your own shipping ticket in no time.

Because the shipping ticket is usually a duplicate of the invoice (except that it often does not include price information), you need only alter your standard invoice form slightly to produce a new form that can be used as your shipping ticket. You'll find detailed information about designing and customizing forms in Chapter 17, "This Is YOUR Program," in the section "Creating Nice Looking Forms," but for our purposes, here is a crash course on creating your own shipping ticket form.

1. Open the Lists menu and choose Templates to open the Template window, shown in the next figure. This window shows all the forms currently available in your QuickBooks file.

The Templates window reveals a list of available templates.

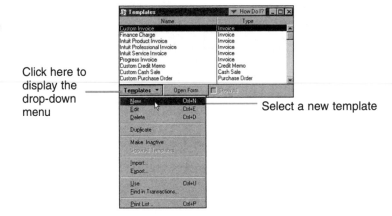

Click here to display the drop-down menu

Select a new template

2. Press **Ctrl+N** (or click the **Templates** button and choose **New**). This opens a box called Select Template Type, as shown in the next figure.

Choose the Invoice template type from this box.

3. Make sure the **Invoice** type is selected, then click **OK**. The Customize Invoice window will appear (see the next figure).

If QuickBooks doesn't have the form you need, you can create your own.

Enter a name you will use to refer to the form

This title will appear on the actual form that you print

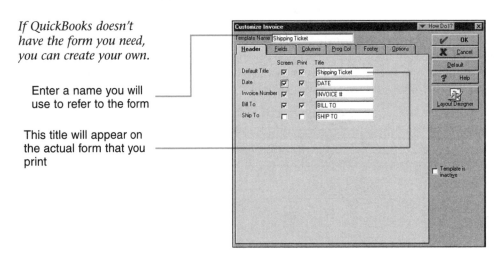

124

4. Now you can start creating your shipping ticket. At the top, where it says Template Name, enter **Shipping Ticket**.

5. On the Header tab, in the Default Title field, enter **Shipping Ticket**, or whatever title you want to actually print on this form.

6. Click the **Columns** tab and uncheck the boxes for Rate and Amount in the Print column only.

7. Click **OK** to save this form.

From now on, when you enter an invoice (see the next section), you can print a shipping ticket to go with that invoice by changing the Custom Template to Shipping Ticket (see the following figure). Simply click the **Custom Template** drop-down arrow and select **Shipping Ticket** from the list.

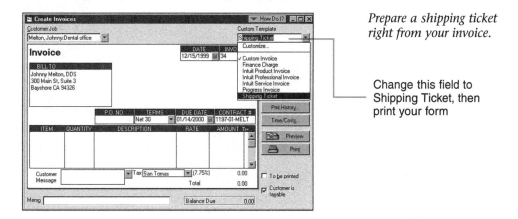

Prepare a shipping ticket right from your invoice.

Change this field to Shipping Ticket, then print your form

Enter all the appropriate information on this form, just as you would for an invoice, then click the **Print** button. Once you have printed the shipping ticket, return the Custom Template to your regular invoice form (click the **Custom Template** drop-down arrow and choose **Intuit Product Invoice** or whichever invoice you want to use). You can click **Next** or **OK** to enter this invoice in your QuickBooks file.

Creating an Invoice

Before there was the money in your hand, there was the invoice. The invoice is the form you provide to your customer so that he knows how much he owes you and for what. The invoice can also tell him when payment is due and how the goods were shipped. Even more importantly from your perspective, the creation of the invoice places the revenue from the sale into your QuickBooks records.

Create an invoice by following these steps:

1. Press **Ctrl+I**, or open the Activities menu and choose **Create Invoices**. If you prefer navigating from QuickBooks Navigator, click the **Sales and Customers** tab and click **Invoices**. The Create Invoices window appears, as shown in the next figure.

Use the Create Invoices window to whip up an invoice to give to your customer.

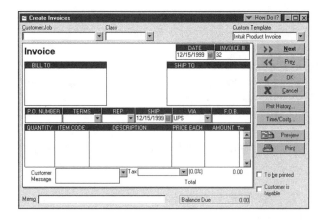

Are You a Cash-Basis Company?

Invoices are used by accrual-basis businesses to reflect the income they earn when they earn it, before they actually receive the payment. If you are a cash-basis company, you may use a cash summary statement instead for entering revenue into your company's records.

2. Use the **Customer:Job** drop-down arrow to enter the customer (and, if applicable, job) name.

3. Verify the date. To change it, click the **Date** icon or type in a new date.

4. Check the invoice number and other pertinent information on the invoice (such as billing or shipping address, purchase order number, terms, shipping method, and so on).

5. At the bottom of the invoice form, enter the item(s) being sold and verify description and price information. To begin, click inside the **Quantity** column. Use the Tab key to move to the next column and continue filling in the information.

6. If you have previously entered time (see the section "Transferring Time to Customer Invoices" in Chapter 15, "Punching the Time Clock") or expenses (as described earlier in this chapter in the section "Your Order Is In!") that specifically relate to this customer, you can apply those amounts by clicking the **Time/Costs** button. This opens the Choose Billable Time and Costs window, where you can check off all applicable amounts. Click **OK** to return to the invoice form.

7. Click **Next** to proceed to the next invoice form, or click **OK** to save your changes and close this window.

What About Defective Merchandise?

There may come a time when you have to record a return of merchandise from your customer. Perhaps the merchandise was damaged. Or perhaps the merchandise that you delivered was not what was ordered (don't you hate when that happens?). Or maybe the customer changed his mind when he got the merchandise (don't you *really* hate when *that* happens?). There can be any number of reasons, but the result is the same: You need to record a credit against the customer's invoice. Since you've already recorded the invoice, which had the effect of adding income into your records, now you're going to remove that income with a credit against the invoice.

Change Your Mind?

Any time you change your mind about completing a form, click the Cancel button to close the window without saving your changes.

To enter returns from a customer or to reflect a credit for any reason, open the Activities menu and choose **Create Credit Memos/Refunds** (or click the **Refunds and Credit** icon on the QuickBooks Navigator on the **Sales and Customers** tab). The Create Credit Memos/Refunds window will appear (see the following figure), in which you'll enter the customer and the job name relating to the returns.

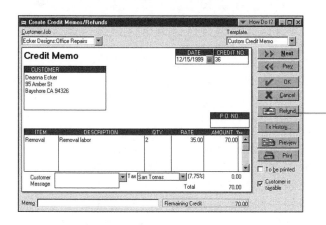

Straighten out your records by entering credits extended to your customers.

Click here to write a refund check

When entering a credit memo, there isn't a way to specifically tie the credit memo to an existing invoice, so you have to make sure you tie the credit memo to the correct customer and job. Then when you record payment from the customer, you will make reference to all invoices and credits reflected by the payment.

When you open the credit memo form, enter the customer name and a job name if applicable (click the **Customer:Job** drop-down arrow and make your selection). In the Item section of the form, fill in the name of the item being returned, the quantity, and the price at which the item was invoiced (the price information may appear automatically).

If you want to create a refund check when you're issuing this credit memo, there is a Refund button right on the credit memo form that opens a Write Checks form (shown in the next figure). All the amounts from the credit memo will be automatically filled in on the Write Checks form, so all you have to do is check the **To Be Printed** box and click **OK** to send the check to the print queue (and the Reminders dialog box). You can leave the To Be Printed box unchecked and click **OK** if you plan to write the check by hand, or click the **Print** button if you want to print the check immediately.

Check this box

Use this window to issue a refund check.

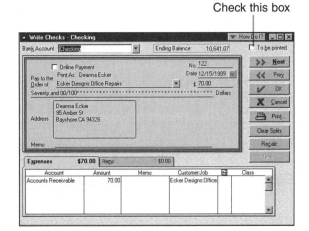

Getting Paid

There are those who might argue that the most important part about a business is the getting paid part. In order to keep your business going and pay for your own expenses, you need to receive money from your customers. When you receive that money, you need to record the information in QuickBooks.

When you receive money that relates to an invoice you have issued in QuickBooks, you'll link that money to the invoice so that the invoice will no longer be recorded as outstanding. If you are a cash business, stay tuned until later in this chapter. The section called "The Cash Business" will give you the scoop on recording income at the time you receive it instead of using invoices.

To record a payment, follow these steps:

1. Click the **Receive Payments** icon on the **Sales and Customers** tab of the QuickBooks Navigator, or open the Activities menu and select **Receive Payments**. Either one of those methods will open the Receive Payments window (see the next figure).

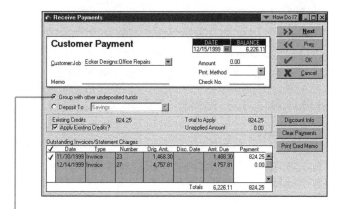

Enter the money you receive from your customers on a Receive Payments form.

Click here if you plan to deposit this money

2. Click the **Customer:Job** drop-down arrow and choose a customer and, if applicable, job name.

3. Verify the date. To change it, click the **Date** icon and choose another, or type in the correct date.

4. Go to the bottom of the window where it says Outstanding Invoices/Statement Charges and check off the invoices against which you've received payment, verifying in the Payment column at the bottom of the screen that the payment received matches the payment on the invoice.

5. If there are outstanding credits available to this customer, click the **Apply Existing Credits?** check box in the middle of the window. This causes the total amount of existing credits to appear in the Payment column at the bottom of the window.

6. Once you've entered all appropriate information on the Receive Payments form so that the amount listed agrees with the amount you actually received, click OK to record the payment and close this window. If you have more payments to record, click Next to open a clean Receive Payments form.

Grouping Payments?

The Receive Payments window also has an option to either group this amount with undeposited funds or indicate to which account this money is going to be deposited. If you want to group with other undeposited funds, you'll have an option of preparing a deposit and a deposit slip through QuickBooks, (covered in Chapter 9, "Quick Guide to Banking with QuickBooks," under the section "Time for a Deposit").

Paying Your Bills

Now that you've collected money from your customers, you may want to think about paying some bills. Before you actually pay your bills, you need to record the bills that you've received. This section explores your payment options.

Recording Amounts You Owe

The mail has just arrived and you've got bills! You'll want to record those bills in QuickBooks as soon as they arrive, so that your QuickBooks financial statements will be completely current and up to date, reflecting all amounts you owe.

To record a bill that you've received, click on the **Purchases and Vendors** tab of the QuickBooks Navigator, and click the **Enter Bills** icon, or open the Activities menu and choose **Enter Bills**. The Enter Bills window will appear, as shown in the next figure.

Use the Enter Bills window to record bills.

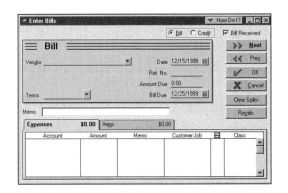

Use the **Vendor** drop-down arrow to choose the name of the vendor. If you enter a vendor for whom a purchase order already exists in your QuickBooks records, you'll get a message onscreen saying that you have received items with which you may want to link this bill (see the figure below). You can indicate that you want to record this bill as it applies to the existing purchase order.

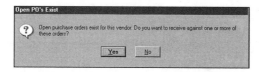

You can link directly to an existing purchase order.

Note that if you enter the name of a vendor and you've already entered items that you've received from this vendor—that is, you entered the items when they arrived in advance of receiving the bill—you'll get a message saying that, instead of going to the Enter Bills window, you should open the Activities menu and choose **Inventory, Enter Bill for Rec'd Items** (see the next figure). This was covered earlier in this chapter under "Your Order Is In!"

If you get this message, you need to enter this payment by requesting the Receive Items with Bill window instead of the Enter Bills window.

If you indicate that you want to receive against an existing purchase order, the Open Purchase Orders window will appear. Check off the corresponding purchase order(s), then click **OK**, and the information from the purchase order will be filled in on the Enter Bills screen. You need only to verify that this information agrees with the bill you've received.

If there is a difference between the amount you're being billed and the amount on your original purchase order (for example, you didn't receive as many items as you ordered, or the price has changed), you'll need to make an adjustment on the purchase order form. You can do that from the Enter Bills form. Click the button at the bottom of the screen called **Show P.O.** The original purchase order form appears onscreen. You can make adjustments on that purchase order for any changes that have occurred since the original order was issued. Click **OK** when you've finished entering any necessary changes on the purchase order screen, then click **OK** to close the Enter Bills screen.

Deciding Which Bills to Pay

When your bills have been entered in QuickBooks and it's time to make some payments, you will need to indicate to QuickBooks which bills you're going to pay.

To pay bills from the QuickBooks Navigator, click the **Purchases and Vendors** tab and then click the **Pay Bills** icon. You can also open the Activities menu and choose **Pay Bills**. Either route brings you to the Pay Bills window, shown in the next figure.

All outstanding bills are shown here—just check off the ones you intend to pay and QuickBooks will do the rest.

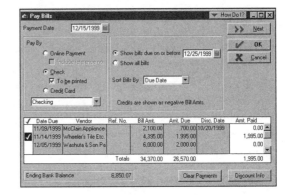

Verify that the payment date at the top of the window is correct. Verify if you are going to make an online payment or pay by check and if the check is to be printed by QuickBooks or not. Verify if this is to be a credit card payment and the account from which the payment will be made.

You can click the **Show All Bills** option to see every bill that has been entered in QuickBooks, including those that are not yet due. At the bottom of the Pay Bills window you'll see a list of all the outstanding bills that are currently due. Check off the bills you intend to pay in the left column, verifying the amount you intend to pay in the column on the right. Adjust amounts if you are not paying a bill in full at this time, then click **OK**.

Writing Checks

You can use QuickBooks to actually write your checks for you, right down to printing the checks on actual check forms. To use QuickBooks to write checks, open the Write Checks form, shown in the next figure. To do so, press **Ctrl+W** or open the Activities menu and choose **Write Checks**. If you prefer to use QuickBooks Navigator, click the **Checking and Credit Cards** tab and click **Checks**. The Write Check form looks like an actual check onscreen.

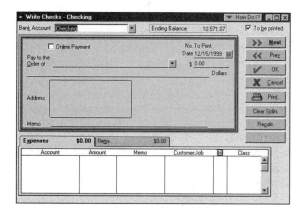

Use the Write Checks form to write an actual check that you can print on specially designed paper.

On the check form, fill in the blanks just like you would on a regular check that you write by hand. If you have signed up for online banking, there is a check box at the top of the form to indicate if this will be an online payment. For more information about making online payments, see the section "Performing Bank Transactions Without Leaving Your Keyboard" in Chapter 9.

Indicate the name of the payee where it says "Pay to the Order of." As soon as you indicate a payee, the address of the payee will be filled in automatically on the check.

If you have previously entered bills for this payee, a little warning window will appear onscreen (see the next figure), indicating that you have outstanding bills for this vendor. If you see this warning, instead of paying the bill on the Write Checks window, you are told to go to the Pay Bills window (see the previous section) and enter your payment from there. That way your payment will be linked directly to the bill to which it relates.

Oops! Should have gone to the Pay Bills screen!

When creating checks in QuickBooks, you may also see a message called Auto Recall. This message asks if you want to recall the last check you wrote to this payee. If you answer Yes, QuickBooks will automatically fill in all the information on the new check that was on the last check you wrote to this payee. This can be handy for recurring payments such as rent or utilities.

Be sure to verify at the bottom of the Write Checks window that the amounts describe exactly what you are purchasing or paying for with this check. Use the **Items** tab if you are purchasing materials that will go directly into your inventory. Use the **Expenses** tab for non-inventory expenses to which this check relates (such as supplies, equipment, or utilities).

When you've finished writing the check, you need to decide if it is going to be printed by QuickBooks or not and if it is going to be printed immediately or later. If you want QuickBooks to print the check, be sure to check off the box at the top right corner that says **To Be Printed**. You have the option of printing the check immediately by clicking the **Print** button or simply clicking **Next** (to write another check) or **OK** (to exit the form). If you indicate the check is to be printed later, it will be completed and stored.

The Cash Business

If yours is a cash business, you make a sale and you get paid at the same time. You get a bill and record it when you make the payment. Retail stores often operate as cash businesses, and so do restaurants. Rather than issuing an invoice, putting it in the mail, and waiting for your customer to get around to paying you, with a cash business you get paid on the spot.

The accounting process in QuickBooks is a little different for a cash business because you don't enter invoices in advance of receiving the payment, and you don't enter bills until you are ready to pay them. The following sections explain how to record payments and pay bills for cash businesses.

Need to Ship?

If you make cash sales but arrange to ship the goods at a later time, you may want to customize your cash sales form to include an area for shipping information. If you are interested in more information about customizing forms, see the section "Creating Nice Looking Forms" in Chapter 17.

Getting Paid Without an Invoice

Even though you don't issue an invoice for your sales in a cash business, you still need to record the sale in QuickBooks. That is how your QuickBooks records will reflect your income. QuickBooks provides you with a Cash Sales form for entering sales that occur without invoices.

To view the form, open the Activities menu and choose **Enter Cash Sales**. If you prefer to use QuickBooks Navigator, click the **Sales and Customers** tab, then click the **Cash Sales** icon. The Enter Cash Sales window will appear, as shown in the next figure. This window looks very much like an invoice form, except there is no place to enter terms or shipping information.

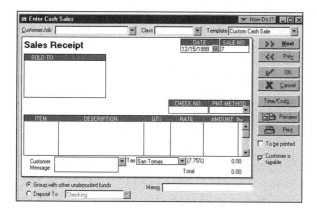

Use this form to enter cash sales information into QuickBooks.

When you enter a cash sale, the customer name is optional. Many cash businesses don't keep track of customer names. You can enter the customer name if you like, or you might just enter something general such as Cash Sale in the Sold To area.

Instead of recording each cash sale individually, you may want to record a day's worth of sales at one time. Perhaps you use a cash register, and at the end of the day you want to enter the sales for the day into QuickBooks. You can enter the daily sales all at once as a single cash sale. Use a text description such as Daily Cash Sales, make sure the date indicates the current date, then list a summary of what you sold for the day at the bottom of the screen. Enter the amount you collected, enter sales tax you collected, then click OK to close this window or click Next to move on to the next Cash Sales window.

Paying Bills on a Cash Basis

If your business is a cash-basis business, you don't record your bills before you pay them. Instead, you record the bills at the same time you make the payment. Go to the Pay Bills screen by displaying the Activities menu, choosing Other, then choosing Pay Bills. The Pay Bills window appears. Enter the amount you are paying, a reference number if applicable, and to whom you are making the payment, and then enter specific information about what the payment is for, so that the payment will be recorded properly in your books. Click the Next button to advance to the next bill, or click OK to close the window, saving your entries.

Bill and Pay

A cash-basis business has the option of entering a bill, then recording the payment of the bill (a two-step process, described in the accompanying text), or simply opening the Activities menu and choosing Write Checks, and entering all the information from the bill on the Write Checks form. The main difference is that the Enter Bills window provides you with an opportunity to enter a reference such as the bill number, whereas the Write Checks window does not.

Now You've Done It

This chapter covers all the regular, ongoing transactions that keep your QuickBooks records up to date on a daily basis. Here's what you learned:

➤ Create and enter purchase orders. See "Purchasing and Receiving Merchandise to Sell."

➤ Sell your goods and reflect all the money you earned in QuickBooks. See "Selling Merchandise and Services."

➤ Keep your records up to date by recording how much your customers have paid you. See "Getting Paid."

➤ Stay in good stead with your suppliers by paying your bills on time. See "Paying Your Bills."

➤ Forget about entering invoices before you get paid or bills before you're ready to pay them if you are a cash business. See "The Cash Business."

Quick Guide to Banking with QuickBooks

I think it's safe to say that there isn't a business that doesn't have a bank account. The bank account is the clearinghouse where all cash comes and goes. The income that you earn makes its way to your bank account, and the payments that you make to operate your business are taken from your bank account.

Keeping track of your back account records and making sure that they are accurate will be two of the most important aspects of your QuickBooks routine. This chapter shows you all the ins and outs of setting up and using your bank account in QuickBooks. You'd better get busy!

Have You Got a Bank Account?

Each bank account owned by your company needs to be set up separately in QuickBooks. Your regular cash checking account, payroll account, savings account, petty cash account—each of these requires separate bookkeeping.

You may have already set up bank accounts when you went through the EasyStep Interview (see Chapter 1, "Doing the EasyStep Tango"). If you acquire a new bank account after the Interview is completed, you'll need to go through the setup steps covered in this portion of the chapter.

Changing Bank Account Info

If you have already created a bank account in QuickBooks and then find you need to change information relating to that account (the account number changed or you want to alter the way in which the name appears on your financial statements), open the Lists menu and choose Chart of Accounts (or press Ctrl+A). Click the name of the account you wish to edit, and then click the Account button at the bottom of the Chart of Accounts window and choose Edit. Make any necessary changes, and then click OK to close the Edit Account window. There, that was easy.

Setting Up Your Bank Account

Follow these steps to set up a bank account in QuickBooks:

1. Open the Chart of Accounts List (press Ctrl+A), and press Ctrl+N to open the New Account window (see the figure below).

Set up a new bank account by entering the name you want to see on your financial statements.

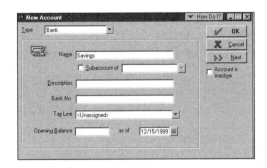

2. Click the Type drop-down arrow and choose Bank as the account type.
3. Next, click inside the Name text box and enter the name of this account. The name you enter, such as *Checking*, *Savings*, or *Cash*, is the name that will appear on your financial statements.

4. If this account is to be a sub-account of another account, click the **Sub-account of** check box and indicate the account.

5. Click inside the **Description** text box and enter an optional description for this account.

6. Use the **Bank No.** box to enter an optional bank number.

7. If you plan to prepare tax reports (see the section "Calculating and Paying Your Income Tax" in Chapter 13, "The Tax Man Cometh"), click the **Tax Line** drop-down arrow and choose the line of your tax return on which the bank account appears (this will apply only to partnerships and corporations—proprietorships don't include their cash account on their income tax returns).

8. If there is a balance in this account, enter that amount and the corresponding date in the Opening Balance area.

9. When you've created the account, click **OK** to add this account to your Chart of Accounts.

How Banking Transactions Are Entered

When you use QuickBooks, most of your transactions are entered on forms such as invoices, purchase orders, bills, cash sales, and so on. Any entry on one of these forms that affects your bank account balance will cause an adjustment to your account. For example, if you receive income from a customer, you'll enter the amount on the Cash Receipt form. That has the effect of debiting, or increasing, the balance in your cash account at the same time it decreases the amount of accounts receivable for your company.

For former Quicken users, this is a change that may take a little bit of getting used to. If you used Quicken in the past, you're accustomed to entering bank transactions in a register. In QuickBooks and QuickBooks Pro, you can view the register associated with your bank account by opening the Chart of Accounts and double-clicking the name of the account whose register you want to open (see the figure below).

The register for a cash account looks a lot like your personal checking account register.

You can make entries in this register, as you did in Quicken, but making entries in the register is generally not recommended. QuickBooks prefers that all entries be made directly on the forms, and the entries you make on the forms will transfer directly to this register. For example, if you enter a bill payment in QuickBooks and then open your bank account register, you will see where the payment was recorded and your cash balance reduced.

Putting Money into the Bank

There are two steps involved in getting money into the bank. One is getting the money to the bank physically, the other is recording the transaction in QuickBooks. QuickBooks can't help you with the first step (at least not until someone programs QuickBooks with wheels), but you can count on QuickBooks to make a record of the deposit and increase your bank balance by the amount you deposit.

Checks in the Mail

Here's a common scenario: You opened the mail this morning and were greeted with a pile of checks from customers who have paid you for work you performed or for purchases they made from you (hooray!). You need to record the receipt of this money in QuickBooks so that the invoices that were issued to your customers will no longer be recorded as outstanding.

To indicate the receipt of cash, open the Activities menu and choose **Receive Payments** (or, in the QuickBooks Navigator, click the **Sales and Customers** tab, and then click the **Receive Payments** icon). The Receive Payments window will open (see the following figure). For each payment that you receive, you'll enter the name of the customer and, if applicable, the name of the job. When you enter the name of the customer, any invoices outstanding for that customer will appear on the lower part of the window.

Enter a customer name and then the amount received in payment.

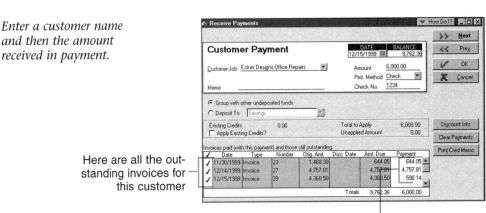

Here are all the outstanding invoices for this customer

You can change these amounts, making sure that the payment applies to the correct invoices

Enter the amount received in the Customer Payment area of this Receive Payments window. You can fill out the fields in this area like a check. Click the **Customer:Job** drop-down arrow to choose a customer, specify a date for the payment, an amount, payment method, and check number (if applicable). Now you're ready to check off which invoices are included in the payment.

When you enter the amount in the Amount field in the Customer Payment area, notice that QuickBooks makes assumptions at the bottom of the window about the invoice(s) to which this payment applies. You can override these assumptions by entering exact payment amounts in the Payment column for each invoice. The payments you enter in the Payment column cannot exceed the amount in the top Customer Payment area. If you do exceed this amount, QuickBooks will give you an error message.

Use the options in the middle of the window to designate whether the money received is to be deposited in a single deposit or grouped with other undeposited funds. For example, if it's a single deposit, click the **Deposit To** option and then specify which account you're depositing to; click the drop-down arrow and make a selection from the account list.

When you've finished entering information and checking which invoices the amount applies to, you're ready to exit the window or move on to record another payment. Click **Next** to move to another window to enter another payment received, or click **OK** if you've entered all of your payments.

What next? The money you received somehow needs to be transported to your bank. The next section covers the procedures for making bank deposits in QuickBooks.

Recording Bank Deposits

When you've entered all of your income in QuickBooks, you need to create a bank deposit. QuickBooks enables you to indicate which funds are being deposited and to which bank and lets you choose how the amounts will be grouped for depositing.

Time for a Deposit

When you're ready to create a deposit, follow these steps:

1. Open the Activities menu and choose **Make Deposits** (or click the **Deposits** icon on the **Sales and Customers** tab of the Navigator). This opens the Payments to Deposit window (see the next figure).

The Payments to Deposit window lists all money that has been received.

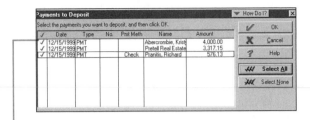

Check off each
payment you want to
deposit at this time

2. All amounts that you have received and recorded in QuickBooks are listed. On this list, you check off all amounts to be deposited in this particular deposit by clicking each one.

3. If you plan to group amounts into separate deposits, for purposes of depositing either on separate days or in separate bank accounts, just check the amounts that are for one deposit. You cannot change amounts in this window. If Mr. Jacobson paid you $2,000 and you only want to deposit $1,000 in your checking account, you cannot make this adjustment—you'll have to record a deposit of the full $2,000.

4. Click **OK**, and the Make Deposits window will appear (see the following figure), listing all the items you checked.

All amounts you checked in the Payments to Deposit window appear in this window, ready to be deposited in your bank account.

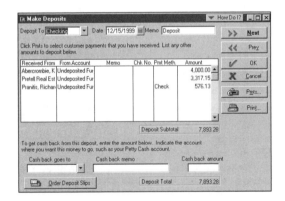

5. Verify the bank account listed in the Deposit To field (click the drop-down arrow to change it) and the date of the deposit shown in the Date field (click the **Date** icon to change it).

6. If you plan to request cash back from the bank when you make the deposit, you can indicate this at the bottom of the window.

7. There is an option to print either a deposit slip or a deposit summary with this deposit. Click the **Print** button to make a choice from these options, and then click **OK** to open the Print Lists box. Click **Print** to print the deposit slip and return to the Make Deposits window.

8. Back in the Make Deposits window, click **Next** if you want to prepare another deposit, or click **OK** if you are finished.

Depositing Plastic Money

If you receive payment from your customers by credit card, these payments need to be recorded just as if they were checks or other forms of cash. The Receive Payments window has a Pmt. Method field where you can indicate credit card payments; simply click the drop-down arrow and select the credit card type. (Refer back to the "Checks in the Mail" section earlier in this chapter to learn how to use the Receive Payments window.)

When you enter deposit information as you did in the previous set of steps, you will see credit card payments listed along with the other payments you received. The Pmt Meth (Payment Method) column of the Payments to Deposit window will indicate a credit card payment.

Typically, all credit card payments are deposited separately from cash, with a separate deposit slip (check with your bank about their rules for making credit card deposits). You may even bank with a separate financial institution for your credit card transactions.

Taking Money Out of the Bank (Legally!)

They say, whoever "they" are, that you have to spend money to make money, and most business owners will verify that is a fact. In the beginning of this chapter, you learned about how to get money into your bank account. This section of the chapter explains how you can get money out of the bank.

When you enter a bill payment on the Pay Bills screen (see the next figure), there's an option to indicate whether or not you want QuickBooks to write the check for you. If you plan to write your checks yourself by hand, uncheck this option. If you want QuickBooks to write the checks for you, leave the option checked. As you enter bill payments on the Pay Bills screen, the checks go into a queue waiting to be written, but they don't actually get written until you make such a request. (For more information about paying bills, see the "Paying Your Bills" section in Chapter 8, "The Daily Grind.")

Show the bills you plan to pay on this screen.

Check this box if QuickBooks is to print the check

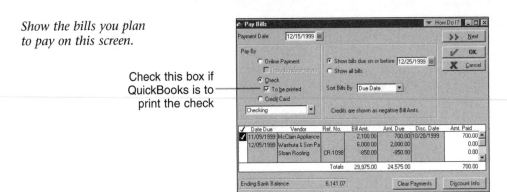

If you take a look at your Reminders List, you'll see that any checks you have indicated QuickBooks should print are listed in the Checks to Print section (see the figure below). Every time you indicate there is a check to be printed, QuickBooks adds that information to your Reminders List. See "Printing Checks," later in this chapter, for the instructions on how these checks get printed.

These checks won't be written until you give QuickBooks the go-ahead.

Your Very Own Reminder List

QuickBooks provides its users with a Reminders List, which shows all items waiting to be printed, bills that are due to be paid, and invoices for which payments should have been received by now. QuickBooks displays this list by default whenever you open the program. To display it any other time, just open the Lists menu, choose **Other Lists**, and then choose **Reminders**. (You also can click the **Reminders** icon on the **Company** tab in QuickBooks Navigator.) Double-click any entry on the Reminders List to see the details of that entry (for example, double-click **Bills to Pay** to see the complete list of bills that are currently outstanding), or click the **Detail** button at the bottom of the list to see the complete details of every topic on the list. The **Summary** button at the bottom of the list returns the list to titles only, with no details.

Add your own personal reminders to the Reminders List (such as your best friend's birthday or a dentist appointment) by opening the Lists menu and choosing **To Do Notes**. Press **Ctrl+N** to enter a new To Do note and set a date on which you want to be reminded. Click **OK** when the note is completed, and QuickBooks will remind you of the event on the date you indicated.

Writing Checks

In addition to the checks that need to be written when you indicate that you plan to pay a bill, you have the option of going right to a check writing screen and issuing checks without a related bill payment.

For example, you may need to issue a check to pay your rent, or perhaps you've been asked to donate money to a local civic group. There is no bill associated with the expense; you simply want to write a check.

Close Your Windows!

It's easy to forget to close feature windows from time to time, but when your screen gets too cluttered, you know it's time to close a few things. To close any window, click the window's close button (X), located in the upper-right corner of the window.

Follow these steps to write a check in QuickBooks:

1. Open the Activities menu and choose **Write Checks**, or just press **Ctrl+W** (or click the **Checking and Credit Cards** tab of the Navigator and choose **Checks**). A check will appear onscreen in the Write Checks window. It looks very much like a real paper check (see the following figure).

Write checks directly on the check form.

Choose a payee; QuickBooks will fill in the address information below

Check here if QuickBooks is going to print the check

Click here if this is an online payment

Show what the check is for here

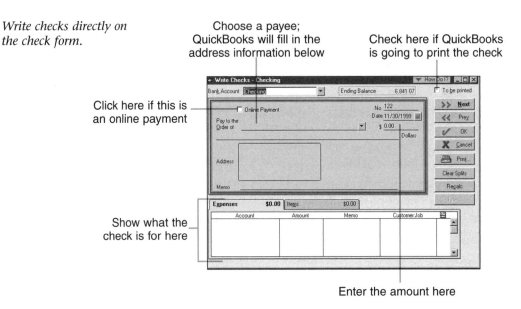

Enter the amount here

2. Verify the bank account at the top of the Write Checks window (click the **Bank Account** drop-down arrow to change it, if needed).

3. Enter the date that should appear on the check in the Date field (click the **Date** icon to change the date, if needed).

4. Click the **Pay to the Order of** drop-down arrow and choose the name of the payee.

5. Enter an amount in the Amount field.

6. If you have already entered a bill from this payee, QuickBooks will remind you that you should use the Pay Bills window to make a bill payment, instead of using this check window.

   If there are purchase orders outstanding for this vendor, QuickBooks will tell you and ask if you would like to pay against an outstanding purchase order. If you indicate yes, QuickBooks will display a list of outstanding purchase orders. Check off the order(s) against which you wish to pay, and then click **OK**. The amount due from the purchase order(s) you checked will appear in the Amount field of the check. You can change this amount if you are not paying the full amount at this time. If you are not paying from a purchase order, enter the amount you intend to pay in the Amount field.

7. Enter a description of what the payment is for at the bottom of the window, in either the **Expenses** or **Items** tab (depending on whether you are paying an expense or purchasing inventory items). Also enter an account to which this payment should be charged.

8. If you plan to have QuickBooks write the check for you, click the **To be printed** check box at the top of the window. Leave the check box unchecked if you're going to write the check by hand.

9. Click **Next** to continue to another check, or click **OK** to close this window and save your changes.

Printing Checks

If you plan to print checks with QuickBooks, you will need to obtain special check form paper. Intuit provides such paper; it can be ordered from the Intuit Web site at www.intuitmarket.com, or you can call Intuit at 800-433-8810. You can also find check form paper at office supply stores. Once you've obtained some check form paper, you're ready to print checks with QuickBooks.

Testing Your Printer

Before sending real checks through your printer, you probably want to run a test to make sure everything is going to line up properly (no sense wasting good checks on a dry run). Before placing checks in the printer, open the File menu and choose **Printer Setup**. In the Form Name area choose **Checks/Paychecks**. Click the **Align** button, and then in the Align Checks window indicate how many checks you plan to print on a page. In the Fine Alignment window that appears next, click **Print Sample**. QuickBooks will print a sample check page on whatever paper you have in your printer.

Hold this page up to your check form to see how everything lines up. If you need to make some adjustments, go back to the Fine Alignment window and enter incremental horizontal and vertical measurements for moving the text on the check. Continue testing in this manner until you are satisfied that the checks will print properly. Click **OK** when you are finished with Printer Setup.

Follow these steps when you're ready to print checks:

1. Make sure you have the check form paper in your printer, and then open the File menu and choose **Print Forms**, **Print Checks**.

2. In the Select Checks to Print window that appears (see the next figure), indicate which checks you want QuickBooks to write by checking them in the left column.

Place a check mark next to each item for which you want QuickBooks to write a check.

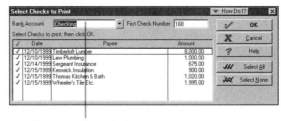

Make sure this is the
correct bank account

3. Make sure you have the correct checking account showing. (Make sure one more time that you put the check paper in the printer!) Click **OK** to print checks.

4. The Print Checks window will appear, as shown in the figure below. Verify the name of the printer (if you have an option for more than one) and the style of checks. There's an **Options** button next to the Printer Name field that lets you request color or black-and-white printing and portrait or landscape orientation.

*Click the **Print** button and QuickBooks will print all the checks you selected.*

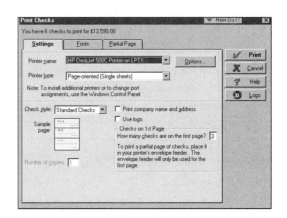

5. Click **Print**. The Print Checks window will close, and checks will start flying out of your printer.

Transferring Funds from One Account to Another

From time to time you will need to move money from one account to another. You may have money in an interest-bearing account that you want to move into your checking account when it's time to write checks. Or perhaps you have a surplus of cash in the checking account and you want to transfer that money into an interest-bearing account.

To transfer money from one account to another, follow these steps:

1. Open the Activities menu and choose **Transfer Money**. If you prefer to use QuickBooks Navigator, click the **Checking and Credit Cards** tab, and then click **Transfer Money**. The Transfer Funds Between Accounts window will appear (see the following figure).

Show which accounts you are transferring from and to in these areas

Tell QuickBooks you want to transfer funds from one account to another.

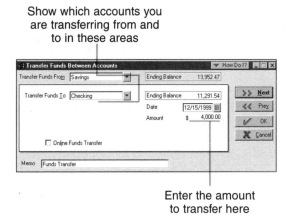

Enter the amount to transfer here

2. Use the **Transfer Funds From** drop-down arrow to select the account you want to move funds from.

3. Use the **Transfer Funds To** drop-down arrow to choose the account you want to move the funds to.

4. Enter a date in the Date field and the amount of the transfer in the Amount field.

5. Check the **Online Funds Transfer** check box if you want to transfer funds between online bank accounts. Both of the accounts have to be online accounts for this to work.

6. Click **OK** and you're in business (or click **Next** if you want to record another transfer).

Entering Dates in QuickBooks

You'll notice the Date icon on numerous QuickBooks forms. A click on the icon will display a pop-up calendar. You can use the calendar to select a date; simply click a date, and it's immediately inserted into the form's Date field. To change the month displayed, click the arrows at the top of the pop-up calendar.

If this is an online transfer, see "Performing Bank Transactions Without Leaving Your Keyboard," later in this chapter, for more info on moving money through cyberspace.

Paying with Credit Cards

When you make a payment with a credit card, it's easy to forget to record that information in QuickBooks. It's up to you to make a regular practice of recording your credit card payments in QuickBooks so that QuickBooks will reflect up-to-the-minute amounts that are owed to the credit card companies.

Your credit card debts are treated as accounts payable by QuickBooks, so when you record a new charge, QuickBooks will update the amount that you owe to the credit card company.

Setting Up Credit Cards

Set up a new credit card account by opening the Chart of Accounts window (press **Ctrl+A**) and pressing **Ctrl+N**. The New Account window will appear. Click the **Type** drop-down arrow and choose **Credit Card** as the type of account. Then enter the name of the credit card, an optional description, the card number (also optional), the tax line if you plan to prepare tax reports in QuickBooks, and the opening balance on this account, if any. Click **OK** to close the window and officially establish your credit card account.

To record amounts charged on credit cards, follow these steps:

1. Open the Activities menu and select **Enter Credit Card Charges**. The Enter Credit Card Charges window will magically appear (see the following figure).

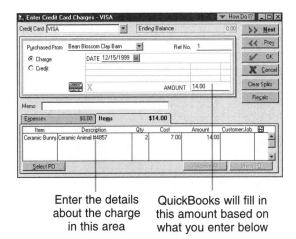

Enter amounts charged on your credit card so that your accounting records in QuickBooks will be up to date.

Enter the details about the charge in this area

QuickBooks will fill in this amount based on what you enter below

2. Use the **Credit Card** drop-down arrow to display a list of credit card accounts. Pick the credit card you used (VISA, American Express, Frederick's of Hollywood...).

3. Click inside the **Date** field and enter the date of the charge.

4. In the bottom part of the screen, enter a description of your purchase, along with the amount. QuickBooks will fill in the total amount at the top of the screen.

5. Click **OK** to close the window (or **Next** to enter another charge).

Oops! I Have to Void That Check

Every now and then you may encounter a situation where you have a check that needs to be voided. Perhaps you wrote a check twice in error or wrote a check for the wrong amount. No matter what your reason is for voiding a check, you need to do more than tear the paper check in two. You must change your QuickBooks records to reflect the void.

Follow these steps to void a check:

1. Open the check register by displaying the Lists menu and choosing **Chart of Accounts** (or press **Ctrl+A**) and double-clicking on the account in which the check needs to be voided.

2. Find the unwanted check in the register. Right-click the check and a pop-up menu will appear (see the next figure).

Choose the **Void** *option from the pop-up menu in the register to void a check.*

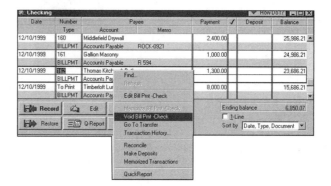

3. Choose **Void Check**, or **Void Bill Pmt-Check** if there is a bill associated with this check. QuickBooks will change the check amount to zero, note that the check has been voided, and go to the associated bill and change the amount paid to zero. The amount of the bill will return to your accounts payable account.

4. Click the **Record** button to finalize this action.

If you void the wrong check, open the **Edit** menu and choose **Revert.** QuickBooks will reinstate the check amount and the paid bill. For this Revert process to work, it must be done right away. You can't perform other transactions and then try to revert the voiding process.

The Dreaded Bank Reconciliation

One of the banes of mankind seems to be the monthly bank reconciliation. Being an accountant type, I'm one of those people who anxiously awaits the monthly delivery of my bank statement, hurries to reconcile as soon as it gets in the door, and insists that everything balance exactly to the penny (and, of course, it always does). But that's me.

Most people set the statement aside and perform a reconciliation only when every other conceivable chore has been completed. And they don't mind a discrepancy of a few cents.

With QuickBooks, your bank reconciliation experience can be just like that of the accountants (I know, a gruesome thought…)—simple, painless, and accurate.

When your bank statement arrives in the mail, follow these easy steps:

1. Open the Activities menu and choose **Reconcile** (or click the **Checking and Credit Cards** tab in the Navigator window and then click the **Reconcile** icon). The Reconcile Checking (or whatever account you're working on) window will appear (see the following figure).

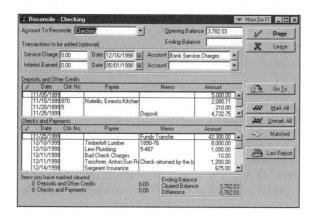

Reconcile your bank account on this screen, checking off each item that appears on your bank statement.

2. Verify that you are reconciling the correct account in the Account To Reconcile field.

3. Compare the opening balance on your bank statement to the balance shown in the Opening Balance field. The opening balance must agree with the amount on your statement.

4. Enter the ending balance from your bank statement in the Ending Balance field.

5. In the Transactions to Be Added area, fill in any other information from your statement, such as service charges or interest earned. *add!*

6. Check off each item in the **Deposits and Other Credits** list and the **Checks and Payments** list as they appear on your bank statement. Make sure the amounts agree (to the penny!). If there is an amount that is different from the statement, figure out which is right. If you're right, contact the bank and let them know they made a mistake. If the bank is right, click the item and the **Go To** button, or double-click the amount in question. QuickBooks will take you right to the original source document, where you can enter a change.

7. When every item has been entered and the amounts all verified, the Difference area at the bottom of the screen will show a zero balance. If there is something other than zero here, go back and compare amounts between your statement and the amounts listed on this screen. When you find the discrepancy, correct it.

8. Click **Done** to finish the job.

If your reconciliation takes longer than you anticipated, you can click the Leave button on the reconciliation screen and return at a later time. QuickBooks will save everything you've entered up to that point, and you can pick up right where you left off when you return.

Performing Bank Transactions Without Leaving Your Keyboard

Online banking is sweeping the country, or so the banks would have you believe. Many companies are taking their time switching to online banking, but the banks are all in favor of it and are offering interesting incentives to get companies to try the service.

What can you do with an online bank account? You can transfer funds between accounts, you can check your balance, and you can pay bills. The banking part and the bill-paying part don't necessarily go hand in hand—at most banks you can sign up for one service or the other or both.

If you decide to give online banking a try, shop around a bit. There are banks all across the country offering online services—you don't necessarily have to use your hometown bank.

Choosing a Bank for Online Transactions

When considering a bank that can provide online services, you should ask a lot of questions. Here's a sample checklist of some questions you can ask when you inquire about signing up for online services:

- ➤ Does the bank take accounts from your state and city?
- ➤ What is the minimum deposit for a new account?
- ➤ Will a minimum monthly balance in either a checking or savings account affect the monthly fee?
- ➤ Does the bank pay interest on funds held in the account?
- ➤ Is there a transaction fee for writing checks?
- ➤ Will you have access to an automated teller? If so, are there fees associated with this service?
- ➤ What online features does the bank offer?
- ➤ Does their service interact with QuickBooks software?
- ➤ What is the monthly fee for online services? (Unfortunately, this stuff isn't free.)
- ➤ Is there a maximum number of transactions that are covered by the online fee?
- ➤ Does the monthly fee take effect immediately, or is there a grace period for new account holders?

➤ Does the fee increase with increased online usage?

➤ Is the online service available 24 hours a day?

➤ Does the bank provide telephone support for online services and, if so, what are the hours of service?

➤ How long does it take for a bill paid online to reach the recipient? Is there a guarantee associated with this? Will the bank pay any penalties that relate from a late online payment?

As you can see, there are many factors to consider when thinking about going online.

Curious About Online Banking?

If you would like to experiment with the online banking screens before actually setting up your own online account, open the sample company file that comes with your QuickBooks program (open the File menu, choose **Open Company**, choose **Sample**, then click the **Open** button. You can explore the online banking options with the sample company's bank account, which is set up for pretend online banking. When you are ready to return to your own company file, open the File menu, choose **Open Company**, click your company filename, and click **Open**.

Setting Up Your Online Account in QuickBooks

So you've decided to give online banking a try, eh? First you'll need to establish an online account with your bank and wait for verification that your online account is available for use. Once you've done that, you're good to go. Here's how you get started in QuickBooks.

Open the Online menu and choose **Online Banking**, **Getting Started**. In the window that appears, choose **Enable Accounts**. The Online Banking Setup Interview window will appear, where you will find step-by-step instructions for setting up your account. Fill in the information about your bank and your account name and number, and click **Next** after each screen is completed. Click the **Leave** button on the last screen to exit from this window.

You can set up as many online accounts as necessary by going through this Interview process multiple times.

What Can You Do with an Online Account?

If you have established an online bank account and set up the account in QuickBooks, you will see check boxes on various forms, indicating an option for online payment whenever you make a transaction where cash is expended (such as paying bills or writing checks). If you plan to use the online banking feature to make a payment, check this box on the transaction form.

Believe it or not, you actually have to be online in order to *send* an online payment. Wishing doesn't make it so. Not only do you have to be online, but you have to ask QuickBooks to send the payment.

Open the Online menu and choose **Online Banking**, **Online Banking Center**. The online world will open up to you via the Online Banking Center window (see the next figure). Check off any transaction you want to perform in the **Items To Send** list, and then click the **Send** button and watch the sparks fly out of your computer! (Well, we hope not....) Clicking **Send** will cause your computer to jump online, if it isn't already there, and follow all of your online banking and bill payment instructions.

*Click the **Send** button when you are ready to dispatch your transactions to your bank.*

Check off any transaction you want to perform

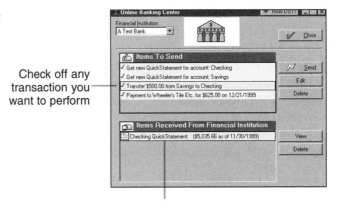

Items your bank sends back to you (like account balances or email messages) will appear here after you make the online connection

Your bank will send your current bank statement when you contact them online. You can also send messages to your bank. Open the Online menu and select **Online Banking**, **Create Message**, and your email message will be dispatched along with your other online transactions. Click the **Close** button when you have finished your online activity.

The Supreme Decadence: Online Bank Reconciliation

When you receive a bank statement from your online account, it appears in the Online Banking Center window (see the previous figure). Click the bank statement, and then click the **View** button to see the statement. You should make sure all transactions match those in your registers. Unmatched transactions are noted at the top of the form. Click an unmatched transaction, and then click the **Match** button, and QuickBooks will enter the transaction in your register.

The next time you reconcile your bank statement, click the **Match** button on the reconciliation screen, and any amounts that were noted on the online statement will be automatically matched up with items on your reconciliation screen. This should make your reconciliation a breeze!

Paying Bills Online

Click the **Online Payment** check box on the Pay Bills window if bills are to be paid via an online transfer. The payment information will appear in the Online Banking Center window, where you will need to go to dispatch the payment.

When you request online payment of a bill, QuickBooks will check the date you have indicated, to see if there is enough time to get the bill paid electronically. You will be advised of an automatic date change if more time is needed for the electronic transfer.

Now You've Done It!

Money is important to your business—there's no income and no cash flow without it. The information in this chapter will help you keep track of your money in QuickBooks.

➤ Set up a bank account, and QuickBooks will do the rest, entering your receipts and payments right into the account so your balance is up to date. See "Setting Up Your Bank Account."

➤ Make deposits with the help of QuickBooks. See "Putting Money into the Bank."

➤ You can write checks, transfer funds, and make credit card payments, with QuickBooks in the background getting everything recorded in the right accounts. See "Taking Money Out of the Bank."

➤ Clean up those bank records by reconciling regularly. See "The Dreaded Bank Reconciliation."

➤ Consider the world of online banking and bill paying—it's the direction of commerce in the twenty-first century. See "Performing Bank Transactions Without Leaving Your Keyboard."

Chapter 10

Getting Useful Information Out of QuickBooks

In This Chapter

➤ Create quick reports with QuickReports

➤ How to use QuickBooks' standard reports

➤ Customize reports to fit your needs

➤ Create your own reports using Excel

You send your child to college, pay the bills for four years (maybe longer) and never see a grade card, right? Wrong. Theoretically, you look to the grade card as a measuring stick to analyze the child's success—and as a sanity check to ensure you've not wasted your money.

QuickBooks reports allow you to generate your own grade card to show you what's going on in your business. You can analyze business activities for specific periods, summarize things that have happened, explain to others how your business is doing, and generate lists of transactions about a vendor, a customer, an item, an employee, or an account.

This chapter looks at the vast array of standard reports, many of which will suit your business needs exactly. Then, for those times when you need to create your own report or simply tweak an existing one, we'll show you that, too. But we'll start with creating a QuickReport—the fastest report in town!

Speedy Reports with QuickReports

With QuickBooks reports, all you have to do is tell QuickBooks that you want a report, and it produces one for you. It's a great time saver, and it gives you the opportunity to boss around your program a little bit.

The quickest way to generate a report is through QuickReports. You can make a QuickReport for any item on any QuickBooks list or from any account or customer register.

For example, display a vendor, customer, item, employee, or account list and press **Ctrl+Q.** You can also click the **Reports** button in the list window and select one of the QuickReport choices. If you display a register such as Accounts Receivable, Accounts Payable, Checking, or Sales Tax Payable and click the **Q-Report** button, QuickBooks generates a QuickReport for an entry in the register. The figure below shows a QuickReport for an inventory item from the Item List.

When you create a QuickReport for an inventory item, you'll see all the invoices, receipts, and purchase orders that include that item.

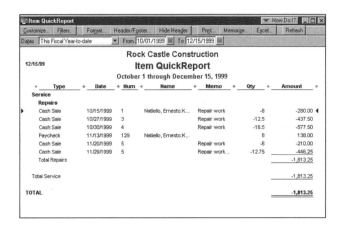

When you're finished with a report, you have several choices. You can close it (click the close button (**X**) in the upper-right corner), print it (see "Printing and Previewing Reports," later in this chapter), customize it (see "Customizing Your Reports," later in this chapter), or memorize it for use at a later time (see "Memorizing Reports," later in this chapter).

Besides generating QuickReports, the Reports menu on the main menu bar offers more than 100 different reports. By clicking **Reports** and going down the list, you can see the categories of reports and the names of the reports in each category. The next figure shows the Reports menu, with the Profit and Loss reports submenu. To view a report, select the name of a report, and it opens onscreen.

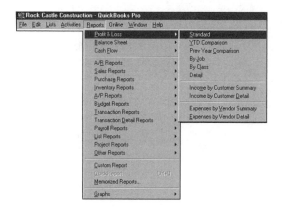

Most of the topics on the Reports menu include sub-menus that list the standard reports available in each category.

There are other opportunities for preparing reports. Notice on the QuickBooks Navigator that on each of the navigator topics there is a list of related reports at the bottom of the Navigator screen. Click a report topic and select one of those listed to generate a report.

The formatting and filtering buttons at the top of each report window enable you to customize the report. We'll cover this in the "Customizing Your Reports" section, later in this chapter.

A Word About Your History

A report is only as good as the information that goes into it. If you haven't entered complete information in QuickBooks, your report is not going to be complete, either. If you haven't entered historical information and this is your first year of using QuickBooks, you won't be able to create reports that compare your company's activity from one year to the next. If this is the first year you're using QuickBooks and your start date is not January 1, your reports will not include an entire calendar year of activity.

Printing and Previewing Reports

Now that you've created your reports, the logical thing to do is to print them. Before you do this, you might want to change the orientation of the paper, resize the margins, change the fonts, or fit the report to one page.

To print a report, click the **Print** button at the top of any report window. You'll see a Print Reports dialog box, shown in the next figure, that allows you to change settings, fonts, and margins for the report. If you won't be changing the report in any way, simply click the **Print** button and you're done.

Click here to print

The Print Reports dialog box offers all kinds of options for controlling how your reports are printed.

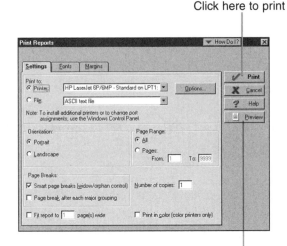

Click here to preview the report first

First Time Use?

The first time you print a report, you may see a prompt box that describes QuickBooks' new and improved printing features. Click **OK** to ignore it and go on. If you don't want to see it again, click the **Do not display this message in the future** check box.

Preview your new creation before it goes to print by clicking the **Preview** button in the Print Reports box. This opens the Print Preview window, as shown in the next figure. The preview displays one page at a time. To see other pages, click the **Next Page** or **Prev Page** button at the top of the preview window.

Enlarge the preview area by clicking the **Zoom In** button. Notice that the mouse pointer becomes a magnifying glass icon when in the Print Preview window. You can also use this to zoom in and out; simply click to zoom. When you're finished previewing the report, click the **Close** button to return to the Print Reports dialog box.

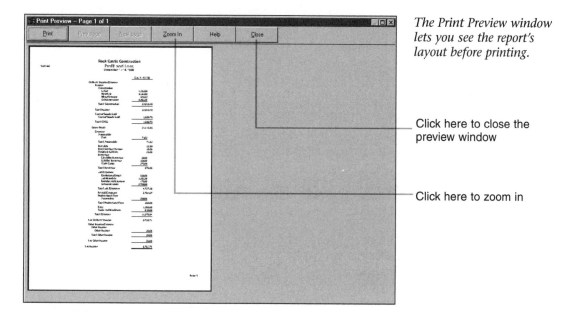

The Print Preview window lets you see the report's layout before printing.

Click here to close the preview window

Click here to zoom in

If you saw some things in the preview screen that didn't look exactly the way you want, you can reshape your report layout. Here are a few tips for changing report elements:

➤ From the Settings tab in the Print Reports dialog box, you can change the Orientation option from Portrait ($8\frac{1}{2}" \times 11"$) to **Landscape** ($11" \times 8\frac{1}{2}"$).

➤ From the Margins tab in the Print Reports dialog box, you can alter your report margins. Increasing the margins makes for more whitespace on the report. Decreasing the margins allows you to fit more information on the page.

➤ Click the **Fonts** tab in the Print Reports dialog box, then click the **Font** button to change fonts for the current report. In the column labeled Change Font For, select the area of the report to change, such as Report Title or Report Data, then click the **Change Font** button and select a new font. Once the font is selected, click **OK** until you return to the Print Reports box.

It's a Tight Squeeze

Ask QuickBooks to fit the report to one page by checking the **Fit report to 1 page(s) wide** check box on the Settings tab. QuickBooks automatically reduces the size of the font to attempt to fit the report on one page. Don't try to fit a five-page report into one—you won't like the result! Instead, use this for reports that are slightly too long or too wide.

Now that your print choices are set, don't forget to click the **Print** button to print your masterpiece.

Reports You Will Use Regularly

Let's take a few minutes to look at some of the reports that you will find your company needs to produce on a regular and frequent basis. We'll examine the standard reports, and later in this chapter we'll talk about how you can customize your reports to make them more useful to your particular company.

Are We Making Money Yet? The Profit and Loss Statement

Is your company making or losing money? It seems like a simple question, and it's a question that can be readily answered by producing a profit and loss statement. The profit and loss statement shows whether your company has made a profit or a loss over a particular period of time.

Many companies produce a profit and loss statement each month, summarizing the activity from the beginning of the year to the end of that month. Some companies produce profit and loss statements quarterly instead of monthly. Publicly held companies are expected to publish their profit and loss statements quarterly, making them available to their shareholders and any interested investors.

The profit and loss statement lists all of the income the company has earned and all of the expenses the company has incurred over the designated period of time.

To produce a profit and loss statement, open the Reports menu and choose **Profit and Loss**, **Standard**. The Profit and Loss report appears onscreen, as shown in the next figure. You can adjust the time period that this report covers by clicking in the **Dates** area at the top of the report window.

Close It!

To close any report window, click the window's close button (**X**) located in the upper-right corner of the window.

When you're looking at the Profit and Loss report, or for that matter any report, you might notice that if you hover your mouse pointer over any of the numbers in the report, the arrow pointer turns into a little mark-of-Zorro icon (the Z actually stands for Zoom). If you double-click a number when you see the Zoom icon, QuickBooks will display the detailed information that makes up that number. On that new report, you can double-click with the Zorro Z and see the form (such as an invoice or a bill) from which the number originated.

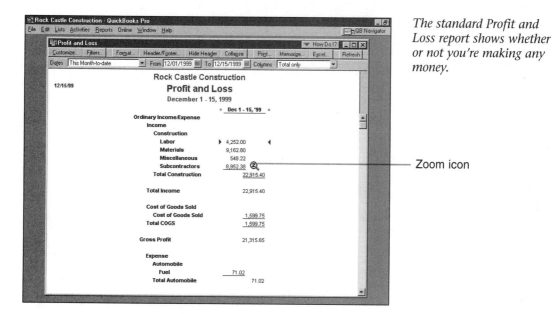

The standard Profit and Loss report shows whether or not you're making any money.

Zoom icon

What Am I Bid for This Company? The Balance Sheet

Unlike the profit and loss statement, which covers a particular time period, the balance sheet is effective as of a particular date. The balance sheet tells you how much your company is worth as of the date you've chosen, and it does this by listing all the company's assets and liabilities and subtracting the liabilities from the assets. The difference is called Net Worth, or Equity. Whichever term you use, it stands for the value of a company. This is one of many ways to value a company, and certainly not the only way, but it does give you a dollar amount that you can use to describe how much your company is worth.

To display the balance sheet (see the next figure), open the Reports menu and choose **Balance Sheet**, **Standard**. You can adjust the date if necessary, and you can double-click any of the numbers with the Zoom pointer to see the source of those numbers.

When Are These Customers Going to Pay Us? The Accounts Receivable Aging Summary Report

If your company is an accrual-basis company, another report that is useful is the Accounts Receivable Aging Summary report. If your company is a cash-basis company and you don't send invoices to your customers (and therefore don't have to cross your fingers and hope they'll pay you on time), then this report is meaningless to you.

Financial analysts like to examine a company's balance sheet to determine how much the company is worth.

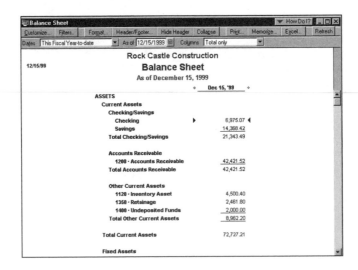

The A/R Aging Summary report shows how much your customers owe you as of the current date, and it breaks down the amounts owed to you in 30-day increments, so you can see which customers are more than 30 days overdue, which customers are more than 60 days overdue, and so on (see the figure below).

Use the A/R Aging Summary report to find out who's been naughty and who's been nice when it comes to making payments on time.

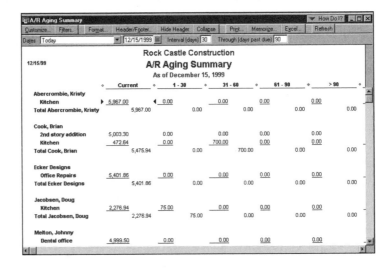

The report gives you an idea of who needs to pay you and who you might need to follow up on. It also gives you a sense of how your company's doing in the collection business. If the majority of your accounts are more than 30 days old, then obviously your customers for one reason or another don't feel the pressure to pay you within a 30-day time period (or whatever time period is important to you).

Business decisions about how to collect receivables from customers are based on the information gleaned from reports like this.

To display an A/R Aging Summary report, open the Reports menu and choose **Accounts Receivable Reports**, **Aging Summary**.

Tell Me EVERYTHING About My Transactions! The General Ledger Report

Another useful report is the General Ledger report, which lists all the transactions that have occurred in your company, in every single account. It is a very thorough, detailed report that allows you to examine all the transactions that have been going on in your company.

To produce a General Ledger report, open the Reports menu and choose **Other Reports**, **General Ledger**. The General Ledger report is arranged alphabetically by account, with the asset accounts first, followed by liabilities, equity, income accounts, and finally expense accounts. The figure below shows an example of a General Ledger report.

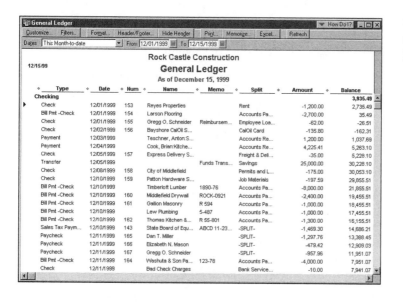

Use the General Ledger to check all the transactions you made.

Reports You'll Use Once in a While

Besides the biggies, there are a number of other interesting reports available to you in QuickBooks, some of which you may never use and some of which you may use only occasionally. It's certainly worth your time to take a look at the reports that are available, so that you'll know what kinds of reporting options are already established for your use in QuickBooks.

Remembering Report Names

After generating a report, print it with the report name at the top so that you have a record of the report. You might even jot yourself a note on the printed report indicating to which report category the report belongs.

There are comparative reports available that show the current year's activity compared to the same time period of the previous year. For example, a comparative income statement is available by opening the Reports menu and choosing **Profit and Loss** and **Prev Year Comparison**. A comparative balance sheet is produced by choosing **Reports**, **Balance Sheet**, **Comparison**.

Comparative reports enable you to see how your company has changed over a period of time.

There are sales reports available in QuickBooks that give you information such as how the sales of each of your individual inventory items are progressing. You can also produce the sales report by vendor so that you can see how much business you're getting from each one of your customers.

You can produce inventory reports that show you how much inventory you have in stock (or how much inventory QuickBooks thinks you have in stock). An inventory report can be used as a reference when you're trying to determine which inventory items sell well and should be ordered in greater quantity or which items you can remove from inventory without greatly affecting your revenue.

There is an array of tax reports available to you in QuickBooks that can help you produce your tax returns. These reports are covered in detail in Chapter 13, "The Tax Man Cometh."

QuickBooks will also produce for you a number of payroll reports that give you details on how much you've spent on payroll for each employee.

Reports You'll Wish You Had That QuickBooks Won't Give You

As vast as the list of standard reports can seem, there are still some reports that are not available automatically in QuickBooks. However, you can create your own reports to meet this shortfall by performing some customizing techniques.

You start with a standard report in QuickBooks, one that comes close to providing the information you want, then alter the report so that it contains more of the information that you need to obtain from it.

Customizing Your Reports

Besides showing report data, the report window includes many controls and data boxes across the top of the screen that can be used to customize the report.

Perhaps the quickest change to make is to alter the reporting period. Just choose a time frame from the Dates drop-down menu (click the drop-down arrow to view the list), such as **Last Week** or **This Fiscal Year To Date**. As soon as you make your selection, your report data will change according to the new dates. Or select specific dates from the **To** and **From** boxes and click the **Refresh** button to update the report.

Another common reason to customize is to add or remove the columns that appear in your report. Click the **Customize** button at the top of the report window. This opens the Customize Report window, as shown in the next figure.

Use the Customize Report dialog box to indicate exactly what types of information you want to include in your report.

By checking or clearing the check boxes, you can add or remove columns of information, change the reporting period, and choose the Cash or Accrual method for compiling the data. Click the **Advanced** button to hide rows or columns that have zero balances or that don't show any activity for the current reporting period, or to change the reporting year used in the report.

There's also a Filters button in the Customize Report window (this button is available on the actual report as well) that lets you filter out certain data, so that only data meeting particular requirements appears on your report. For example, you might want to show only amounts over $1,000 on your reports, or you might want to include only certain accounts on your report.

There are many choices for filtering your reports (as shown in the figure below). The choices that appear in the filter window depend on the filters that you choose. Follow these steps to filter report data:

1. Click the Filters button to open the Report Filters window (you can click the Filters button in the Customize Report box or on the report window). The Report Filters dialog box appears, as shown in the figure below.

2. Select an item to filter from the Filter list at the left of the box.

3. By choosing from pop-up lists, check boxes, or option buttons, or by typing data into a text box in the middle of the window, set the criteria for the filter items. The options will vary, depending on the filter you choose.

Choose a filtering option, then describe how you want to limit the items you see on your report.

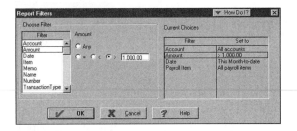

4. The filter and its criteria are added to the Current Choices listing on the right side of the window. You can remove any filter from the Current Choices area by clicking on the item you want to remove and pressing the **Delete** key on your keyboard.

5. Select another filter from the Filter list if another filter should by applied to the report.

6. When you are ready to apply the filters, click the **OK** button to see the report results.

When a filter is applied, the results are temporary unless the report is memorized with the filter options. See the section "Memorizing Reports," coming up next.

Memorizing Reports

You've gone to all the trouble of customizing a report to make it work for you, and it would be a shame to have to take the time to re-create this report each time you need it. In particular, if this is a report you will need to prepare frequently, you ought to consider memorizing the report.

To memorize a report, click the **Memorize** button at the top of the report window. QuickBooks asks you to type a report name, then click **OK**. The report will be remembered by that name. Don't make the name too obscure—you want to be able to find this report again in the future.

To display a report after you've memorized it, open the Reports menu and select **Memorized Reports**. QuickBooks will display a list of reports that you have memorized (see the figure below).

Look at all these reports I've memorized!

Sick of one of your memorized reports? From the Memorized Report List window, click the one you don't want and press the **Delete** key on your keyboard (or press **Ctrl+D**).

Working with Reports Outside of QuickBooks

Eventually you'll find that QuickBooks reports have their limits. When this happens, start with a report that gives you some of the basics, customize as best you can, then consider sending the report to Excel.

A good example of this is a report many people wish QuickBooks would produce—one that helps with computing state unemployment tax.

In most states, the state unemployment tax applies to the first $7,000 of each employee's wages. You need a report that will show you all employee wages up to $7,000. While you're at it, you might as well feed in the state unemployment tax rate that you pay and have all the calculations you need for this tax payment done on the report for you.

Reports in Excel

Our example here introduces you to the idea of working with QuickBooks reports in Excel. Learn more about how QuickBooks works with Excel in Chapter 19, "Making Friends with Microsoft."

To create a state unemployment report, first create in QuickBooks a payroll report that lists all of your company's employees and how much they have been paid year-to-date. You can start by showing the year-to-date earnings summary for each employee. Use the Employee Earnings Summary report (open the Reports menu and choose **Payroll**, **Employee Earnings Summary**).

Display the report in Excel by clicking the **Excel** button at the top of the report. (Note: If you are using a pre-Office 97 version of Excel or a different spreadsheet program, use the Print option to print the report to a file that can be read by your spreadsheet program.)

Once you're in Excel, delete any extraneous information (for example, you need only payroll amounts, you don't need withholding amounts for this example). Total the wages paid to each employee. Next to each employee's total wages, enter a formula that will present the information necessary for the unemployment report (see the accompanying Tip), as shown in the next figure.

Using Excel Formulas

In order to prepare the state unemployment report, create a formula in Excel that compares the employee's year-to-date salary or wages to $7,000 and prints the lesser number. For example, if an employee's total year-to-date salary is in cell M3, enter a formula such as this one in cell O3: =IF(M3>7000,7000,M3). This will place 7,000 in cell O3 if M3 is greater than 7,000 but otherwise will place the contents of cell M3 in cell O3.

Use Excel to provide you with the power to create a report that gives you exactly what you need.

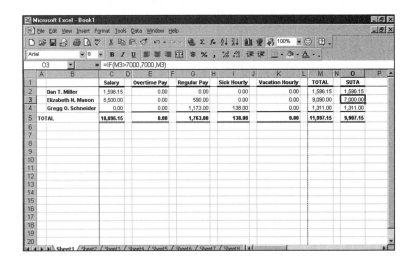

This is just one example of a report that you can spend hours sweating over in QuickBooks, attempting to find a way to create it, or you can spend five minutes creating in Excel. The Excel option gives you a speedy way to cut to the chase and customize reports beyond the restraints of your QuickBooks program.

Now You've Done It!

You should be well-versed in reports now, ready to extract all kinds of useful information from your QuickBooks program. You learned

➤ QuickBooks offers plenty of reports that don't take any effort on your part other than to click the name of the report and bring it up onscreen. See "Reports You Will Use Regularly."

➤ QuickBooks has a whole slew of reports that you may only use once or twice, but you can certainly experiment and see what's available. Check out "Reports You'll Use Once in a While."

➤ Sometimes QuickBooks just can't accomplish what you want in reports, but you can easily go one step beyond the standard reports with the help of a spreadsheet program. See "Reports You'll Wish You Had That QuickBooks Won't Give You."

Part 3

Special Features of QuickBooks

This section of the book covers features that are unique to QuickBooks Pro, such as estimates, time tracking, and multiuser functions. You will also find information here about particular areas of business accounting that probably affect every business in one way or another: depreciation, amortization, income taxes, and inventory.

Every accounting program has special ways of dealing with these special areas. Learn how QuickBooks treats these topics, and learn about alternatives to using QuickBooks to accomplish accounting feats that are beyond the scope of this program.

Special Treats for QuickBooks Pro Users

Did you spend a few extra bucks to spring for QuickBooks Pro? If so, what do you get that the regular QuickBooks users don't get? This chapter gives you the low-down on all the special features that only you QuickBooks Pro users can enjoy.

All of the features covered in this chapter relate to QuickBooks Pro. If you own the standard version of QuickBooks, you may want to read this chapter to satisfy your curiosity about what the "other guys" have. Just remember, the features described here, unfortunately, are not available in your version of the program.

What Does QuickBooks Pro Have to Offer?

Both QuickBooks and QuickBooks Pro have a lot to offer—no doubt about that. However, there are some major differences between the two programs. Knowing about those differences can help you if you are still trying to decide which program is best for you.

Here's the low-down on all the unique features of QuickBooks Pro:

➤ **Estimates** Submit proposals on jobs with estimates—forms that look a lot like invoices but are really just proposals. When you get the job, the estimate magically communicates with your invoice so you don't need to re-enter all the amounts.

➤ **Progress Billing** If you use estimates, you can choose to bill the client for all or a portion of the estimate by simply checking which items should be billed or indicating what percent of the estimate should be billed.

➤ **Time Tracker** QuickBooks Pro provides you with a little timer program that you can give to your employees and contractors. Just turn it on, and the clock starts ticking, keeping track of time spent on a job. Best of all, they don't need to have QuickBooks Pro in order to run the timer on their computers.

➤ **Multiple Users** Up to five computers can use QuickBooks simultaneously on a network, accessing the same data.

➤ **Best Buddies with Microsoft Word and Excel** An outstanding interface with Excel sends your reports dashing over to the world's most popular spreadsheet program, where you can massage the numbers to your heart's content. Create dazzling professional-sounding (and looking) form letters by integrating your Customer and Vendor Lists with Microsoft Word.

The remainder of this chapter will focus on the invoicing and timer features available in QuickBooks Pro.

Job Tracking in QuickBooks Pro

If you perform more than one job for a customer, you can keep track of the jobs separately, just as if they are subaccounts under a customer's name. You can prepare reports based on the total activity for a customer or for individual jobs for each customer.

To keep track of jobs in QuickBooks Pro, you first must set up a customer. Once a customer is entered into your QuickBooks file, you can create jobs for that customer.

The way you set up a job in QuickBooks Pro is to open the Lists menu and choose **Customers:Jobs** (or just press **Ctrl+J**). If you're using QuickBooks Navigator, click the **Sales and Customers** tab and then click the **Customers** icon at the top of the window. Any of these routes opens the Customer:Job List window. Click a customer name to select it from the list.

Where's That Customer?

If the name of the customer isn't on the list, click the Customer:Job button at the bottom of the Customer:Job List window and select New (or press Ctrl+N) and enter information about the customer, such as name, address, whether or not subject to sales tax, and so on.

Click the Customer:Job button, and choose Add Job. A window will appear called New Job (see the figure below). In the New Job window there are three tabs across the top.

Enter the name of the job here

Click here to enter information about this particular job

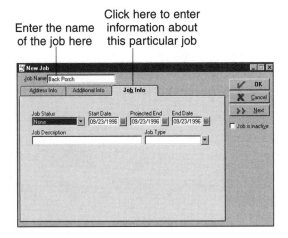

Enter information about a new job for an existing customer.

Enter the job name at the top of this window. You can have duplicate job names from one customer to the next, but each job for a particular customer should have a unique name. For example, if this is the second job you have done on this customer's back porch, make the job name more descriptive—something like Back Porch Job 2, or Second Back Porch, or Back Porch Windows.

The first tab, Address Info, contains address information about this customer and should not require any changes. The second tab, Additional Info, contains information about the customer such as account number, email address, and so on.

It is the third tab, Job Info, that you will use to provide details regarding this particular job. The information on the Job Info tab relates to this specific job, as opposed to the customer in general. Click the tab, and then enter a job status (Pending, Awarded, In progress, Closed, Not awarded), start and end dates, and miscellaneous memo information relating to this job.

When you've finished entering job information, click Next if you want to enter another job, or click OK to close the window.

Creating and Using Job Estimates

Probably the main reason people choose QuickBooks Pro over QuickBooks is to take advantage of the job estimates feature. In QuickBooks Pro you can create estimates, which are proposals or bids for jobs wherein you determine how much you think it will cost to do a job. The estimate stays in your QuickBooks Pro file. When you start performing the job, you can relate back to the estimate as you prepare invoices.

To create an estimate in QuickBooks, follow these steps:

1. Open the Activities menu and choose Create Estimates. (You can also click the Estimates icon on the Sales and Customers tab of QuickBooks Navigator.) The Create Estimates window will appear (see the figure below).

Create an estimate for a job to use as a proposal and a guide while the job is in progress.

Use the drop-down arrow to select the name of the customer and the job

2. Enter a customer and job name at the top of the estimate in the Estimate For text box. The address information for this customer will fill in automatically if you've previously entered this information when setting up the customer.

3. Enter items for this estimate (see Chapter 4, "What Are These Items, Anyway?," for more detail about items). Items include pieces of inventory, subcontracting costs, permits, the cost of your labor, and anything else you expect to sell to this customer. Descriptions and amounts may fill in automatically for the items you enter, or you may need to enter specific information in these columns.

Protect Yourself on Estimates

The estimate is just that—an estimate. Sometimes it's difficult to know in advance exactly how much a job is going to cost. When you create an estimate, you may plan to meet the exact amounts that are listed. But you might find that, once you begin the job, circumstances change, and the actual job cost might differ from the estimate. Because changes can happen, you will want to protect your right to alter an estimate. You should include a message on the estimate form that goes to the customer, describing the fact that you reserve the right to change the esti-mate, or that if there are changes in the estimated amounts, you will contact the customer for approval before performing any work beyond the costs shown on the original estimate.

4. Verify any sales tax that might appear, and then click Next to advance to the next estimate form, or OK to close this form.

The Beauty of Progress Billing

Once you have an estimate in your QuickBooks file, you can refer back to that esti-mate when you prepare invoices for the customer. When you prepare an invoice on a job that has been estimated, you have the option to reflect 100% of the estimate or a different percentage, or you can request that the invoice be prepared for specific items on the estimate.

This process of creating invoices based on a portion of the estimate is known as *progress billing*. The idea behind progress billing is that you bill the customer as por-tions of the job are completed, instead of waiting until the entire job is finished.

Progress Billing

The act of billing for a job as the job progresses, rather than waiting to bill when the job is completed.

Invoices are really easy to create when an estimate exists. Open the Activities menu and choose **Create Invoices** (or press **Ctrl+I** on the keyboard), and then enter a job name. QuickBooks will give you an alert message indicating that an estimate already exists and offering to let you build the invoice based on information from the estimate (see the figure below).

When this message appears, you can choose to create the invoice based on the estimate or not. If you create the estimate based on the invoice, you will see a window that asks you if you want to apply a percentage of the estimate to the invoice, or if you want to select specific items from the estimate (see the next figure).

Choose Yes to let QuickBooks create an invoice based on your estimate.

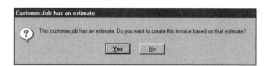

Choose the terms of your progress invoice.

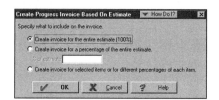

Enter a percentage, if that's the way you want to bill this job, or click **Create invoice for selected items or for different percentages of each item** to choose specific items that should appear on the estimate. Click **OK** when you have made your choice.

A window will appear, showing you the specific items that have been listed on the estimate, and you can check off the ones you want to appear on this invoice. You can also alter the amounts of items you are billing at this time. For example, if you are ready to bill for only a portion of the items at this time, you can enter the exact amount that should be billed for each item (see the following figure).

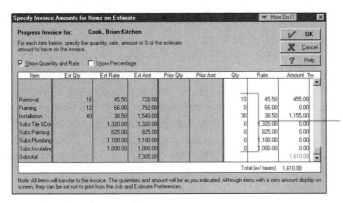

Choose which items you want to include in the progress invoice for this job.

Notice the specific quantities being billed at this time

When you're billing for an estimate, the invoice that you see onscreen lists all the items from the estimate, not just the items that you indicated you want to bill. However, when you print the invoice, only the items you requested will appear. You can verify this by clicking the Preview button in the Create Invoices window; you'll see that only the items you're actually billing will appear on the printed invoice.

No Zeroes

In order to ensure that only the items for which you are currently charging the customer appear on the invoice, open the File menu and choose Preferences, Job & Estimates. On the Company Preferences tab, check the box that reads Don't print items that have zero amount. Click OK to close the Preferences window.

Using the QuickBooks Pro Timer

It's not always easy keeping track of the amount of time you spend on a specific job. Wouldn't it be sweet if you could take an actual time card, stick it in a slot in your computer to punch in to start a job, and then punch out at the end of a job? Guess what—QuickBooks Pro comes with a built-in time clock! Well, you have to install it first, but it's there. The QuickBooks Pro Timer doesn't work exactly like a time-punch clock, but it's very close.

When you turn on the timer and indicate the job you're working on, you can leave the timer running in the background on your computer and go to work, whether the job requires working on the computer or running around the building. Whatever you do on the job, the timer keeps track of the time for you. You can also enter specific time allotments on the timer instead of running it as a time clock.

What's the point of the timer? By entering time in the timer, you keep an accurate record of time, and you save headaches for the person who figures out the payroll for your company. The payroll person needs only to call up your timer file, and all of your time will transfer into QuickBooks Pro. Also, time can be billed directly to jobs from the QuickBooks Pro Timer.

You can give the timer program to your employees, to contractors who perform work for you, or to anyone else you pay on the basis of the amount of time worked. The worker can enter information about time worked on a job into the timer program, and when the time file is returned to you, it can be imported directly into QuickBooks. Pretty slick!

Installing the QuickBooks Pro Timer

If you haven't installed the timer yet and want to use it, insert the QuickBooks Pro CD-ROM into your computer's CD drive. When the QuickBooks setup window appears onscreen, choose the **Install Timer** option to install this program on your computer.

When asked if you want to place the timer item on your desktop, choose **Yes**. This way the timer is easily accessible. If the timer has already been installed on your computer without a desktop icon, you can choose **Start**, **Programs**, **QuickBooks Pro**, **QuickBooks Pro Timer** to run the program.

Setting Up the QuickBooks Pro Timer

You don't need to run the QuickBooks Pro program, or even have it installed on your computer, to run the QuickBooks Pro Timer program. The two are independent of one another.

However, in order to use the timer with QuickBooks, you must create a file in QuickBooks Pro that contains the information that the person who will be using the timer will need. All the information required of QuickBooks Pro Timer users is saved in this export file. This includes a complete list of vendors (including employees), a list of customers and jobs, a list of service items, and a list of classes (if you use class tracking).

To create an export file in QuickBooks Pro, open the File menu and choose Timer Activities, Export Lists for Timer. An Export dialog box opens, as shown in the next figure. Here you are asked to indicate a filename, such as *custlist* or *jobnames*. (The QuickBooks Pro Timer uses the old eight-digit file naming convention for this filename—you can enter a longer name, but it will be truncated to eight letters when it is read by the timer.) Enter the name of a file, and then click Save. This file will be saved with an IIF extension.

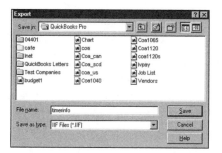

Enter a filename for your export file.

Using the QuickBooks Pro Timer

After creating the file, you're ready to use the timer. The timer is a separate program from QuickBooks Pro, so you don't need to have QuickBooks open when you run the timer. From the Windows desktop, double-click the QuickBooks Pro Timer icon, or open the Start menu and choose Programs, QuickBooks Pro, QuickBooks Pro Timer.

Double-click the desktop icon to run the QuickBooks Pro Timer.

Each person who uses the QuickBooks Pro Timer must create a personal timer file. From the QuickBooks Pro Timer program, open the File menu, choose New Timer File, and enter a name (such as *judytime* or *mytime*). Next, you must import the list file you created in QuickBooks Pro. Open the File menu, choose Import QuickBooks Lists, and choose the name you set up as your export filename in QuickBooks Pro. Click OK, and the lists referred to above will be available to you in the timer.

When the timer file has been created and the list file has been imported, you're ready to use the timer. Click the New Activity button and enter your name, the job name, the type of work you are performing, the class (if applicable), and any notes that seem appropriate to the job (see the following figure). Click OK.

Enter all appropriate job information in this window.

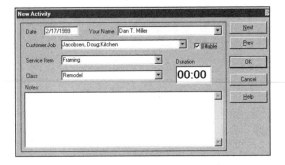

Make sure the correct activity appears in the timer window, and then click the **Start** button to start the clock. Only one activity can be clocked at a time. If you change the current activity, the timer will stop on the former activity and begin timing on the new activity.

To turn off the clock, click the **Stop** button (see the next figure). The buttons share space on the timer. When you click **Stop**, the button changes to Start, and you can continue turning the clock on and off until you're finally finished for the day or get tired of fooling around with the Stop and Start buttons, at which time you should definitely click the **Stop** button.

Choose an activity and click the Start button to activate the timer, and then click Stop when you're done.

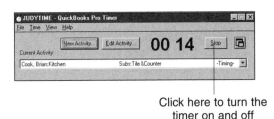

Click here to turn the
timer on and off

It's In the Way!

If the timer box is in your way while you work on the computer, just minimize it. Click the Minimize button in the upper-right corner of the timer window to reduce the timer to an icon on the Windows taskbar.

Sending Your Timer Information Back to QuickBooks Pro

When you've finished using the timer, you need to get the information back to QuickBooks Pro so that it will be recorded in your QuickBooks file. From the QuickBooks Pro Timer window, open the File menu and choose **Export Time Activities**. In the window that appears, indicate the date through which time should be exported (as shown in the next figure), click **OK**, and indicate a filename for your timer file. Click **OK** again, and your time information will be dispatched to QuickBooks.

Choose the date through which your time will be exported to QuickBooks Pro.

To access the timer information in QuickBooks Pro, open the File menu and choose **Timer Activities**, **Import Activities from Timer**. Click the name of the file, and then click **Open**. A summary of time that has been imported will appear onscreen (see the figure below). Click **View Report** to see detailed information about the time that was charged (if there is more than one item listed under Type, click the item for which you want to see a report, and then click **View Report**). Click **Close** when you have finished with this Import Summary window.

Using QuickBooks Navigator?

You can easily import the timer file using QuickBooks Navigator. Click the **Payroll and Time** tab, and then click **Timer Import/Export**. Select the file you want to import and click **Open**.

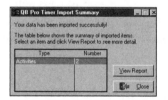

You can view a detailed report of the time that has been imported, or click Close *to close this window.*

Any information that was designated as chargeable directly to a job will be available with the invoice that you create for the job. From the invoice window, click the **Time/Costs** button, and the Choose Billable Time and Costs window will appear (see the following figure). Click the **Time** tab to see all the time that has been charged to this job, and then click in the left column to check off any time you want to place on the invoice. Click **OK** to close the Time/Costs window and return to the invoice.

All billed time is available on the client invoice.

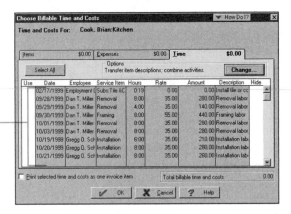

Click here to check off time that is to be billed currently

If you want to provide employees or vendors with a copy of the QuickBooks Pro Timer program to use on their own computers, you can do so by following these steps. You will need three blank, formatted disks for this process.

1. Place the first of three blank floppy disks in your computer.

2. Place the QuickBooks Pro CD-ROM in the CD-ROM drive of your computer.

3. Click the **Start** button, choose **Programs**, **QuickBooks Pro**, **Create Timer Install Disks**. Follow the onscreen instructions to transfer the timer program to the three floppy disks.

4. Give the floppy disks to an employee or contractor, who will then be able to use the timer on his or her computer. To install the timer, the user will click **Start**, **Run**; enter a:/install (where a: equals the floppy drive); and then click **OK**.

Refresh It!

When more than one person is using the company QuickBooks file at the same time, you should get very friendly with the Refresh button on the top of your report screens. If you're viewing a report and someone else has made a change that affects that report, clicking Refresh will bring the up-to-date info onto your screen.

Using QuickBooks Pro on Multiple Computers

Here's another feature fairly new to QuickBooks Pro—the ability to use your QuickBooks file on up to five separate computers simultaneously. You'll find this feature to be extremely cool if you've suffered the frustration of several people trying to use the QuickBooks company file on the same computer (one chair gets mighty crowded when five people are trying to sit on it at once). Now you can all sit at your own desks (unless you truly prefer the lap method) and work in the same QuickBooks file at the same time.

The QuickBooks Pro program gets installed on each of five computers, and you can purchase QuickBooks Pro in a 5-pack to make this process easier. You must have a separate copy of the program to install on each computer.

When you purchase the 5-user QuickBooks Pro program, you receive five separate CD-ROMs, each with its own registration number. Each computer participating in the multiuser option must install QuickBooks Pro from a separate CD-ROM. Each user may access the same QuickBooks data file.

Once QuickBooks Pro has been installed on each computer, the company file should be placed in a location where each computer can have access to it (such as a common network drive).

Now You've Done It!

I'll bet you're glad you're a Pro user now! Here are the special things that you can brag about to all your friends who purchased the standard edition:

➤ You can create estimates for the jobs that you're going to perform. See "Creating and Using Job Estimates."

➤ You can create invoices based on all or part of the estimates you've created. See "The Beauty of Progress Billing."

➤ You can give the QuickBooks Timer to your employees and let them use their computers as time clocks. See "Using the QuickBooks Pro Timer."

➤ You get to use QuickBooks Pro on more than one computer in your office, with everyone having access to the same company file. See "Using QuickBooks Pro on Multiple Computers."

Chapter 12

Everything You'd Rather Not Know About Depreciation

In This Chapter

➤ What's this depreciation stuff?

➤ Why do we have to use depreciation?

➤ How do you figure out depreciation?

➤ How do you record depreciation?

Depreciation? Yuk! If you've ever tried to figure out depreciation, you know what I mean. Depreciation is a fake expense. According to the depreciation rules, if I buy a piece of equipment that costs $3,000, then its depreciation in the year of purchase is $429. I don't want to say I only spent $429 this year and next year say I spent $738, and so on, when in fact I know I spent $3,000, and I have $3,000 less cash to show for it.

Just see what happens if I try telling the equipment store manager that I only want to give him $300 this year and that I'm going to pay for this equipment over the course of the next five years. The world of commerce doesn't work that way, but the world of financial statements requires that you confront the depreciation beast. This chapter shows you how.

What Is Depreciation and Why Do We Need It?

Techno Talk

Depreciation

A method of equating the cost of an asset with the useful, income-producing life of the asset. It's also what happens to a new car the second you drive it off the dealer's lot.

The theory behind depreciation is that the cost of major expenditures relates to a period of time longer than the current year. If I purchase a piece of equipment, say for $3,000, there is an assumption that I'm going to use the equipment to generate income for several years, so I should spread the cost of the equipment over those years in order to present a fair picture of my income, offset by appropriate expenses.

In point of fact, you and I know that I spent $3,000 this year, and that seems like it is the true fair picture of my financial distress. But accountants and the IRS all agree that we have to play this depreciation game and spread the cost of major purchases over the lifetime of the item(s) we purchase.

With that in mind, let's proceed to what we have to know about depreciation so that we can figure out how to account for it. Technically speaking, depreciation expense represents the wearing down or the usage of major purchases over a period of time. That period of time is supposed to equate roughly to the period of time during which you will use the asset to produce income.

Fortunately, you don't have to guess how long an asset is going to last, nor do you have to go back and redo your depreciation calculations if it turns out the asset lasts way longer than you predicted. There are tables that assign a life expectancy to various typical asset purchases that companies make. See the accompanying table, which sets out many common asset types and their designated life expectancies.

Life Expectancies of Common Assets

Type of Asset	Life Expectancy
Breeding hogs, racehorses (at least 2 years old), and old horses (at least 12 years old when placed in service)	3 years
Automobiles and light purpose trucks, computer equipment, and office equipment such as typewriters (remember those?), calculators, and copiers	5 years
Office furniture, tools, carpeting, business equipment that doesn't fit in the 5-year group, and horses that don't fit in the 3-year group	7 years

Type of Asset	Life Expectancy
Trees and vines bearing fruits or nuts and assets used in petroleum refining	10 years
Land improvements, sewers, treatment plants, drainage ditches, fences, telephone distribution plants, and communication equipment	15 or 20 years
Residential rental property	27.5 years
Commercial real estate property placed in service before May 13, 1993	31.5 years
Commercial real estate property placed in service after May 12, 1993	39 years

When entering the purchase of a computer in QuickBooks, for example, you'll enter the computer as an asset. That asset will appear on your balance sheet when you prepare your financial statements. The full cost of the computer will appear as an asset on your balance sheet for as long as you use that computer in your business.

You'll record the deterioration of that asset on a regular basis, in the form of depreciation expense. By a regular basis, I mean monthly, quarterly, or annually, depending on how often you produce financial statements. You should record updated depreciation expense each time you issue financial statements for your company. So if you prepare company financial statements on a quarterly basis, you should record your depreciation expenses quarterly.

Why do we need depreciation? Because it's the rule. You are required to spread the cost of assets over the anticipated life of the asset. You are required to do so by the IRS, which dictates the way in which tax returns are prepared, and you are required to do so by Generally Accepted Accounting Principles—rules that dictate the way in which financial statements are prepared. In other words, we're all stuck with depreciation.

Hiring an Accountant

Depreciation is an extremely complicated area, and you shouldn't be at all hesitant to consider hiring an accountant or tax advisor to help you with the calculation of depreciation expense. There is information in this chapter that can help you calculate depreciation on your own, but there are exceptions and special considerations with regard to the depreciation rules that are not covered here and that your tax professional can help you with.

Calculating Depreciation with QuickBooks

This section contains no useful information. Why? Because there is no provision for calculating depreciation with QuickBooks. You need to perform the calculation on your own or request assistance from an accountant or a tax professional. There's no place where you can calculate depreciation within the QuickBooks program. What a bummer.

You can, of course, calculate the depreciation yourself. In this case, read the next section to learn how.

Calculating Depreciation Yourself

To calculate depreciation, you first must know the cost of the asset and the useful life of the asset (see the Life Expectancies of Common Assets table that appeared earlier in this chapter). To figure out the amount of depreciation expense, refer to depreciation tables prepared by the IRS. You can get a copy of the complete IRS guide to depreciation by contacting the IRS at 1-800-TAX-FORM and requesting Publication 946, "How to Depreciate Property." You can also download this publication from the IRS Web site at www.irs.ustreas.gov.

This publication is about a quarter the size of this book—it's really lengthy. There's a lot of published material about depreciation, much of which won't apply to you. But just looking at this publication, you'll see how ridiculously complicated this area of tax law is.

Tables in the next section can help you calculate depreciation in most circumstances.

Entering Depreciation in QuickBooks

You may have noticed, if you entered assets during the EasyStep Interview, that you were asked for the total of depreciation you had deducted previously on any assets you entered. If you entered depreciation in the Interview, you already have some accumulated depreciation relating to these assets in your QuickBooks company records.

This depreciation entered in the EasyStep Interview is not current year depreciation expense, but depreciation that has accumulated over prior years.

When you enter depreciation in QuickBooks, there are two areas that are affected:

➤ There is a depreciation expense account, in which you record the current period cost of the asset being expensed.

➤ The depreciation expense is offset with an accumulated depreciation account, which is an account that appears on your balance sheet in the asset section and which summarizes all the depreciation expense taken on your assets over the life of the assets (see the next figure). Accumulated depreciation is actually referred to as a *contra asset* because, instead of adding to the value of your asset, it decreases the total value of your asset.

Use Account Numbers!

QuickBooks likes things orderly. So orderly, in fact, that it insists on alphabetizing your account names on your balance sheet. If you name your accumulated depreciation account "Accumulated depreciation" (a logical choice) and your asset cost account "Cost," QuickBooks will place Accumulated depreciation before Cost on the balance sheet—an accounting faux pas. In the accompanying figure, I've circumvented this problem by using account numbers (which get placed in neat, numerical order).

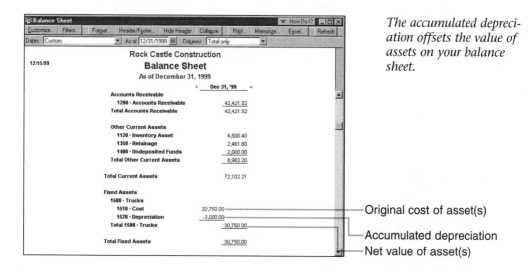

The accumulated depreciation offsets the value of assets on your balance sheet.

Original cost of asset(s)

Accumulated depreciation

Net value of asset(s)

To enter depreciation expense for an asset, you need to make a general journal entry. You can find detailed information about general journal entries in Chapter 6, "Charting Your Accounts and General Journal Entries." The journal entry for depreciation is one of the most common journal entries businesses make in QuickBooks.

There is no specific form for entering depreciation in QuickBooks. When you know how much depreciation expense you intend to deduct (see "Calculating Depreciation Yourself," earlier in this chapter), you can make a journal entry by following these steps:

1. Open the Activities menu and choose **Make Journal-Entry**.

2. In the General Journal Entry window that appears (see the following figure), assign a number to your journal entry and verify the date.

3. Enter your depreciation expense account and a debit amount for the depreciation expense, then enter your accumulated depreciation account and a credit for the same amount.

4. Click **OK** to execute the entry.

Enter depreciation expense with a journal entry.

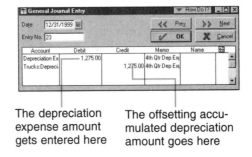

The depreciation expense amount gets entered here

The offsetting accumulated depreciation amount goes here

The Section 179 Deduction

There's one other thing to keep in mind with regard to depreciation. Under certain restrictions, the IRS allows businesses to take a full deduction for the cost of some assets purchased each year without spreading the cost of the asset over the useful life. This can be particularly helpful to small businesses. This rule is referred to as a Section 179 deduction because that's the section of the Internal Revenue Code that authorizes it.

The maximum yearly amount of a Section 179 deduction is dictated by Congress, and it changes each year. For 1998 tax returns, the maximum deduction under Section 179 is $18,500. For 1999 tax returns, the maximum deduction is $19,000.

There are a few sticky rules about taking a Section 179 deduction, so listen up:

➤ The election to take this deduction must be made by the due date (including extensions) of the tax return for the year in which the qualifying property is placed in service.

➤ For a business automobile, the maximum deduction under Section 179 is $3,060 for a car placed in service during 1999 (this amount changes annually).

➤ The property must be purchased and placed in service during the year in which you take the deduction and must be tangible personal property, such as computers, office equipment, machinery, a car, or a truck. The deduction does not apply to buildings, furniture, or equipment previously used for personal purposes.

➤ If you use the asset for both business and personal use, the business portion of the asset must exceed 50% for this deduction to apply.

➤ The total cost you deduct can't exceed the taxable income from the business. In other words, you can't take a Section 179 deduction and show a tax loss on your business tax return. If this rule takes you out of the running for the Section 179 deduction, all is not lost. You can carry over the unused portion of your Section 179 deduction to the next year.

For example, if you purchased $20,000 of equipment in 1999 and the equipment qualifies for a Section 179 deduction, you may take a deduction for up to $19,000 of the cost of that equipment. The remaining $1,000 must be depreciated over the useful life of the equipment.

When you prepare your tax return, no matter what form of depreciation you take, and no matter what kind of tax return you are required to file, you'll fill out a Form 4562, "Depreciation and Amortization." The Section 179 deduction is figured at the top of page one of this form. Other depreciation is listed in the body of the form.

If you're taking a Section 179 deduction, the journal entry in QuickBooks will probably be for the same amount, but not necessarily. You're entitled to take a Section 179 deduction for tax purposes and spread the cost of the asset over its useful life for financial statement purposes. By all means, you should contact an accounting professional if you're considering this kind of treatment of your assets, because the area is complicated, and there are special rules that need to be followed.

Handy Depreciation Tables

You can use the amounts in the following table to compute depreciation for your assets (but it is recommended that you check with a pro to make sure you're doing this correctly).

For example, if you own an asset that cost $3,000 and is classified as 5-year property, and this is the third year in which you are depreciating the asset, your depreciation would be $3,000 × 19.20%, or $576.

Depreciation Expense for 3-, 5-, 7-, 10-, 15-, and 20-Year Personal Property

Recovery Year	3-year	5-year	7-year	10-year	15-year	20-year
1	33.33	20.00	14.29	10.00	5.00	3.750
2	44.45	32.00	24.49	18.00	9.50	7.219
3	14.81	19.20	17.49	14.40	8.55	6.677
4	7.41	11.52	12.49	11.52	7.70	6.177
5		11.52	8.93	9.22	6.93	5.713
6		5.76	8.92	7.37	6.23	5.285
7			8.93	6.55	5.90	4.888
8			4.46	6.55	5.90	4.522
9				6.56	5.91	4.462
10				6.55	5.90	4.461
11				3.28	5.91	4.462
12					5.90	4.461
13					5.91	4.462
14					5.90	4.461
15					5.91	4.462
16					2.95	4.461
17						4.462
18						4.461
19						4.462
20						4.461
21						2.231

For residential rental property, use the table below to determine the depreciation expense for the first year. The expense varies, depending on the first month in which you place the property in service. After the first year, calculate depreciation by multiplying 3.636% times the depreciable cost of the property (which would not include the value of land that was purchased with the property) each year for the next nine years. In the tenth through twenty-eighth years, alternate between using 3.636% and 3.637%. In year 29, the depreciation deduction is whatever is left that hasn't yet been depreciated.

Depreciation Expense for Residential Rental Property in the Year of Acquisition

Month of Acquisition	First-Year Deduction
January	3.485%
February	3.182%
March	2.879%
April	2.576%
May	2.273%
June	1.970%
July	1.667%
August	1.364%
September	1.061%
October	0.758%
November	0.455%
December	0.152%

Now You've Done It!

This depreciation stuff is confusing, and if you don't understand it, you're in good company. Most people leave this stuff to the pros. With the knowledge you've gained in this chapter, you now know

➤ How frequently you need to calculate depreciation. See "What Is Depreciation and Why Do We Need It?"

➤ How to enter depreciation into your QuickBooks file. See "Entering Depreciation in QuickBooks."

➤ How to calculate depreciation, or at least who to ask for help in this area. See "Calculating Depreciation Yourself."

➤ About the Section 179 deduction, which enables you to deduct some of the cost of your assets in the year in which you purchase them. See "The Section 179 Deduction."

Chapter 13

The Tax Man Cometh

In This Chapter

➤ Collecting and paying sales tax

➤ Where to find sales tax reports

➤ Working with tax line assignments

➤ Dealing with income tax reports and tax returns

➤ Quarterly estimated income tax payments

Since the beginning of recorded history, mankind has found itself confronted with taxes: taxes on income, taxes on property, taxes on agriculture production, taxes on prostitution, taxes on importing, taxes on exporting, taxes on tea, taxes on liquor and cigarettes, taxes on hotel rooms, taxes on estates and gifts, taxes on highway use, and more and more and more.

Records of tax payments dating as far back as 3300 BC have been discovered. In ancient times, representatives of the rulers came to the doors of the peasantry, examining resources and deciding on a worthy amount to claim as tax. Early tax evaders would attempt to hide their possessions to keep their tax burden low.

This taxation process has evolved into what can be described as either more civilized or more bizarre—in today's tax ritual, taxpayers willingly submit forms admitting to the value of property they own and the income they earned and then equally willingly send the government a percentage of the take. Pretty wacky, huh? QuickBooks has a few tricks up its sleeve to help you handle your company's taxes.

Collecting and Paying Sales Taxes

First up in our explanation of taxes and QuickBooks is sales tax. Sales tax is a pass-through tax. The tax is owed by your customers, but you collect the tax when you make a taxable sale. Then you pay the government on behalf of your customers. Isn't that nice of you? I guess the theory is that it's less paperwork if the business pays the tax for lots of purchases, instead of each of the consumers paying the tax individually. I think our friends in the government feel it's also more likely that the government will get the tax if the business is responsible for making the payments instead of individuals.

Ultimately, it would be hard to determine whether or not individuals made purchases that were subject to tax and institute collection procedures against all those individuals. Instead, the government can focus on the business end of the deal and strong-arm the business owner into coughing up sales tax in lieu of facing criminal prosecution.

Did You Know Sales Tax Is an Item?

Sales tax should be set up as an item in your company's QuickBooks file. You may have already done this during the EasyStep Interview. To see if you have set up a sales tax account, open the Lists menu and choose **Items**. (Alternatively, click the **Sales and Customers** tab of QuickBooks Navigator, and then click **Items & Services**.) This opens the Item List, shown in the following figure. Look for a sales tax item on the Item List.

The types appear alphabetically, so
scroll down to find a Sales Tax Item

Oh where, oh where, is
my sales tax item?

If you need to create a sales tax item, press **Ctrl+N**. In the New Item window that appears (see the figure below), click the **Type** drop-down arrow and choose **Sales Tax Item**.

Next, enter the name of the sales tax—this is the name that will appear on your sales forms as part of a drop-down list from which you can choose sales tax items. If you pay only one type of sales tax, you can use "Sales Tax" as the name of the item. If you pay more than one type of sales tax, you should distinguish between the taxes, such as "Food/Bev Tax," "Cook County," or "Indiana Sales." Be succinct, because you are limited to 13 characters, including spaces.

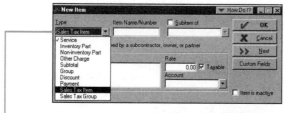

Use the New Item window to create a sales tax item.

Selecting **Sales Tax Item** will cause certain fields to appear and others to disappear in the New Item window

Click inside the Description text box and enter a description for the sales tax (see the following figure). This is the description that customers will see when they purchase taxable items from you.

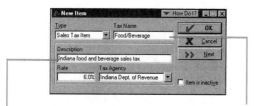

When you create a sales tax item, you must describe the sales tax.

This area is for a descriptive name that will appear on sales forms

Enter the short name for your sales tax

Click inside the Rate text box and enter the rate for this tax and the name of the agency to whom you pay the tax (if this agency is not already on your Vendor list, you will be asked to add this new vendor). When you're finished filling out the New Item window, click **OK** to save the information you entered and exit the form. From this point forward, this sales tax rate is available to you on your sales forms (estimates, invoices, cash sales).

I've Charged Sales Tax to My Customers—Now What?

Collecting the sales tax is only half the game—and the lesser half, as far as the government is concerned. You are not required to collect the sales tax from your customers, but you are required to pay the sales tax on your customers' purchases. Usually companies collect the tax owed on sales from their customers, but if you prefer to pay the sales tax yourself, that is certainly your prerogative.

Based on the rules set out by your state taxing agency, you are required to file a report showing your company's sales and the amount of tax owed on those sales. When you submit this report to the taxing agency, you are expected to include a payment for the sales tax shown on the report.

When Is This Tax Due?

Each state is entitled to make its own rules regarding the required tax rate and the frequency with which reports and payments are due. Usually reports and payments are due 30 days after the close of each month, but you should check with your state taxing agency for more precise information. A complete list of state taxing agencies is provided in Appendix B, "Tax Agencies," at the back of this book.

Getting Sales Tax Information Out of QuickBooks

QuickBooks provides you with the reports you need to help you fill out your sales tax forms. The Sales Tax Liability report, for example, is extremely useful.

To find your way to this report, open the Reports menu and choose A/P Reports, Sales Tax Liability Report. (If you prefer using QuickBooks Navigator, click the Taxes and Accountant tab, and then click Tax in the Reports to find the Sales Tax Liability Report.) QuickBooks displays a report that gives a breakdown of all of your taxable and nontaxable sales for whatever time period you select, similar to the one shown in the next figure. If your company's sales are subject to sales tax at more than one rate, you will see a separate line for each of the different rates.

You can choose the dates that this report will cover by clicking a drop-down arrow or by inserting the specific dates

You can see a complete summary of all sales tax owed on the Sales Tax Liability Report.

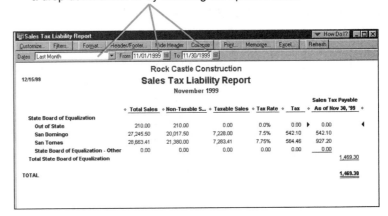

Calculating and Paying Your Income Tax

QuickBooks is not a tax program. It will not prepare your income tax forms. (Sorry!) But this doesn't mean it can't help you with your taxes. If you let it, QuickBooks will take you all the way up to the preparation of your income tax forms and even take your numbers right into a tax program that *will* prepare your returns.

QuickBooks provides reports that show you the numbers you will need for your income tax return. It even shows you which lines of the tax return will receive those numbers. Granted, QuickBooks doesn't actually prepare your tax return—but it gets you pretty close.

Do-It-Yourself Sales Tax Forms

The Sales Tax Liability Report *is* only a starting point for preparing your sales tax return. QuickBooks is not equipped for preparing these tax returns, because every state has a different form and different rules. Use this report as deep background—the information you need to get pointed in the right direction for filling out your tax forms yourself.

Assigning Tax Lines

QuickBooks is smart, but it's not psychic. You have to tell the program which of your accounts should appear on which line of your income tax return. The way you do this is by assigning a *tax line* to each account.

You can assign tax lines when you create account names, although you don't have this opportunity for accounts you set up during the EasyStep Interview. Probably the easiest way to assign tax lines is to use the Edit Account window. First display your Chart of Accounts (press **Ctrl+A**, or click the **Company** tab of the QuickBooks Navigator and click **Chart of Accounts** at the top of the window), and then click an account and press **Ctrl+E** to edit the account. The Edit Account window appears (see the next figure). At the bottom of the window is a Tax Line field. Click the drop-down arrow to display a complete list of all tax lines from the tax return that is appropriate for your business. (See "What Type of Business Do You Want to Be when You Grow Up?" in Chapter 1, "Doing the EasyStep Tango," for more information about the type of tax return your business should file.)

Assign tax lines to get the most out of the tax reports QuickBooks has to offer.

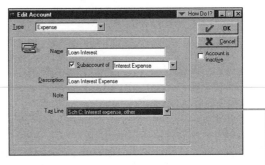

Click here for a complete list of all tax lines
from the tax return your company will file

Incorrect Company Setup

If you are trying to assign tax lines and the lines that appear in the Tax Line field of the Edit Account window don't go with the right tax return for your company, you may need to change the company information in QuickBooks. To do this, open the File menu and choose **Company Info**, and then correct the information in the Income Tax Form Used field. Watch out! If this setting has been incorrect while you've been making entries in QuickBooks, there may be some errors in your company's equity accounts. You may want to check with an accounting professional before making this kind of change.

To exit the Edit Account window, click **OK**. After you assign one tax line, keep going right down the Chart of Accounts list and assign tax lines to each account.

One nice feature about tax lines is that, once you take the time to set up all your accounts with tax line assignments, you never have to go through the process again. Tax lines stay with the accounts forever. What a relief!

QuickBooks and Income Taxes

There are two nice income tax reports provided by QuickBooks. Between the two of them, you'll be all set to prepare your company income tax return. Here's a description of each:

➤ **Income Tax Summary Report**   This report lists all the lines on your tax return (see the figure below), with the numbers already filled in—what could be easier? To view the report, open the Reports menu and choose **Other Reports**, **Income Tax Summary**.

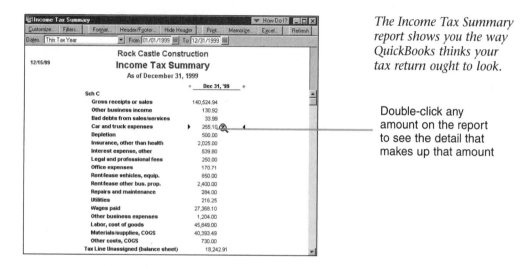

The Income Tax Summary report shows you the way QuickBooks thinks your tax return ought to look.

Double-click any amount on the report to see the detail that makes up that amount

➤ **Income Tax Detail Report**   This report (see the next figure) shows the trees instead of the forest that appeared in the previous report. This report gives you all the detail that you have to double-click for on the other tax report. Each tax line is listed in order as it appears on your tax return, with the complete listings of every transaction that affects this tax information. To view this report, open the Reports menu and choose **Other Reports**, **Income Tax Detail**.

If you prepare your own tax returns, or even if you send your material to an outside tax preparer, the information in these two reports will be priceless in putting together tax returns.

The Income Tax Detail report provides you with a list of every transaction that occurred in each account.

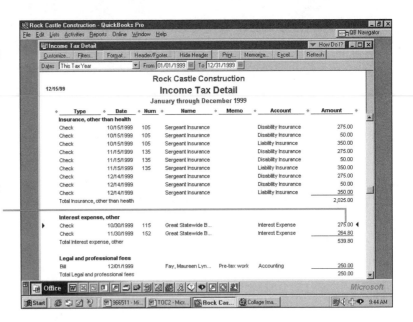

Double-click any amount on the report to see the original document or entry from which that amount was created

QuickBooks and TurboTax Are Buddies

If you are a TurboTax (tax software made by Intuit) user, you'll find your job is even easier. Account balances from QuickBooks transfer directly into TurboTax for immediate processing of business tax returns. You must still assign tax lines for the transfer to work but, once you've assigned the tax lines, TurboTax will prepare a complete business tax return for you.

Pay as You Go—The Estimated Tax Payments

Employees pay their taxes through the system of tax withholding—an employer takes tax out of every one of their paychecks and sends it to the government. At the end of the year there is a reckoning between the tax owed and the tax paid. If the tax paid is higher, the employee gets a refund. If the tax paid is too low, the employee sends a check with his tax return.

But what about businesses? There's no employer to take out the taxes from a business's income and diligently send payments to the government. No, businesses are out there on their own, responsible for figuring out how much to pay and required to "voluntarily" submit payments on a frequent basis.

These frequent payments are referred to as quarterly payments, estimated taxes, extortion (depending on whom you're talking to), and no doubt plenty of other names as well. Whatever you call them, as a business you are required to make these payments at regular intervals. The actual payment due dates vary, depending on if your business is a corporation or if the business income gets reported on the individual tax returns of the business owners or partners. The following table sets out the due dates for income tax returns and estimated payments for businesses and individuals.

Table 13.1 Federal Income Tax Due Dates

Date	What's due today
January 15	**Individual estimated payment** Fourth quarter estimated payment for individuals.
March 1	**Income tax return** Farmers and fishermen are required to file their income tax returns.
March 15	**Corporate income tax return** Federal form 1120 for corporations is due. Federal form 1120S for S-corporations is due.
April 15	**Individual and partnership income tax return; individual and corporate estimated payments** Federal income tax form 1040 for individuals is due. Federal income tax form 1065 for partnerships is due. First quarterly estimated tax payment is due for individuals and corporations.
June 15	**Individual and corporate estimated payments** Second quarterly estimated tax payment is due for individuals and corporations.
September 15	**Individual and corporate estimated payments** Third quarterly estimated tax payment is due for individuals and corporations.
December 15	**Corporate estimated payment** Fourth quarter estimated tax payment is due for corporations.

Due Dates for Fiscal Year Taxpayers

Corporations with fiscal years that are different from the calendar year need to adjust the dates in the accompanying table to fit their business calendar. For a fiscal year corporation, the annual income tax return is due on the fifteenth day of the third month following the last day of the fiscal year. Quarterly estimated payments are due on the fifteenth day of the fourth, sixth, ninth, and twelfth months of the fiscal year.

The IRS has set out special rules for calculating estimated payments, designed to approximate 25% of the annual tax liability. The rules for individual taxpayers are as follows:

➤ Estimated payments are required if the tax owed on the annual tax return, after reducing the tax by withholding and other credits, exceeds $1,000.

➤ The individual is to pay at least 90% of the current year tax liability prior to the due date in the form of tax withholding or estimated payments.

➤ Alternatively, the taxpayer may pay 100% of the prior year income tax through withholding and estimates.

➤ If a taxpayer's income fluctuates during the year, he may calculate his quarterly estimated tax requirements according to a method of annualizing the current year income. The rules for annualizing income accompany the instructions for form 1040-ES, Estimated Tax Payment Voucher.

Check the Mailing Address

Be careful where you mail your estimated tax payments! The estimated payments do not go to the same address as your regular income tax return, so check instructions carefully for the correct mailing address.

Each quarterly payment is to represent one quarter of the total amount of estimated tax due. Estimated payments are paid by individuals on form 1040-ES and are mailed to the Internal Revenue Service at the address shown on the instructions accompanying that form.

The rules for corporate taxpayers are as follows:

➤ Estimated payments are required if the tax owed on the annual tax return exceeds $500.

➤ The corporation is to pay the lesser of 100% of the actual tax due for the year or 100% of the tax for the prior year.

➤ If a corporation's income fluctuates during the year, annualized income can be calculated, and the estimate can be based on the appropriate percentage of this calculation.

Corporations pay their estimated tax payments by making a tax deposit at a bank or other financial institution that accepts federal tax payments. The payments must be accompanied by form 8109, which is available from the IRS.

Don't Forget the State!

The feds aren't the only ones hungry for your tax dollars. Don't forget about filing tax returns and making estimated payments in your state. Each state has its own rules, and there are some states where there is no income tax. (But there are trade-offs—there may be no income tax in Texas, for example, but they have big, scary bugs...)

The due dates for filing tax returns and estimated payments vary by state as well, even though they closely approximate the federal dates.

Spend a pleasant evening by the fire reading up on your state tax rules so you won't be surprised by a missed due date or overdue tax payment.

Now You've Done It!

Like it or not, taxes are a way of life for all of us. One way or another, you can count on some of your hard-earned profits being siphoned off for the tax man. At least you can be fully prepared for the inevitable, because you know

➤ How to collect sales tax by adding it to the invoices of customers, and how to figure out how much tax you owe (see "Collecting and Paying Sales Taxes").

➤ How to assign tax lines to your accounts so that you can prepare meaningful tax reports (see "Assigning Tax Lines").

➤ How to collect all the right information for preparing your income tax returns (see "QuickBooks and Income Taxes").

➤ Corporations and individuals are required to pay estimated taxes to the extent that withholding doesn't cover their income tax liability (see "Pay as You Go—The Estimated Tax Payments").

Chapter 14

Tracking Inventory (Or Not...)

In This Chapter

➤ What is inventory, and have you got any?

➤ Setting up inventory in QuickBooks

➤ What to do with QuickBooks inventory features

➤ How to take a physical inventory count

➤ Using a program other than QuickBooks to track your inventory

You are going to either love or hate accounting for your inventory in QuickBooks. The precision that QuickBooks offers and the up-to-the-minute accurate inventory information can keep your company humming and make you constantly aware of inventory that you have in stock and inventory that you need to order.

On the other hand, there are several weaknesses in QuickBooks when it comes to accounting for inventory. These weaknesses will be addressed in this chapter, along with ways to deal with these weaknesses.

Keeping Track of Inventory in QuickBooks

Inventory is the tangible things you sell. Some companies don't have inventory. A law firm, for example, sells legal services, not cans of soup, so there are no inventory records to keep.

Keeping track of inventory means knowing how many items you have available for sale, knowing the value of those items, and knowing when you need to order or produce more items. QuickBooks handles inventory this way: Every time you make a sale, your inventory supply is decreased; every time you make a purchase, your inventory supply is increased.

Inventory

This term refers to the tangible items quantified and sold by your company. If you keep items in stock and keep track of how many you have, they're inventory. If you purchase an item and resell it without keeping it in stock, it's not inventory.

When an item of inventory is sold, QuickBooks immediately revises all of your inventory accounts to take that sale into account. This, in turn, reduces the quantity of inventory items you show in your reports. And every time a new piece of inventory is received at your place of business, QuickBooks immediately revises all of your inventory accounts to show the addition to your inventory supply.

This kind of accuracy provides you with confidence that your inventory records are always up to date. Plus, you are able to get information in the form of inventory reports that are current and up to the minute, too.

Now here's something interesting—the cost of items in your inventory is calculated on a weighted average basis. This means that every time you add or subtract items from inventory, the entire inventory value is recalculated so that the value of an individual item in stock equates to the average cost of all pieces of that item in stock.

Want to see this principle in practice? Let's say you purchase 10 ceramic bunnies for $7 each. This makes the total value of your inventory $70. The average value of a bunny is $7. Okay, but what if you then purchase 15 ceramic bunnies for $8 each? QuickBooks tallies the total value of your inventory as $70 + $120 (or $190). The average value of a bunny is $190 divided by 25, or $7.60. If you turn around and sell three of your ceramic bunnies for $15 each, your remaining inventory will be 22 bunnies valued at 167.20, or 7.60 per bunny. (Of course, when dealing with bunnies, the inventory may repopulate your warehouse without any help from you or QuickBooks.)

Buying and Selling Inventory

With QuickBooks, you don't need to make adjustments to your inventory accounts. Preparing forms such as bills and invoices will take care of all the adjustments you need to make to inventory on a day-to-day basis.

For unusual adjustments to inventory, see the section titled "I've Counted My Inventory, Now What?" later in this chapter.

When you make a purchase of inventory items, you might issue a purchase order. To illustrate, let's use that ceramic bunny example again. Let's say you create a purchase order for 10 ceramic bunnies. Your inventory records are not immediately increased by 10 ceramic bunnies. Only when you indicate the bunnies have been received—either by issuing an Item Receipt (see the next figure) or by entering a bill—is your inventory increased. For more information on recording the receipt of items, see the "Your Order Is In!" section in Chapter 6, "Setting Up Accounts and General Journal Entries."

In the Create Item Receipts window, you can enter merchandise records into your QuickBooks file before the bill for the merchandise has been received.

When you sell inventory items in QuickBooks, you issue an invoice form, shown in the next figure. When you create that invoice, QuickBooks removes from inventory the number of items you sold. For more information on this subject, see the section titled "Creating an Invoice," in Chapter 8, "The Daily Grind."

Hey! Let's Add a New Inventory Line!

Perhaps your sales of ceramic bunnies have been doing so nicely that you've decided to get into the ceramic burro business as well. (Good move, according to Wall Street experts.) Each type of product that you sell is referred to as an item, according to QuickBooks law. (For the lowdown on all sorts of item lore, see Chapter 4, "What Are These Items, Anyway?".) An item represents a line of information on a form, such as an invoice, a purchase order, or a bill.

Estimates and Inventory

You can issue an estimate form prior to issuing the related invoice. Issuing an invoice will decrease the quantity of an inventory item in your records; an estimate does not.

When you sell items on an invoice, QuickBooks looks at the quantity reflected on the invoice and makes a reduction in your record of the quantity of inventory items on hand.

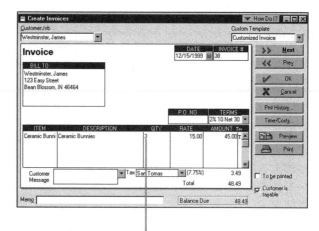

Issuing this invoice will result in your inventory records being reduced by three ceramic bunnies.

Before you can purchase or sell an inventory item, you have to enter that item in QuickBooks. You can see a list of all the items that have already been entered in your company file. Just open the Lists menu and select **Items** (see the figure below). Or, from QuickBooks Navigator, click the **Purchases and Vendors** tab, and then click the **Items & Services** button.

All of your company's items appear on the Item List.

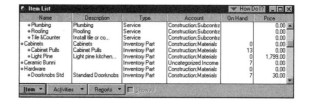

There are a couple of ways to add a new item to your inventory. One way is to open the New Item window. Simply press **Ctrl+N** from the Item List window, or click the **Item** button and choose **New**. This will open a New Item window, shown in the next figure.

Another way is to add an item "on the fly," directly from a purchase order or bill form. If you attempt to purchase an item that has not been set up in your inventory, you will see the box shown in the next figure. Click **Set Up** to open the New Item window.

Choose Inventory Part
to add an Inventory item

Name as it appears on
your customer invoices

Name of the item

Open the New Item window by one of the methods described, and you can add items to your inventory.

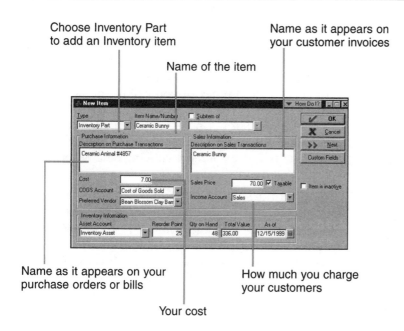

Name as it appears on your
purchase orders or bills

How much you charge
your customers

Your cost

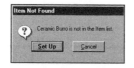

QuickBooks hasn't heard of this inventory item yet.

With the New Item window open (refer back to the New Item figure), click the **Type** drop-down arrow to display a list of item types. Choose **Inventory Part** as the item to add. In the Item Name/Number field, enter the item as you want to see it on your Item List. You can use a short narrative description (such as Ceramic Burro) or a numerical description (such as a part number).

In the Subitem of field, you can check the box if this item is to be a subitem of a larger category of items (such as Ceramic Figures).

In the Purchase Information area, you can enter a description that will appear on purchase transactions (such as purchase orders or bills). You have room to enter a lengthy description, so you can elaborate on the merits of your burros.

Under the Description field, enter the standard cost for this item in the Cost field. If your cost varies each time you purchase this item, you can leave this field blank and fill in the correct amount on your bill form when you make a purchase.

It's Not Written in Stone

When entering an item on an invoice or purchase order form, you always have the right to override the description or the cost amount. Simply delete the information on the form and enter the description and amount as you want them to appear.

There's also a place for a description in the Sales Information area of the form. This is the description that will appear on your sales forms (such as estimates and invoices) when you sell this item to customers. Often this description will be the same as the description you entered for Purchase Information, but not necessarily. You might describe the item by part number when ordering it from a supplier but give it a more enticing description when selling the item to your customer.

Enter a Cost of Goods Sold (COGS) account. This is the account to which your purchases of this inventory item will be charged when you make the purchases. Normally you'll choose an account called something like Cost of Goods Sold, or Cost of Sales. If there is an account called Cost of Goods Sold in your Chart of Accounts, QuickBooks will automatically choose this account for you.

Preferred Vendor is an optional entry. You can enter the name of the vendor from whom you typically purchase this item. If you enter a vendor in this field, that vendor name will appear on some of the inventory reports that you prepare.

Enter the typical sales price at which you sell this inventory item in the Sales Price field. If this price varies from customer to customer, leave this area blank and enter the price directly on the invoice form when you make a sale. In the Income Account field, you must enter the name of the account into which you want your sales revenue for this item to be recorded; use the drop-down arrow to select an account.

In the Inventory Information area at the bottom of the New Item window, enter the asset account that will contain the value of your inventory (click the drop-down arrow and select an account). This is not an optional field. However, the other fields in this area are optional. You can enter a reorder point in the Reorder Point text box. If the number of this item that you have in stock drops below the number you enter here, QuickBooks will give you a reminder, indicating that it's time to order more of this item. (That can come in handy, huh?)

If you have some of these items on hand when you set up this new inventory item, enter the quantity in the Qty on Hand box. QuickBooks will calculate the total value, based on the cost you entered earlier. If you are entering a quantity on hand, enter the date at which that quantity is available.

Click the **OK** button to save all the information you've entered about your new inventory item.

Secret Code Names and Other Special Information

If there's any additional information you want to keep track of about your inventory items—such as weight, color, or warehouse location—there is a button in the New Item window called Custom Fields that might meet your needs. If you click the **Custom Fields** button and then click **Define Fields**, you'll find you can assign up to five additional fields of information that will be available to each inventory item (see the figure below).

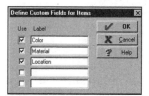

Enter up to five custom fields for use with your items.

For example, you might want to create a Location field that will indicate a row and shelf number in the warehouse where the inventory item is stored. Enter the name *Location* as your label. Keep adding field labels as needed. If you want to use two or more of these fields for this inventory item, be sure to click the **Use** check box in front of each label. Click **OK** to exit.

Counting Your Inventory

Once a year at a minimum, every company that maintains an inventory should take a physical count of every single item in the inventory. Ideally this count should be performed at midnight on December 31, especially if yours is a calendar year company. Your employees are in their best form for doing accurate work late at night, anyway (particularly on New Year's Eve), right?

The inventory count can be a daunting process if your company has a large (large as in quantity) inventory. For example, a company that sells hundreds of different sizes and styles of nuts and bolts is going to have A LOT more pieces of inventory to count than a company that sells cars or RVs.

Nevertheless, you need to arrange a time, arrange for personnel, arrange for proper forms, and arrange for plenty of pizza and soft drinks (and plenty of strong coffee) to get the inventory counted. For many companies, this count is performed when the business is closed, whether after hours or simply closed to customers while the inventory count is going on.

Who's Going to Count All These Items?

Your company's accounting firm may be able to provide experienced people (also known as bean counters) to help count inventory for you, if you need additional assistance.

Why Do We Need to Count?

The reason you need to take a physical inventory count is to verify the number of inventory items you have on hand and to ensure that your inventory records are correct. Even though QuickBooks does an excellent job of increasing and decreasing your inventory records with each purchase and sale, there are other inventory-related circumstances for which QuickBooks can't account.

For example, some inventory may have been lost, stolen, or damaged, or become obsolete. These factors need to be taken into consideration after you count your physical inventory and compare your totals to the quantities that QuickBooks thinks you should have.

QuickBooks helps with your physical inventory by providing you with a useful worksheet for summarizing your counted items. This worksheet (see the next figure) includes the following information:

➤ The name of every inventory part item

➤ A description of each item, as you entered it in your New Item setup

➤ A preferred vendor, if you entered a vendor in the New Item setup

➤ The quantity on hand, according to QuickBooks, as of the date you created the report

➤ A fill-in-the-blank column where you can enter the actual quantity on hand when you perform your count

Print a Physical Inventory Worksheet

With the Physical Inventory Worksheet displayed onscreen (see accompanying information about how to display the worksheet), click the Print button at the top of the worksheet. The Print Reports window will appear. Make sure the correct printer is selected, if you have a choice among printers, and then click the Print button.

To produce this worksheet, open the Reports menu, choose Inventory Reports, and then choose Physical Inventory Worksheet. You can print out a copy of this report and make as many copies as you need for all those who will be helping with the physical inventory count.

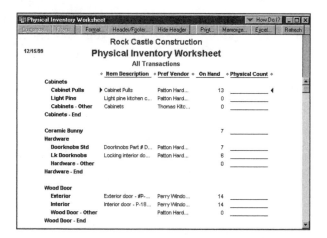

The handy Physical Inventory Worksheet, courtesy of QuickBooks.

I've Counted My Inventory, Now What?

The first thing you may want to do after you've taken the physical inventory count is to lay down and take a nap. After that, you need to compare the quantities that QuickBooks says you have on hand with the actual quantities that you counted, and attempt to determine any differences. So what do you do if there are differences? For example, if you're in the business of selling buttons, and your inventory in QuickBooks says you have 25,252 buttons on hand but your physical count shows you actually have 25,247 buttons, you may not feel that this difference is significant enough to spend your time trying to trace.

If, on the other hand, you're in the business of selling refrigerators, and you find that five refrigerators are missing from your inventory, that's a much more significant difference and one for which you'll want to find an explanation. Maybe it's time to set up that surveillance camera you've wanted to install.

When you encounter differences in inventory count, you may need to make an adjustment in your QuickBooks records so that the number of items QuickBooks shows on hand agrees with the actual quantity that exists on your premises. You wouldn't want QuickBooks to show that you have 12 refrigerators on hand when actually you have only 7. QuickBooks would allow you to create invoices for and sell 12 refrigerators. If you are missing 5, you're going to have difficulty filling your orders.

It's a good idea to have your QuickBooks records agree with the number of inventory items that you actually have on hand. If you do need to adjust your QuickBooks records to reflect a change in the number of items on hand, follow these steps:

1. Open the Activities menu and choose **Inventory, Adjust Qty/Value on Hand**. This opens the Adjust Quantity/Value on Hand window, shown in the next figure.

The numbers on this report should agree with the quantity of items you have on hand.

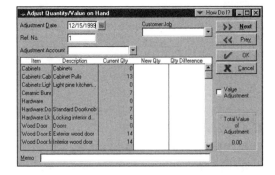

2. In the New Qty column, enter adjusted totals for any inventory items where your physical count disagrees with the quantity QuickBooks shows on hand. QuickBooks will calculate the difference between the original quantity and the new quantity in the Qty Difference column.

3. Click **OK** to save this information and exit the window. QuickBooks will apply the change to your inventory accounts.

Notice also that there's a Value Adjustment check box in the Adjust Quantity/Value on Hand window. If you check this box, two more columns will appear, as shown in the figure below. In these columns, you can enter adjustments to the actual value of your inventory. The Current Value column displays the value of each of your items, according to QuickBooks (using the weighted average method of valuing inventory). You can make adjustments in the New Qty column if you need to. This can be useful if you use a program other than QuickBooks to calculate your inventory and then transfer the adjustment information into QuickBooks. (See "What Are My Choices for Tracking Inventory?" later in this chapter.)

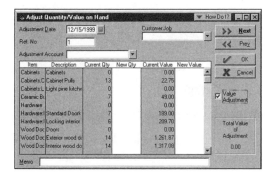

Enter changes to the value of your inventory items in this window. Be sure to keep a record (outside of QuickBooks) of the reasons for your changes.

Shortcomings of QuickBooks when It Comes to Inventory

QuickBooks is a great program for almost every aspect of accounting for your company, but when it comes to inventory, you might find QuickBooks lacking. You just have to face it. There are certain aspects of accounting for inventory that QuickBooks simply cannot do. Here are a few to consider:

➤ If your company is a manufacturing company, QuickBooks *recommends* that you not use the inventory feature in this program, because there is not the capability to record the complete manufacturing process, from goods acquired to the work in process to the finished product.

➤ If you have an inventory with lots and lots of pieces, you may find QuickBooks to be limiting there as well. You are limited to 14,500 different items that can be entered in your QuickBooks file.

➤ One other factor that might affect your decision to use QuickBooks for inventory is that QuickBooks accounts for inventory using the weighted average method. This means that the cost of all pieces of a particular item of inventory is averaged to determine the cost of each individual piece.

You may want to account for inventory in a different method, using a LIFO, FIFO, or Specific Identification method of valuing your inventory. These methods are not available in QuickBooks, so you may find yourself seeking an alternative to QuickBooks for calculating the value of your inventory, while using QuickBooks for your other accounting needs. You can account for inventory outside of QuickBooks, and then make general journal entries to reflect any changes that need to be made to your inventory accounts at the end of the year.

FIFO? LIFO? What's the Difference?

There are three popular methods of valuing inventory, none of which is readily available to you in QuickBooks. The methods are FIFO, LIFO, and Specific Identification.

FIFO stands for First In, First Out, a method of valuing inventory wherein it is assumed that inventory is sold in the order in which it is purchased. The first items you purchase (First In) are the first items you sell (First Out).

LIFO stands for Last In, First Out, a method of valuing inventory wherein it is assumed that the most recently acquired inventory items (Last In) are the first to be sold (First Out).

Specific Identification describes a method of valuing inventory wherein each inventory item is tracked separately, so you know the cost of each individual item as you sell it.

A QuickBooks Alternative to Valuing Inventory

I know, I know—I just told you QuickBooks doesn't do a very good job of tracking inventory. But here's one way you might be able to make the program work for you.

If you want to use a LIFO or FIFO method of valuing your inventory, you can force QuickBooks to account for your inventory in price layers, sometimes called *tiers*. Say, for example, you keep an inventory of ceramic bunnies, and over the course of the year you purchase five lots of ceramic bunnies, all at slightly different prices.

You can set up an Inventory Part Item for ceramic bunnies with no associated cost. Each time you purchase a lot of ceramic bunnies, set up a new part item as a subitem of the original ceramic bunny. As you sell ceramic bunnies, you can sell from the earliest lots to the latest (for FIFO) or from the latest lots to the earliest (for LIFO), thus forcing QuickBooks to create a FIFO or LIFO system for you.

What Are My Choices for Tracking Inventory?

There are several software programs on the market that provide inventory accounting and give you the numbers you need to correctly account for your inventory in QuickBooks, based on the method you use. I've found that a simple Internet search for INVENTORY AND SOFTWARE results in several inventory programs, some of which provide demos with which you can sample and experiment.

You might want to check with an outside accountant for recommendations for inventory tracking software. You can also set up an inventory system in a spreadsheet, using a program such as Microsoft Excel, Corel Quattro Pro, or Lotus 1-2-3; keep track of your own inventory in the spreadsheet; and then transfer any adjustments to your own QuickBooks program.

A database program such as Access, Paradox, or Oracle can also work especially well to accommodate a large collection of inventory records. A database program can provide you with the means of tracking inventory through the entire manufacturing process, which is not a capability of QuickBooks, as was mentioned earlier.

Now You've Done It

You've learned what QuickBooks can and cannot do regarding tracking inventory records. This chapter provided you with detailed information about

➤ Recording inventory on sales forms and purchase forms. See "Buying and Selling Inventory."

➤ Setting up inventory as items in QuickBooks. See "Hey! Let's Add a New Inventory Line!"

➤ The weaknesses of using QuickBooks to keep track of your inventory. See "Shortcomings of QuickBooks when It Comes to Inventory."

➤ Taking a physical inventory count. See "Counting Your Inventory."

➤ Alternative programs for tracking inventory. See "What Are My Choices for Tracking Inventory?"

Part 4

Tracking Time and Paying Employees

The cost of paying your employees and contractors may well be one of your largest business expenses. You need a program that can keep track of all the information that accompanies making payments to others for their time. You also need to be able to produce all the right tax forms and financial statements related to those payments.

Check out this section for the scoop on keeping track of everybody who works for you. You'll also find out how to stay square with the IRS and state governments to whom you must pay your payroll taxes.

Punching the Time Clock

Time is money, so they say (whoever *they* are). As it turns out, they're right, and QuickBooks Pro can help you track the time you spend on the job. QuickBooks Pro's time tracking features can help you or your employees gauge how much time is spent on a particular project or daily task. For example, if you bill time for your customers, let QuickBooks Pro help you keep track of that time.

Not to be confused with the Time Tracker feature (a separate program packaged with QuickBooks Pro, covered in Chapter 11, "Special Treats for QuickBooks Pro Users"), time tracking in QuickBooks Pro is a feature you don't have to use. However, you may find it thoroughly addicting. It's an efficient and effective way of accounting for time, as this chapter will show you.

Unfortunately, only QuickBooks Pro users have access to the time tracking feature. If you use the standard version of QuickBooks, the information in this chapter doesn't apply to you. Bummer!

Why Bother Tracking Time?

QuickBooks Pro gives you the option of keeping track of time worked by yourself and your employees right in your QuickBooks Pro program. With the timekeeping features provided, you can use your QuickBooks Pro program like a stopwatch. You can keep track of current time, turning the stopwatch on when you are working and off when you take a break. Or you can enter time on a QuickBooks timesheet form, entering up to a week's worth of hours worked.

By using the time tracking features described in this chapter, you can expedite the processing of your company's payroll. The QuickBooks Pro payroll feature draws information from the time information that has been entered, so the hours you or your employees work only need to be entered once.

The timer features are used both for recording time for which employees are to be paid and for recording time that is to be billed to a client. Often this is the same time—hours worked on a job for which a client will receive an invoice and the employee will receive a paycheck.

As an employee using the QuickBooks Pro timing features, you can elect to turn on the timer and leave it running, recording the time you are working on a project. That time can be associated with your payroll and billed directly to a client.

Employees can also keep track of their time on paper, away from the QuickBooks Pro program, and then enter up to a week's worth of time all at once on the QuickBooks timesheet.

Entering Time in QuickBooks

Time that you need to record for customer billing or employee payroll can be entered in QuickBooks Pro in two ways:

➤ As a single activity, such as the time worked for a particular job.

➤ By filling out a weekly timesheet window in QuickBooks Pro, where you can enter up to a week's worth of time at once and indicate jobs to which the time should be charged (if applicable).

When entering time, employees may enter their time as it is completed, such as on a daily basis or after each job, or they may fill out a paper timesheet and then enter their time for up to one week all at once. The employees may enter their time themselves into QuickBooks Pro's Timesheet window, or someone else who has access to QuickBooks Pro can enter the time for them.

Frequency of Entering Time

If you're going to pay your employees from the timesheets and don't intend to bill time directly to customers, your employees can wait until the end of the pay period to enter their time or submit it to someone who will record the time into QuickBooks Pro.

If employee time is going to be billed directly to customers from the employee timesheets, waiting until the end of the pay period may be too long. You might have invoices that need to be issued before a pay period ends. If there is employee time to be charged to customers, this time must be entered in QuickBooks Pro before you prepare the invoices. Therefore, you might want your employees' time to be entered on a daily basis or every couple of days, instead of waiting until the end of the time period. Whichever you choose, the process of entering information is the same.

Entering Time on a Per-Project Basis

Follow these steps to enter time for a single activity:

1. Open the Activities menu and choose **Time Tracking**, **Time/Enter Single Activity** (or, from the Navigator, click the **Payroll and Time** tab and choose **Time/Enter Single Activity**). The Time/Enter Single Activity window will appear, as shown in the following figure. Time is entered on this form for a single project.

2. In the Date field, verify that the date corresponds to the time being entered.

3. Click the **Name** drop-down arrow to display a list of vendor and employee names. Click the name of the person whose time is being entered.

4. Click the **Customer:Job** drop-down arrow and select the customer name (and job, if applicable), if this time is to be billed to a customer.

Time Feature Not a Requirement

For employees whose work is not billed to clients, the QuickBooks Pro time feature may not be of importance. Use the time feature if it is necessary to keep track of the kind of work performed and the customer for whom the work is being done.

Pay Period

The *pay period* is the number of days covered by one paycheck. Some companies pay their employees biweekly, so the pay period is two weeks. Employees who are paid weekly have a pay period of one week. Employees who are paid semimonthly have a pay period that goes from the 1st to the 15th of a month and from the 16th to the end of the month.

Click here to minimize the window

This form accommodates one employee's time for a single project.

Time/Enter Single Activity

Date 12/15/1999

Name Dan T. Miller
Customer:Job Abercrombie, Kristy:Kitch
Service Item Installation

Duration
5:00

Not Billed
☑ Billable

Payroll Item Regular Pay

Notes

>> Next
<< Prev
✓ OK
✗ Cancel
Timesheet

Start
Stop
Pause

Enter actual time here, or click **Start** to turn on the time clock

Enter optional notes about the job here

5. Enter the type of work being performed in the Service Item field. (A click on the drop-down arrow provides a list of all items that have been set up in QuickBooks.)

6. In the Duration area of the window, enter the exact amount of time to be recorded. If you want to use the feature to track time for you, click the **Start** button to turn on the stopwatch, which will keep track of elapsed time until the Stop button is clicked. Just don't forget to click **Stop** when you're finished.

Get It Out of the Way!

If you click **Start** to turn on the stopwatch, you can move the window out of the way while you work by clicking the **Minimize** button at the top right corner of the window (see the previous figure). This reduces the window to a small bar with buttons and places it at the bottom of the QuickBooks window. The clock will keep running, but the window will be out of your way. Double-click the bar to restore the window to its original size, or click the **Restore** button (the middle button).

7. If this time is being recorded for an employee who has been set up to transfer time from the timer to payroll records (see the following tip), choose the type of pay (such as Regular Pay or Overtime) using the Payroll Item drop-down list.

8. Click in the **Notes** text box and enter any information pertinent to the time being charged.

Set Up Employees for Time Transfer to Payroll

Before you can use the QuickBooks time feature to record time for payroll purposes, the employee must be set up properly. Open the Lists menu and choose Employees. Click the employee name in the Employee List that appears, and then press Ctrl+E to edit the employee's information. On the Payroll Info tab of the Edit Employee window, click the Use time data to create paychecks option. Click OK.

9. Click Next to enter time for another employee or activity, or click OK to save your changes and close this window. Note that the stopwatch aspect of the timer can be used to record time for only one person at a time.

Entering Time on the Timesheet

If you want to enter up to a week's worth of time at once, follow these steps:

1. Open the Activities menu and choose Time Tracking, Use Weekly Timesheet. The Weekly Timesheet form will appear (as shown in the following figure).

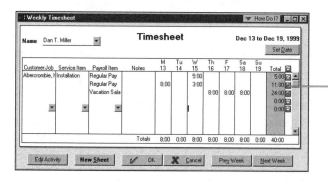

Enter time for an entire week on the Weekly Timesheet form.

Click here to place an "X" over the invoice form if this time is not to be billed to a customer.

2. Verify the time period, or click the Set Date button to change to a different week.

3. Click the Name drop-down arrow and select the employee name from the list.

4. If applicable, enter the customer and job names for time that is to be billed to a customer. Click the Customer:Job drop-down arrow to view a list of all customers and, if applicable, jobs.

5. In the Service Item column, enter the type of service performed, or use the drop-down arrow to select a service type from the list.

6. Click the **Payroll Item** drop-down arrow and enter the type of pay (such as Regular Pay or Overtime).

7. Use the Notes column to enter miscellaneous information about the work that was performed.

8. In the days of the week columns, enter the time that correlates to the jobs, service items, or payroll items listed in the first three columns. For example, if you worked eight hours on Monday and three hours on Wednesday on the Abercrombie job, enter an 8 in the M column and a 3 in the W column, on the Abercrombie job line. QuickBooks automatically totals the hours for each day at the bottom of each column and totals the time across for each job.

9. Click **Next Sheet** to proceed to the next week's timesheet for this employee, **New Sheet** to open a timesheet for another employee, or **OK** to close this window.

Notice that you don't have to enter billing or payroll rates on either the Enter Single Activity window or the Weekly Timesheet window. The billing rate and the payroll rate are already entered in the system and will be automatically calculated by QuickBooks (see the following tip).

How Much Is an Hour Worth?

QuickBooks can figure out how much to charge a client for the time you spend on a job if you provide that information when you set up the service item. For example, if you are setting up a new service item, *Painting*, you will open the Lists menu and choose **Items**. Press **Ctrl+N** to create a new item, and choose **Service** from the **Type** drop-down list. In the Item Name/Number field, enter *Painting*. In the Rate field, enter the rate at which time for this item will be billed. This is the rate QuickBooks Pro uses to carry over to invoices. Click **OK** to exit the window.

To set up hourly rate information in QuickBooks Pro for employees, open the Employee List, choose **Employees**, click an employee and press **Ctrl+E** to edit an existing employee, or press **Ctrl+N** to enter information for a new employee. In the employee window that appears, click the **Payroll Info** tab, and then enter an hourly rate in the Hour/Annual Rate column. This is the amount QuickBooks Pro will use when calculating payroll for employees who submit timesheets. Click **OK** to exit the window.

The billing rate is determined by the type of service item chosen for the time. For example, if you set up a service item for a painting service and enter $20 as the rate for this service (see the previous note for information about setting up rates on service items), when an employee bills three hours of time to a customer for painting the customer's kitchen, there will be a charge on the customer's invoice for $60 (three hours times $20 per hour). If a service item is billed at different rates, depending on the employee performing the job, you will need to fill in the appropriate rate on the invoice for the customer.

The employee pay rate is set up when you set up the employee payroll information. You can view employee time rates and change this information if necessary. To do so, open the Lists menu and choose Employees, and then click an employee name and press Ctrl+E to bring up the Edit Employee window. Click the Payroll Info tab (see the next figure) to view pay rates. You can refer to Chapter 16, "Figuring Out Your Payroll," for more information about payroll.

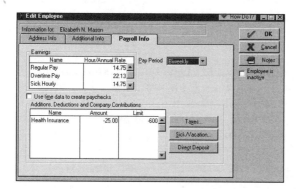

Pay rates are recorded when you set up employees.

Entering Non-Billable Time on Timesheets

Your employees probably have to record time that is not billable to customers. You can enter non-billable time as "Regular Pay" without recording a reason for the time. But what if you want to keep track of how your employees are spending their non-customer time?

You can set up service items that don't get billed to customers but are available only to track non-billable time. For example, you may want to track time devoted to continuing education, cleaning the warehouse, reading professional publications, or training employees. Follow these steps:

1. Open the Lists menu and choose Items, and then press Ctrl+N to open the New Item window.
2. In the New Item window, click the Type drop-down arrow and choose Service as the item.
3. Enter a brief name (such as Training) in the Item Name/Number field.

4. Leave the Rate field blank, and click the **Account** drop-down arrow to select an account where the expense of this amount will be tracked.

5. Click **OK** to exit the window.

You can produce a report showing the amount of time charged to non-billable service items such as training and continuing education. To do so, open the Lists menu and choose **Employees**. Click the **Reports** button in the Employee List window, and choose **Reports on All Employees**, **Project**, **Time Activity Detail**. Use this report to keep track of how employees are spending their time, and how much time from all employees is being devoted to non-billable activities.

Charging Time to Customers

Any time that has been entered and that relates to customers is available on the invoices that you create for your customers. Interestingly, when you create an invoice on which time has been charged, you receive no message from QuickBooks Pro indicating that billable time exists for this customer, nor does the time flow directly into the invoice.

In order to assess a customer for time that has been billed to that customer (and, if applicable, a particular job), open an invoice form and enter the name of the customer for whom you want to create a bill. Click the **Time/Costs** button on the invoice form (see the first figure below), and the Choose Billable Time and Costs window will appear (see the second figure below).

There is no indication on an invoice that time has been billed to this customer or job.

Click here to open the Billable Time and Costs window, where you can indicate time to be billed to this customer.

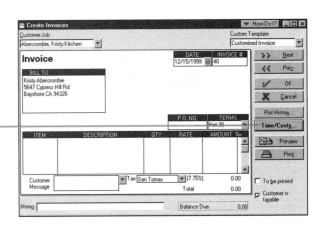

On the Choose Billable Time and Costs window, all employees who charged time to this job will appear, along with the amount of time they charged and the services they performed. Check the time that you want to include on this invoice, and then click **OK**. QuickBooks Pro returns you to the invoice, and the time you checked will now appear as a billable item on the customer invoice (see the next figure).

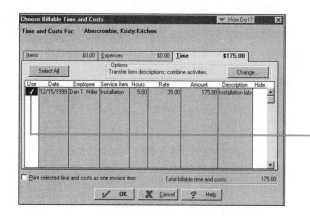

Click the Time *tab to view all time available to be billed to this customer.*

Check off any items you want to bill at this time.

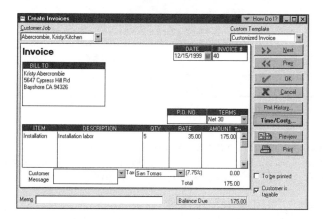

Amounts from the Billable Time and Costs screen flow through to the invoice.

Paying Employees Based on Time Entered

Time entered in timesheets flows through to employee payroll records. This really comes into play when issuing paychecks. To see what I mean, open the Activities menu and choose **Payroll, Pay Employees** (or, from the Navigator, click **Create Paychecks** on the Payroll and Time tab). The Select Employees To Pay window will appear (see the figure below).

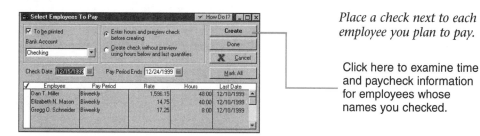

Place a check next to each employee you plan to pay.

Click here to examine time and paycheck information for employees whose names you checked.

To view the payroll information for an employee, click the **Create** button after checking off the employee name. Any time charged on timesheets flows right into the employee's payroll records (see the next figure).

Time charged to customers appears in the Earnings section of the Preview Paycheck screen.

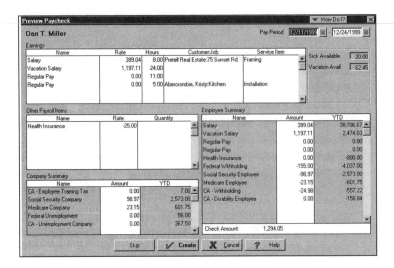

Note that you don't have to check anything off on the Preview Paycheck window—the time is automatically recorded for the employees. If there is an error in the amount of time recorded, you can make a correction on the Preview Paycheck window. You don't have to return to the timesheet to change this information.

When you are satisfied with the information on this screen, click the **Create** button, which will return you to the Select Employees To Pay window. Clicking the **Done** button in the Select Employees To Pay window will issue the paychecks.

For more detailed information about creating paychecks and performing other payroll tasks in QuickBooks, see Chapter 16. You may also want to take a look at the Time Tracker information in Chapter 11 if you have the Pro version of QuickBooks.

Now You've Done It!

Timekeeping is a breeze in QuickBooks. You need only to enter employee time once, and the time flows through to all appropriate locations in the program.

➤ You can enter time directly on employee timesheets. See "Entering Time on the Timesheet."

➤ Time that is charged to customers appears on customer invoice forms, ready for you to bill to the customers. See "Charging Time to Customers."

➤ Time from the timesheets flows right into the employee payroll information. See "Paying Employees Based on Time Entered."

Chapter 16

Figuring Out Your Payroll

In This Chapter

➤ Setting up employees in QuickBooks

➤ Accounting for vacation and sick time

➤ Accounting for benefits

➤ Creating paychecks for employees

➤ Creating payroll reports and payroll tax forms

If your company doesn't have any employees, you don't need this chapter. But if you have a payroll to maintain and payroll tax people to placate, this is the place for you. QuickBooks will calculate the withholding on your paychecks, prepare nice reports to show you how much you've spent on payroll, and help you with payroll tax reports so that you get all your tax forms prepared correctly and filed on time. (Well, okay— you are still the one who has to get the stamps and put the tax forms in the mail by the due date. You can't expect QuickBooks to do *everything* for you!)

Setting Up Employees

Got employees? If so, you can count on QuickBooks to help you track employees in all these ways:

➤ Create an Employee List

➤ Prepare paychecks

➤ Keep up to date on payroll tax withholding rates

➤ Track vacation and sick time

➤ Prepare payroll tax forms

To begin using the QuickBooks payroll features, you'll need to set up each one of your employees in QuickBooks. Your employees may already be set up if you entered the employee information during the EasyStep Interview (remember that from Chapter 1, "Doing the EasyStep Tango"?). The EasyStep Interview provides you with step-by-step data entry screens for setting up employee records. In fact, if you have a new employee to set up, you may want to reopen the EasyStep Interview and set up your employee there, using the step-by-step procedure for entering preliminary information about your employee.

Using the EasyStep Interview for a New Employee

If you used the EasyStep Interview to set up your company in QuickBooks, you can return to the Interview screens to set up additional employees. To enter an employee record through the EasyStep Interview, open the File menu and choose **EasyStep Interview**. When the EasyStep Interview opens, click the **Payroll** tab, and then press **Next** until you get to the Adding an Employee window, shown in the following figure. Click the **Add Employee** button, and QuickBooks leads you through a series of questions to help you set up a new employee. Just follow the directions on each screen.

*Click the **Add Employee** button and QuickBooks will lead you through the employee set-up process.*

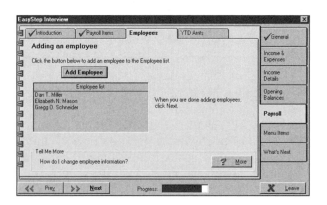

Click the **Leave** button when you've had enough of the EasyStep Interview.

Ignoring the EasyStep Interview for a New Employee

To set up an employee outside of the EasyStep Interview, start by opening the Employee List. To do so, display the Lists menu and choose **Employees**. Next, press **Ctrl+N** to open the New Employee window, as shown in the following figure. Enter the personal information for the employee, including the name, address, phone number, Social Security number, and any other information you need to track. Click inside each field into which you want to enter information; press **Tab** to move from field to field while typing.

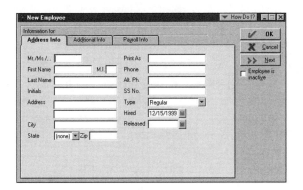

Enter the scoop on your new employee.

Click the **Additional Info** tab at the top of the window to enter miscellaneous information such as an employee number, birthday, dog's name, or any other intelligence you want to keep on your employees.

You can design custom fields to capture all the goods on your employees by clicking on the **Define Fields** button on the Additional Info tab. The Define Fields window appears (see the next figure), and you can add up to 15 new fields to your form. To make sure the new fields are included on every employee-related window, be sure to click the **Employees** check box for each field. With the appropriate check mark, you can also make this information available on your Customer:Jobs and Vendors windows.

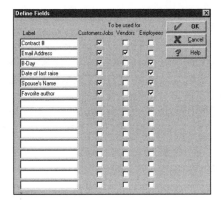

Set up specialty fields for tracking information that's important to you.

Back in the New Employee window, click the **Payroll Info** tab. On this tab, shown in the following figure, you'll fill in important financial information as follows:

➤ Type of pay (Regular, Overtime, Salary, and so on) is entered in the Earnings section. Choose from existing pay types by clicking the drop-down arrow in the **Name** column. If you want to add a new pay type (such as Overtime or Holiday), choose **Add New** from the top of the drop-down list.

➤ Pay rate is entered in the Hour/Annual Rate column.

➤ Choose a frequency of pay periods using the **Pay Period** drop-down arrow.

➤ Deductions and additions to paychecks are entered in the Additions, Deductions, and Company Contributions area. Click the **Name** column down arrow to choose from existing deductions and additions, or choose **Add New** from the top of the drop-down list to set up a new deduction or addition.

➤ Check the **Use time data to create paychecks** check box if this employee will record time on timesheets (see Chapter 15, "Punching the Time Clock").

Enter information about payroll and deductions for this employee.

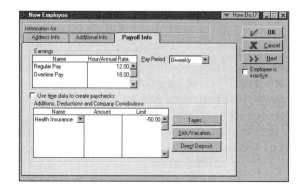

Entering Employee Tax Information

Need to enter tax information about the new employee? That's easy. Click the **Taxes** button on the Payroll Info tab of the New Employee window. This opens the Taxes box, shown in the next figure. From here, you can enter the information related to filing status and withholding exemptions for the employee. This is the information employees fill out on their federal W-4 forms ("Employee's Withholding Allowance Certificate") and the comparable form in your state. Note that each employee is required to file a federal W-4 form.

The W-4 is a form on which an employee calculates the number of exemptions he wants to claim. The number of exemptions controls how much income tax is withheld from each paycheck.

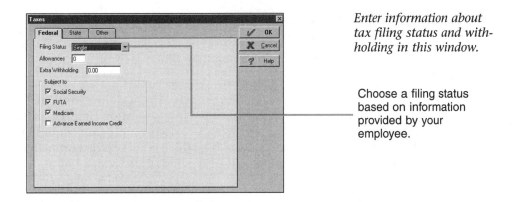

Enter information about tax filing status and withholding in this window.

Choose a filing status based on information provided by your employee.

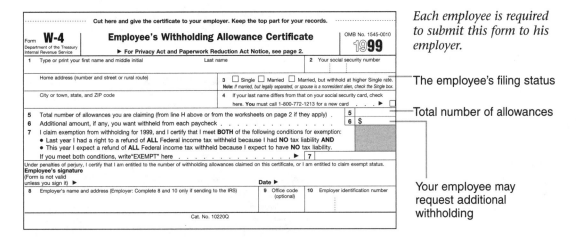

Each employee is required to submit this form to his employer.

The employee's filing status

Total number of allowances

Your employee may request additional withholding

Each employee is required to give the employer a W-4 form at the time he is hired. In addition, employees have the right to file a new W-4 form at any time. Whenever you receive a W-4 from an employee, the revised information must be entered on this screen. QuickBooks refers to this information for calculating paychecks.

There are three tabs in the Taxes window for entering information about Federal, State, and Other taxes. Enter information from the federal W-4 form on the Federal tab, including filing status, number of allowances, and any extra withholding requested by the employee. On the other two tabs, enter information from the comparable state and local tax forms such as filing status, number of allowances, name of local taxing authority, and any other information required by your state or local government.

Click **OK** to return to the Payroll Info tab of the New Employee window.

Accounting for Vacation and Sick Time

The setup for accounting for both vacation time and sick time is the same, so this section will cover accounting just for vacation time. Know that the same rules apply when accounting for sick time.

If you plan to track vacation time for your employees, QuickBooks will enable you to enter the number of hours an employee earns toward vacation time. QuickBooks will accumulate these hours on an ongoing basis and decrease the number of hours when the employee uses vacation time. QuickBooks will also make a determination as to how to account for unused vacation time at the end of the year.

To set up vacation time, follow these steps (use these same steps to set up sick time, but do so in the Sick area of the dialog box):

1. Click the **Sick/Vacation** button in the Payroll Info tab (of the same old New Employee window). The Sick & Vacation dialog box appears (see the following figure).

Fill in the blanks and QuickBooks will keep track of vacation and sick time for your employees.

Indicate whether vacation time is accrued annually or by pay period

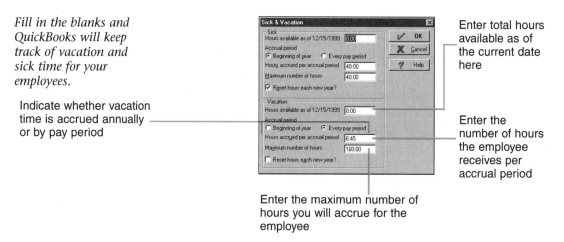

Enter total hours available as of the current date here

Enter the number of hours the employee receives per accrual period

Enter the maximum number of hours you will accrue for the employee

2. In the Vacation area, enter the total number of hours of vacation time available as of the current date in the Hours Available As Of field.

3. Indicate whether vacation time is awarded each pay period (click the **Every pay period** option) or at the first of the year (click the **Beginning of year** option).

4. Show how many hours are awarded at a time (for example, 10 hours per semi-monthly pay period). Enter this number in the Hours Accrued per Accrual Period field.

5. Enter the maximum number of hours that will be accumulated in the Maximum Number of Hours field.

6. There is a check box (Reset Hours Each New Year) to indicate if the accumulated hours are to be reset to zero at the beginning of a calendar year.

7. Click **OK** when you have completed all information.

When you're through working with the New Employee window, click **OK** to exit. You can leave it open if you plan to enter payroll additions and deductions, as covered in the next section.

Accounting for Payroll Additions and Deductions

Many employers provide benefits to their employees in addition to salary or wages. Health insurance is a common benefit, as are contributions to a retirement plan, expense reimbursements, child care plans, and more. All benefits offered to your employees can be tracked in QuickBooks.

In addition, companies often offer programs—such as childcare, optical insurance, and retirement accounts—in which employees can participate at their own cost.

The setup process for employer-paid benefits and employee-paid benefits is essentially the same. The differences are in the account that is charged with the cost of the plan and how the amount is computed.

In this section we'll set up a medical insurance plan that is provided by the employer.

Setting Up Payroll Benefits in QuickBooks

Before you begin to set up a new payroll benefit in QuickBooks, you need to gather information about the benefit: To whom are payments for this benefit made? Is the benefit reflected on the employee's W–2 form? Which accounts are affected by this benefit? Are payments made from employee withholding, or does the employer make all payments? You may want to consult with your accountant or tax advisor before setting up benefits, to make sure you have all the necessary information.

To add an employer-paid item, open the Lists menu, choose **Payroll Items**, and then press **Ctrl+N**. You can also request a New Item on the Payroll Info tab of the New Employee window (if the window is still open on your screen). To do so, click in the **Name** column in the Additions, Deductions, and Company Contributions area of the window. This displays a drop-down arrow. Click the arrow and choose <**Add New**> from the list.

Regardless of which route you take, the goal is to display the Add New Payroll Item window, as shown in the following figure.

Choose Company Contribution *to set up a company-paid medical plan.*

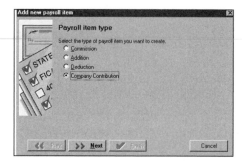

Choose **Company Contribution**, and then click **Next** through the ensuing screens. You will be asked to enter a name that will describe this amount in payroll reports and on pay stubs (Health Insurance, for example), information as to the recipient of payments for this benefit (your health insurance supplier), and the account that you will charge for the expense of this benefit (Insurance Expense, for example). Indicate if this is a pre-tax or a post-tax benefit (company-paid medical insurance typically counts as a pre-tax benefit).

Enter the dollar amount of this benefit if it is to be fixed per employee. If the amount will vary from one employee to the next, leave the amount blank and enter amounts on the employee setup screens. Click **Finish** to complete entry of this new item.

Back at the New Employee window, you can now make this benefit available to the employee by clicking the **Name** column in the Additions, Deductions, and Company Contributions area and choosing the new item from the drop-down list. Enter an amount if the amount isn't automatic.

To exit the New Employee window, click **OK**.

Issuing Paychecks

Payday is approaching and it's time to tell QuickBooks to issue paychecks for your employees. What do you do? Open the Activities menu and choose **Payroll, Pay Employees**. The Select Employees To Pay window will appear (see the next figure).

Start by verifying that the bank account and the dates of the check and the pay period are correct. Check the **To be printed** check box if QuickBooks is to print these checks.

Click the check boxes next to all the employees whose paycheck information you want to review (you can come back later and check off employees whose information you don't need to review).

248

Click here to review the payroll information
for each checked employee

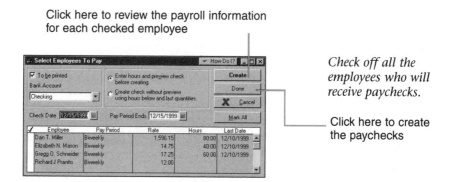

*Check off all the
employees who will
receive paychecks.*

Click here to create
the paychecks

Make sure the **Enter hours and preview check before creating** option is
selected. This indicates that you want to preview checks before creating them.

Ready to review? Click the **Create** button and QuickBooks enables you to view the
paycheck detail information for all checked employees. The next figure gives an
example of what you might encounter. On each individual paycheck preview, make
changes if necessary, and then click the **Create** button at the bottom of the screen to
create the paycheck and advance to the next preview.

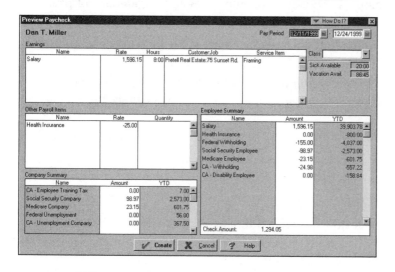

*Here's Dan Miller's pay-
check information.*

When you're finished, you will be returned to the Select Employees To Pay window. If
there are other employees who need to be paid but whose payroll information does
not need to be examined, check those employees, choose the **Create check without preview** option, and click the **Create** button to create the paychecks.

Click **Done** when you are ready to leave this window.

*NOT IN
→ THIS PROGRAM*

If you indicated that QuickBooks is going to print your paychecks, these checks will appear in your Reminders window, letting you know there are checks to print (see the next figure). For more information on using the Reminders list in QuickBooks, see the sidebar, "Your Very Own Reminder List," in Chapter 9, "Quick Guide to Banking with QuickBooks."

Your Reminders list keeps you up to date on paychecks that need to be printed.

When you are ready to print the paychecks, open the File menu and choose **Print Forms**, **Paychecks**.

Payroll Reports

There are payroll reports that you can produce in QuickBooks that show you details or a summary of the amounts you paid your employees and the amount of payroll taxes you have paid or need to pay throughout the year.

To see a list of the six reports that are available, open the Reports menu and choose **Payroll Reports**.

➤ **Summary**   Lists total wages and withholding, with details of the type of wages and all withholdings, on an employee-by-employee basis, for a requested time period.

➤ **Employee Earnings Summary**   Lists each employee, the gross pay, and deductions for the designated time period.

➤ **Liabilities**   Shows the balance in each payroll liability account for the designated time period.

➤ **Item Detail**   Displays a breakdown of every transaction that occurred for each of the payroll items for the designated time period.

➤ **Transaction Detail**   Shows every payroll check issued for the designated time period, with the detail of all amounts.

➤ **Transactions by Payee**   Shows each employee's name, followed by a list of the checks that were issued for the designated time period.

For more information about working with reports in QuickBooks, see Chapter 10, "Getting Useful Information Out of QuickBooks."

Payroll Taxes

The IRS requires employers to file a quarterly payroll tax form, Form 941, indicating the amount of payroll paid during the quarter and the amount of payroll tax withheld from each employee. On this form you also indicate the amount of payroll tax you as the employer owe.

Where Are Those #$%@!& Payroll Features?

Getting frustrated trying to find the Payroll features in QuickBooks? Some features, such as the payroll tax forms, will not be accessible to you if you have not turned on the full Payroll features in QuickBooks. If Payroll is not listed on your Activities menu, open the File menu, choose Preferences, click the Payroll & Employees icon, click the Company Preferences tab, and click Full payroll features. Click OK to save this change, and now you should have access to all payroll features in QuickBooks.

QuickBooks can prepare part of Form 941 (page 1) for you. To prepare Form 941, open the Activities menu and choose Payroll, Process Form 941 (alternatively, from the Navigator, click the Payroll tab, and then click the Process 941 icon). The Form 941 window will appear, as shown in the next figure. If this is the first time you have used this feature, you may have to answer some brief questions, such as in which state you make your deposits and for which quarter this return is being prepared.

You may not need to make any changes in this information at all, but you should click through (click Next to move from screen to screen). Examine each screen to make sure that this information agrees with what you expect to see on your Form 941.

And what should you expect to see? Before entering the Form 941 arena, take a look at the Payroll Liability Report for the same time period. (Open the Reports menu, select Payroll Reports, Liability, and set the date at the top to the same quarter for which you are preparing Form 941 (see the figure below).

Follow along through the Form 941 screens, verifying information as you go.

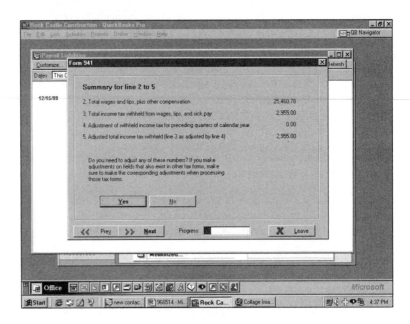

The information in this report should tie in to Form 941. If you want to see the details of any amount, double-click it.

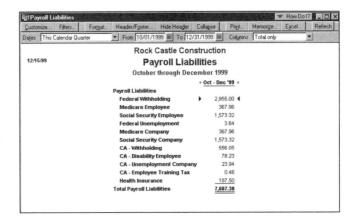

When finished with your Form 941, you can print it out. When you click the **Print** button, QuickBooks will print your form immediately.

Don't Want to Print?

What happens if you choose not to print your Form 941 while the Form 941 window is open? Do you have to start from scratch to create the form again? Nope! If you leave the Form 941 window without printing your form, open the Activities menu and choose **Payroll**, **Process Form 941**. A little window will appear, offering you an option to print your Form 941. Phew!

No Schedule B

QuickBooks does not prepare Schedule B of Form 941. Schedule B is the part of the form that sets out your withholding and tax liability for the company on a weekly basis throughout the quarter. Many companies aren't required to prepare this part of the 941. If you need Schedule B, you'll have to prepare this yourself. You can get the numbers you need by creating the Payroll Liability Report, mentioned earlier in this chapter. Create this on a week-by-week basis in order to get the correct information for your Schedule B.

The quarterly payroll tax reports cover the following periods and are due on the following dates:

Table 16.1   Payroll Tax Return Due Dates

Payroll Period	Tax Return and Due Date
January 1 through March 31	Form 941, due April 30
April 1 through June 30	Form 941, due July 31
July 1 through September 30	Form 941, due October 31
October 1 through December 31	Form 941, due January 31
January 1 through December 31	Form 940, due January 31

As with any tax return, if the due date falls on a weekend or a federal holiday, the next working day becomes the due date. So if January 31 falls on a Sunday, the due date for the January 31 tax report is Monday, February 1.

Tax that is owed during the quarter is deposited with a bank or other authorized financial institution and is accompanied by a little coupon called Form 8109. You must obtain this form directly from the IRS. Tax owed with Form 941 is submitted with the 941 in the same envelope, which you mail to the IRS.

Every state has different requirements regarding unemployment compensation and other state withholding. QuickBooks does not attempt to address issues of state payroll forms. You need to check your state requirements, get forms from your state, and prepare your own state payroll tax forms.

State Unemployment Taxes

You may have noticed that QuickBooks does not prepare any sort of state-level payroll tax reports, including the state unemployment tax report. I recommend preparing the Employee Earnings Summary Report (open the Reports menu and choose Payroll, Employee Earnings Summary), and then exporting the report to Excel by clicking the Excel button at the top. In Excel, you can perform calculations to arrive at the amount you owe for state and unemployment compensation tax.

Year-End Payroll Tax Reports

Employers are required to file Form 940, Employer's Annual Federal Unemployment Tax Return. Form 940 is due each year by January 31. It summarizes federal unemployment tax for the year. Note that the amount you incurred for each quarter is listed on Form 940. If the cumulative amount of federal unemployment tax you owe during the quarter ever exceeds $100, you are required to make a deposit for that amount.

FUTA? SUTA? What's the Difference?

Too many acronyms can make even the most savvy of us crazy. FUTA stands for Federal Unemployment Tax Act, SUTA stands for State Unemployment Tax Act. If you're paying FUTA, you're paying unemployment tax to our federal government. If you're paying SUTA, you're paying unemployment tax to your state government. Most businesses pay both federal and state unemployment taxes.

To prepare Form 940, open the Activities menu and choose **Payroll**, **Process Form 940** (alternatively, click the **Payroll** tab in the Navigator, and click **Process 940**). Just as with Form 941, QuickBooks displays a series of screens that you can click through, verifying information as you go. Compare numbers to the amounts on your Payroll Tax Liability Report that you should prepare for the same time period as Form 940 (usually the calendar year).

Now You've Done It!

You'll find you can use QuickBooks for nearly all of your payroll needs.

➤ Set up your employees in QuickBooks. See "Setting Up Employees."

➤ Account for special payroll features like vacation and sick pay. See "Accounting for Vacation and Sick Time."

➤ Account for employer-paid benefits and employee deductions. See "Accounting for Payroll Additions and Deductions."

➤ Issue paychecks to your employees. See "Issuing Paychecks."

➤ Prepare payroll reports summarizing all of your payroll and payroll tax information. See "Payroll Reports."

➤ Prepare federal payroll tax forms. See "Payroll Taxes."

Part 5

Qualities That Make QuickBooks Unique

Poke around in this section for quick tricks that will make your QuickBooks program seem like it was written just for you. Sure, you can learn fun stuff such as how to change the colors on your screen, but you can also pick up useful tricks, such as how to customize your iconbar, how to take advantage of the little calculator that comes with the program, and how to write clever letters to your customers, plus stay ahead of the game with a working budget.

You'll also learn about some neat places on the World Wide Web that are especially nice for QuickBooks users. Most of all, you'll be able to remind yourself of the fact that there are a lot of good reasons why you bought this program.

Chapter 17

This Is YOUR Program

In This Chapter

➤ Learn how to customize your QuickBooks forms

➤ Fiddle with the program features

➤ Find out how to alter the way numbers appear

➤ Add the QuickBooks calculator to your iconbar

Like many computer programs, QuickBooks has a personality all its own. You'll find quirky little program characteristics, plus menu choices and toolbars that are unique to this program and different from any other program you've used.

A lot of QuickBooks' program characteristics can be changed. For example, you can change the way in which some of the tools are accessed. Which features of the program are available to you can also be altered, and you can make changes in the way numbers are entered (with or without decimal places).

There's a lot you can do to make this program behave the way you'd like it to, so don't think you have to accept everything just the way it comes out of the box. Take a look at this chapter and learn some interesting techniques for customizing your QuickBooks program. There's not enough room here to cover every customizable option, but this information will help you as you explore the many options on your own.

Creating Nice-Looking Forms

As you've learned in the previous chapters, QuickBooks comes with an array of standard forms that go to customers. These include invoices, purchase orders, estimates, monthly statements, credit memos, and cash sales forms. You're not stuck with the default designs of these forms. You can change the standard forms so that they meet the specific needs of your company.

Alternatively, you can create your own forms from scratch so that all the fields you need appear on the form in the order that is most useful to you. You can alter the size of the forms, and you can incorporate graphic features such as your company logo and favorite typefaces.

All these changes can be made to the forms in QuickBooks by following the steps set out in this section. Want to give some a try?

Changing the Appearance of Standard Forms

Perhaps the easiest way to get your feet wet in the area of customizing forms is to change the appearance of one of the standard forms, such as an invoice. Once you get used to working with the features that enable you to customize forms, you can try your luck at creating a custom form from scratch.

To take a look at the standard forms that are available in QuickBooks, open the Lists menu and choose **Template**. A Templates window will appear (see the following figure) showing all of the forms that are currently available in your QuickBooks file (including any custom forms that have been created).

Choose a form to view or customize from this list of templates.

Click a form name, and then click here to open the form

To change a standard form and customize it for your own use, open the standard form that you want to change. Click the form name in the Templates list, and then click the **Open Form** button. Next, in the upper-right corner of the Form window, click the **Custom Template** drop-down arrow and choose **Customize**. The Customize Template window will appear for the form you have chosen (see the following figure). You can choose to edit the form you selected or create a new form based on it. If you choose to edit an Intuit standard form, you will be limited in your editing options. For purposes of this example, we'll look at customizing an invoice form.

Click here
to edit the
existing form

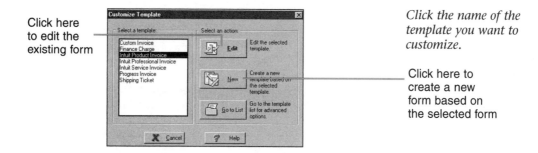

*Click the name of the
template you want to
customize.*

Click here to
create a new
form based on
the selected form

When you click the **Edit** or **New** button, the Customize window will appear, as shown in the next figure. In this example, the Customize Invoice window appears, since I'm customizing an invoice form. Enter a name for your customized form in the Template Name text box in the upper-left corner of the Customize window. Use the various tabs in the Customize window to make changes to the form, as explained in the remaining sections.

Customizing the Header

Use the Header tab to change the information found at the top of the form, such as the name of the form, the date, the form number, and various other elements, depending on the form type.

There are two columns on the Header tab, Screen and Print, with check boxes in each column (see the figure below).

Each item that's checked in the Screen column will appear on the screen when you use the form. Each item that's checked in the Print column will be included when you print a hard copy of the form. There's a separate column for each, so that some information can appear onscreen while the form is being filled out but not appear on the printed copy that goes to the customer.

Or Double-Click

Another way to open the Customize Invoice window is to double-click the **Custom Invoice** form name in the Templates window. As soon as you do, the Customize Invoice window will appear.

You can change any of the information on the Header page. For example, you may want to change the name of the form from *Invoice* to *Bill of Sale*. Or you might choose to include a *Ship To* address on your invoice form.

The Header tab includes options for titles that appear at the top of your form.

Click this column to include these items on the screen version of the form

Click this column to include these items on the print version of the form

Take a Look at What You've Done

While going through the various customizing tabs, if you want to see how your changes are going to be incorporated into your form, you can always click the Layout Designer button, examine the appearance of the form, and then click OK to return to the Customize window. For more information about using the Layout Designer to change the appearance of your form, see the "Previewing Your Form" section later in this chapter.

Customizing Your Form Fields

Click the Fields tab to see a long checklist of information that appears on your form, as shown in the next figure. As in the Header tab, there are two columns: Screen and Print. In the Screen column, place a check in the box next to any item that should appear on the onscreen version of the form. Check the box in the Print column for any information that should appear on the printed form.

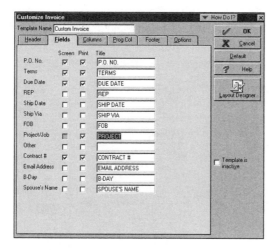

Each item on the Fields tab represents a piece of information that appears on your form.

Each of these items has a title, which is the text that will appear on your form. If you find there is a title that is more descriptive or more appropriate for your business, you can change any of these titles by deleting the title and entering one of your own. For example, you may want the Terms area of the form to read *Payment Terms*, or perhaps you want the Due Date area to read *Payment Due*. Make a change by clicking inside the **Title** box and then editing the text to read the way you want. You are limited to 41 characters (including spaces) for your titles.

Customizing Form Columns

The Columns tab is where you choose which columns will appear at the bottom of the form, on your screen and on your printed form. In the Screen and the Print lists, indicate which you want to appear in each version. Also, check the titles to see if they are as you want them to appear on the form.

There is also an Order list (see the figure below). Here you indicate numerically the order in which you want the columns to appear on the form. The item you mark as number 1 will be the leftmost column, 2 will be next, and so on. Any columns that are not checked to appear in the print or screen version of your form will have an order number of 0.

Change Your Form Titles

Don't feel you are restricted to using the QuickBooks titles for entries on your forms. For example, there is a Project field on the invoice form. If yours is a legal services business, you may want to change this description to read *Case*. Take advantage of the fact that you can change these titles so that your forms will make sense for your business.

Enter the order (1, 2, 3...) in which columns
should appear from left to right on your form

*Choose which columns
should appear on your
form.*

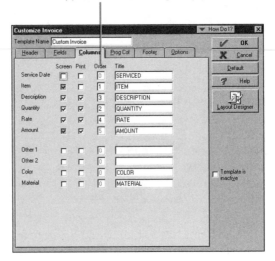

Customizing the Progress Column

If you are working with an invoice form, use the Prog Col (short for *progress column*)
tab to change the form fields for tracking information from estimates relative to progressive invoices. As with the tabs previously covered, each of the items on this tab
can represent a column on your invoice form, as shown in the figure below. Click the
items you want to include on your screen and on the printed form. For example, you
may want the Prior Amount that has been billed to appear on the printed invoice. To
do this, click in the **Print** column next to Prior Amount. You can also edit the field
titles as needed.

*Use the Prog Col tab to
change fields for tracking
progressive invoice information.*

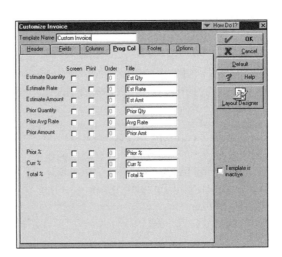

Customizing the Form Footer

The Footer tab contains an area in which you can insert a message that will be printed on all your forms, typically at the bottom of the form. The next figure shows the options available on this tab.

In the Customer Message field, you can enter text that is unique to each customer to be printed on the form. Use the Total field if your forms need totaling (if you sell only one item at a time and there is no sales tax to apply, there will be nothing to total, so you won't need this field).

Where's My Prog Col Tab?

The Prog Col tab in the Customize window appears only if you have QuickBooks Pro and use the Progress Billing feature with estimates.

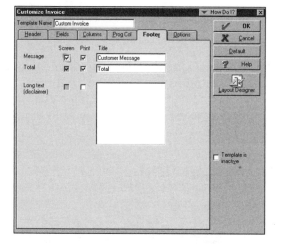

Use the Footer tab to establish text that is printed at the bottom of each form.

Use the Long Text field if you want to enter a message that will appear on every invoice. You could print warranty information in this area, your company's return policy, or information about items that are on sale. The Long Text information appears on the printed form only, not on the onscreen form.

Other Customizing Options

The last tab in the Customize window, the Options tab shown in the next figure, contains options for including information about your company, such as the company name, address, and logo. You also can alter the style and size of the font for various areas of the printed form.

Decide what company information to include on your form and choose your fonts.

Click here to show your company name and address

Click here to give the name and location of the bitmap file you want to use

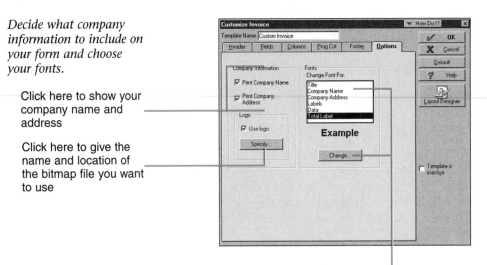

Click an option, and then click the Change button to change the font style or size

To add a logo to your form, the logo must be in a bitmap file on your computer's hard drive. Check the **Use logo** check box to include your logo on the form, and then click the **Specify** button to indicate the name of the file that contains your company logo. In the Logo window that appears, click the **File** button to indicate to QuickBooks the location of the file containing your logo.

Creating a Bitmap File

You may have a company logo that was created in a file other than a bitmap file (bitmap files use a BMP extension). To convert your file to a bitmap that QuickBooks can read, open a graphics program such as Microsoft Paint. (If this program is on your computer, it will be found by clicking Start, Programs, Accessories, Paint.) Resave the file by choosing File, Save As. In the Save As dialog box that appears, change the Save as type option to a bitmap selection. Enter a filename, and click the Save button.

On the Options tab, you can select a typeface and font size for the text that appears on your printed form. Click an item in the list box under Change Font For—for example, the title of the form or the company name—and then click the Change button. A dialog box will appear in which you can select a font, choose the style of the font (such as bold or italic), choose a type size, indicate an effect (such as underlining), or choose another color for the type. Make your changes and click OK to return to the Customize window.

Previewing Your Form

Once you have chosen all the different elements to appear on your form, you should preview the form and check out how everything looks. For example, you may find you need to alter the size of a form element or change the placement of some of the titles on the form.

To preview the form or make changes to its composition or layout, click the Layout Designer button in the Customize window. You'll see a sample version of the form, as shown in the following figure. The sample will show the elements you selected to appear on the form.

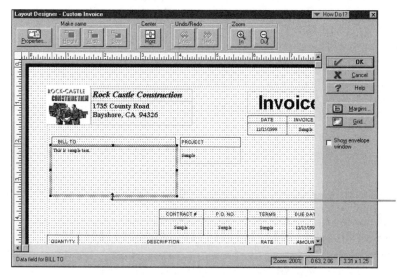

You can click any object and stretch it to a new size or drag it to a new location.

Your mouse pointer becomes a double arrow when you are about to resize an object

You can click any object on this form to select it. When you do so, little black handles will appear in the corners and on the sides of the object. Place your mouse over any one of the black handles and drag to stretch or shrink the object. Or, to move the object to a new location, place your mouse pointer in the center of the object and drag. You can move the fields around or resize them as needed.

Also on the Layout Designer window is an option for changing margins. By clicking the **Margins** button on the right side of the screen, you can enter adjustments to your margins. A Margins window will appear in which you can enter the precise measurements for the margins on all four sides of the printed form.

If you are using preprinted forms that don't match the standard size of the onscreen form (8fi" by 11"), you can resize the screen form to match your paper forms. For example, if your preprinted form is 8fi" by 5fi" and you want a fi" margin on all four sides of the page, you would set your margins at 0.50 inch for left and right, 0.50 inch for top, and 6 inches for the bottom. That gives you a total of 6fi" for the top and bottom margins, leaving you with a 4fi" writing area. Click **OK** to return to the Layout Designer window.

There's also an option for examining the placement of an envelope window. If you mail your forms in window envelopes (with the opening so you can see an address on the bill inside), you want to make sure that the address on the form will align with the window in the envelope. Click the **Show Envelope Window** check box and you'll see an outline of where the envelope window will appear on the form. If necessary, just click and drag the Address field until it's right.

When you have finished working with the Layout Designer, click the **OK** button and you will return to the Customize window. If all necessary changes have been made and you're ready to complete this form, click the **OK** button. Your changes will be saved. The next time you want to use this form, it will be listed on the Customize Template drop-down list on the standard form.

Add a Form to the Iconbar

If you have a form that you use regularly in QuickBooks and you'd like to make that form readily accessible, you can add a button for the form to the QuickBooks iconbar. To do this, display the form onscreen, open the Window menu, and choose **Add Window to Iconbar.** In the window that appears, enter a name (such as the name of the new form) and a description (optional) for your button. Then choose a button design by clicking one of the pictured choices. Click **OK** to exit the dialog box. A button for this particular form will now appear on your iconbar.

Fiddling with QuickBooks' Program Settings

There are many customizable features in QuickBooks, including those that affect the appearance and use of the program. Many of these are addressed throughout the book. This section gives you an overview of some of the more common customizable features in QuickBooks.

To begin customizing features, open the File menu and select Preferences. This opens the Preferences window, as shown in the next figure.

Click a general topic

Click here to change the appearance
of the program and certain features

*Making changes in the
QuickBooks Preferences
window.*

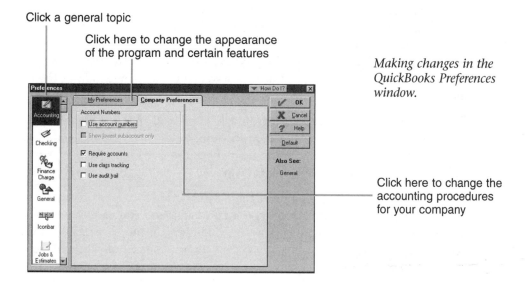

Click here to change the
accounting procedures
for your company

QuickBooks features are organized into categories represented by icons on the left side of the window. Use the scroll arrows to see what's available. When you click an icon, the options on the My Preferences and Company Preferences tabs change to correspond with the category selected. For example, if you click the General icon, the tabs display general program options.

The following sections will explain some of the ways you can change how QuickBooks operates. Take time to explore all the categories and the options for each to see what kind of fine tuning you can perform to suit your needs.

Changing Accounting Preferences

To turn account numbers on or off, click the Accounting icon at the left side of the QuickBooks Preferences window. Then click the Company Preferences tab and the Use account numbers check box option (see the previous figure).

To associate income and expenses with classes, check the Use class tracking box (also found on the Company Preferences tab of the Accounting category).

Using Classes in QuickBooks

QuickBooks provides its users the opportunity to group income, expense, and payroll transactions into *classes*, or separate logical categories. For example, maybe your business operates in three different cities. You could use the class feature to group transactions for each city. Or maybe your company is a law firm that practices both family law and personal injury law, and you want to separate your transactions so that you can produce financial statements for each faction of the law firm.

Turn on the class feature by opening the File menu and choosing Preferences, and then click the Accounting icon at the left side of the Preferences window. Click the Company Preferences tab, and check the Use class tracking check box. Click OK to close the Preferences window.

Set up classes on-the-fly as you need them by choosing Add New in any Class field that appears on a form, or open the Lists menu and choose Other Lists, Classes. Press Ctrl+N to create a new class, indicating in the New Class window the class name and, if applicable, which class this is a subclass of. Click OK to close the New Class window.

From this point forward, your invoices, purchase orders, payroll, bills, and checks will include an area where you can indicate an optional class. At the top of reports, in the Columns area, you can choose Class as the method of grouping report information. QuickBooks will display your report with a column for each class.

Another feature available in the Accounting, Company Preferences area is the audit trail. The audit trail is a feature that enables you to view a report showing every transaction that has been entered in your QuickBooks file, the date on which it was entered, and the name of the user who was logged in when the transaction was entered. If you find that you need to retrace your footsteps, turning on the audit trail will keep an historical record of all of those footsteps. If you work with an outside accountant, he may request that you use the audit trail to give him a guide in figuring out how different transactions are entered in your company records. Turn on the audit trail by checking the Use audit trail check box.

Turning On Automatic Decimal Points

If you're the sort of person who hates to enter that little dot that separates the dollars and cents in an amount, you can ask QuickBooks to take care of this task for you. Click the General icon on the left side of the Preferences window and display the My Preferences tab. Here you'll find an option for automatic decimal points. Click the **Automatically place decimal point** check box.

From this point forward, when you enter 38475, for example, QuickBooks will enter 384.75. Watch out! If you enter a whole number that doesn't have any cents, you need to enter two zeros. Otherwise, QuickBooks is going to place the decimal point and turn 374 into 3.74, even though you meant it to be 374.00.

Fine Tuning the QuickBooks Iconbar

QuickBooks comes with a toolbar called the iconbar, which can be displayed across the top of your screen. You won't see the iconbar unless you request it—QuickBooks doesn't display this bar by default. The iconbar includes several buttons that can execute menu choices quickly. For example, you can click a button to open an invoice or a purchase order. A tip earlier in this chapter discusses creating an iconbar button for a new form.

To display the iconbar, open the Preferences window and click the Iconbar icon at the left side of the screen. Click the My Preferences tab, and then click the option to display the iconbar with or without pictures or text, whichever you prefer. On this screen you can also edit the iconbar, adding or taking away icons.

Finished with Preferences?

After making changes in the Preferences window, be sure to click the OK button to close the window and save your changes. Click Cancel, and the window will close but your changes won't be saved. If you press Esc to exit the window, QuickBooks sends you a message reminding you that you made some changes and asking if you want to save them. Click Yes to save the changes.

Click any button on the QuickBooks iconbar to open a form or perform a task.

I like to add an iconbar button for the QuickBooks calculator. QuickBooks comes with a helpful little calculator that you can use right in the program while you are entering your data. This calculator will perform onscreen mathematical computations for you. By adding a button to the iconbar, you make the calculator easy to find. Otherwise, you have to find it in the Activities menu (open the Activities menu and choose **Other Activities, Use Calculator**).

Add the calculator to your iconbar by following these steps:

1. If the Preferences window isn't onscreen, open the File menu and choose **Preferences**. The Preferences window will appear.

2. Click the **Iconbar** icon at the left of the Preferences window, and then click the **My Preferences** tab at the top of the window (see the next figure).

Click a display option

Set preferences for your iconbar using this window.

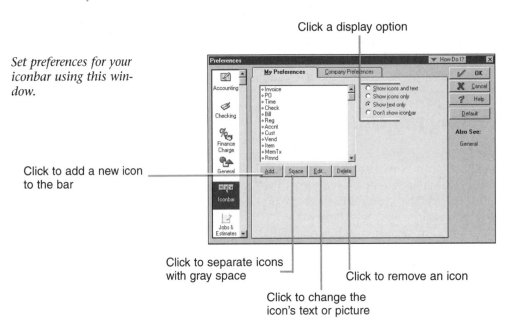

Click to add a new icon to the bar

Click to separate icons with gray space

Click to change the icon's text or picture

Click to remove an icon

3. Click the **Add** button and the Add Iconbar Item window will appear (see the following figure).

Click the feature you want to add

Choose from this list

Add an icon to your icon-bar using this window.

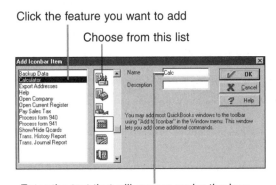

Enter the text that will appear under the icon

4. Click the **Calculator** item in the list of items.

5. In the middle of the window, click an image that you want to use for the picture on your iconbar button. Use the scroll arrows to view the available images.

6. Enter a name to go with the icon in the Name text box. This name will appear as text on your iconbar button.

7. Click **OK** to close the Add Iconbar Item window. Click **OK** again to close the Preferences window. The new iconbar button will appear on your iconbar (as shown in the next figure).

The iconbar wraps to a second line when new icons are added.

New button

Giant Icons

Add too many icons and your iconbar will wrap around to a new line, taking up valuable space onscreen. The QuickBooks icons are larger than those that appear on toolbars in other programs. You can save some space by selecting **Show text only** on the My Preferences tab for the Iconbar category in the Preferences window.

Now You've Done It!

The more you take charge of the way your QuickBooks program works, the more you're going to feel like this really is YOUR program! Here are some of the customization tasks you can now perform:

➤ Create and customize the forms that you give to your customers. See "Creating Nice-Looking Forms."

➤ Attach account numbers to your account names. See "Changing Accounting Preferences."

➤ Turn on the audit trail, and you'll have a record of everything that has transpired in your program. See "Changing Accounting Preferences."

➤ Take advantage of the QuickBooks iconbar—include your own custom-made forms on the bar. See "Fine Tuning the QuickBooks Iconbar."

Making and Saving (and Actually Using) Budgets

You've heard of budgets. You may even have a budget. A budget is often thought of as a wish list of how you'd like your company to perform. In actuality, a budget is a financial statement of projected performance.

Your budget may reflect how you hope your company performs in the future, or it may reflect how you realistically expect to perform in the year ahead. What's the difference? A hopeful budget is a goal, whereas an expected budget is pragmatic. Ideally, you should prepare one of each, using the expected budget as a regular monitor of your performance, and referring to the hopeful budget as a means of keeping your future goals in sight. Then you can compare your actual performance to your expectations and make informed decisions about how your company is performing. This chapter discusses how budgets are used and how to create a budget in QuickBooks.

Why You Need a Budget

Moving through life without a budget for your business is like stepping onto the stage without having studied the script. You have a pretty good idea of how the story is supposed to end (with the boss and all the employees making lots of money and living happily ever after, of course!), but you may not know what you need to do to get there.

Budget

An estimate of revenue and expenses.

You lose the ability to see where you're going when you don't use a budget to help you anticipate future activity. The budget is a compass that helps you point your company in the correct direction. Use a budget to help keep the future in perspective while you're operating in the present.

Once you've created a budget, which you can do in QuickBooks, **don't** make the mistake of sticking it in a drawer and taking it out at the end of the year to see how you've done. **Do** keep your budget with you, post it on the wall, pass out copies to co-workers, refer to it regularly during the course of the year, and use it to help guide you and keep your business on track. Pat yourself on the back when you meet or do better than your budgetary projections. Make corrections in your business activities when you go off track.

Creating a Basic Budget

Usually budgets are created for an entire year, with a breakdown on a month-by-month basis so that you can refer to it monthly and also use it to analyze an entire year's performance.

When you create a budget of projected financial activity, you'll enter amounts that you anticipate you will see on your financial statements in the year ahead. Try to be somewhat realistic about the numbers you choose for your budget. It's fun to think that your income might increase 100% next year and that your expenses will go down 50%—but is there really any chance that this might happen? A budget that shoots for the stars, or even a budget that shows zero growth and zero decline, is not useful unless it is based on reality.

That is not to say that you shouldn't try to reach some goals with your budget. Just the opposite. If your income is not high enough to meet your required (or desired) expenses, you can create a budget that tightens up your expenses a little bit. In this way, even if you don't plan on having your income increase, your can work at reducing your expenses. By using a budget as a tool and as a guide, you can institute rules for yourself to keep your expenses down or to indicate which areas you want to work on improving in terms of raising your income.

Start with Last Year's Financials

When you're ready to create your budget, you need to start with a copy of your financial statements for the prior year. You'll use those statements as an initial guide in creating a budget. Many budgets get their start with the actual numbers from the prior year's income statement (see "Copying Last Year's Budget," below), and then those numbers are fine-tuned to show whatever expectations you have for the year ahead.

For example, you may expect a 5% increase in revenue, so you can start with last year's income statement and increase all your revenue numbers by 5%. Maybe you know your rent's going to go up this year, so at the point in the year when you expect an increase in rent, you'll change your budgeted amount to that new figure.

Get the Whole Staff Involved

Creating a budget should be a group effort. After all, who knows better how the business is running than those people who are out on the front lines every day?

If your business includes more than one person, take the time to discuss the budget with the people who are involved in some financial aspect of the business, such as salespeople and purchasers, and get their input on how the business is expected to perform in the future. Ask about the areas they think can be changed and where they think emphasis can be placed on improvement.

Learn from the Competition

A company like yours, with perhaps a few more years of experience, would provide a great resource for comparing notes and sharing budget information. Maybe you know someone in the same type of business as yours but who is not in direct competition with you. Check with friends in other states to see if they know someone in your line who might be willing to open up a bit. You could try searching for companies like yours on the Internet. Successful business people are always willing to brag a little—maybe you can learn some of their secrets.

Once you have a sense of what numbers you want to use in your budget, you're ready to enter your budget in QuickBooks.

Fill In the Blanks

To create a budget in QuickBooks, open the Activities menu and choose **Set Up Budgets**. (If you don't see this option on your menu, look on the Activities menu under Other Activities.) If you're using QuickBooks Navigator, display the **Company** tab and click **Budgets**. The Set Up Budgets window will appear (see the following figure).

Create your budget, account by account, on this screen.

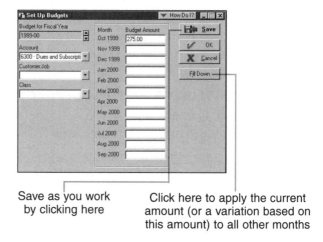

Save as you work by clicking here

Click here to apply the current amount (or a variation based on this amount) to all other months

The first piece of information you're asked for is the fiscal year for which you're creating this budget.

Create More Than One Budget

In QuickBooks you can create only one budget for each fiscal year. But what if you want to have a working budget and a more goal-oriented budget to refer to during the year? If you want to create more than one budget for the year, don't feel you're limited by QuickBooks. You can create a budget in QuickBooks, produce the budget report, and then export it to Excel (or any spreadsheet program), where you can create additional budget columns and experiment with some different scenarios instead of just the one main budget. For more information on exporting reports to Excel, see the section "Exporting Reports to Excel" in Chapter 19, "Making Friends with Microsoft."

In the upper-left corner of your budget screen, choose the year to which the budget will apply. There are three fields beneath the fiscal year box: one for Account, one for Customer:Job, and one for Class. Click a field's drop-down arrow to see the available choices. When you create a budget in QuickBooks, you can choose a maximum of two of these three options for amounts that you are budgeting (or you can choose just one if you prefer). For example, you can choose to budget for accounts, and within the accounts you can budget by customers and jobs, or you can budget by class (alternatively, you can budget just by account without any breakdown by job or class). Make your choices from these three boxes, and then enter the amount you anticipate for the first month of the first account in the Budget Amount column.

You can enter an individual amount in each month. If you anticipate that the amount will be the same in each month or that it will increase or decrease by a fixed percentage or dollar difference, you can enter the amount in the first month and then use QuickBooks to help you fill in the rest of the months.

For example, if you enter $500 as your budgeted amount for the first month and want to use that same amount for each month of the rest of the year, click the **Fill Down** button at the right side of the budget window. The Fill Down box will appear (see the figure below).

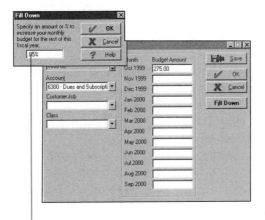

Use the original number you entered to calculate the budgeted amount for each month of the year.

Indicate an amount or a percentage by which you want the budgeted amount to increase or decrease each month

There are three ways in which you can use the Fill Down box.

➤ Click **OK**, leaving the increment set at 0, if you want to apply the same dollar amount to each remaining month in the fiscal year.

➤ Enter a positive or negative dollar amount if you want to increase or decrease the originally budgeted amount by a specific dollar amount each month.

➤ Enter a positive or negative percentage if you want to increase or decrease the originally budgeted amount by a percentage each month.

Then click **OK** to exit the Fill Down box, and QuickBooks will fill in the rest of the budget amounts for this account for the year. After using the Fill Down option, you can still override individual amounts by clicking in the space for the amount for a particular month, deleting the existing amount, and replacing it with a different amount.

You need to go through each of your accounts and jobs one at a time to create your budget. This is an extremely tedious and time-consuming process (have a nice snack nearby or listen to music to help the time pass), and you definitely want to have a financial statement or a list of your accounts or jobs at your side so you can check off each one as you create the budget for that amount.

Click the **Save** button at any time as you work on creating your budget to save your work in progress. When you have finished your budget (or need to take a break), click the **OK** button to close the Set Up Budgets window.

Copying Last Year's Budget

Once you've gone through the process of creating a budget in QuickBooks, you can use that budget as a starting point for creating a budget for a different year. If you have Microsoft Excel, this process is relatively simple, because you can copy the budget into Excel, change the year, and transport the budget back to QuickBooks.

Who Needs Excel?

QuickBooks Pro has this nifty relationship with Excel, whereby you can send secret messages back and forth between the two programs. But who says you need to have two-way communication? You can export a budget report to any spreadsheet program by clicking the report's **Print** button and requesting to print to a file. Keep your budget in your spreadsheet, and don't worry about needing to get it back to QuickBooks.

You can copy a prior year's budget to Excel by following these steps:

1. From QuickBooks, open the File menu and select **Export**. The Export window will appear, as shown in the next figure.

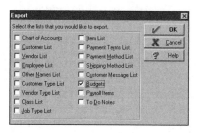

Check Budgets if you want to export a budget to Excel.

2. Click the **Budgets** check box, and then click **OK.**

3. In the Export window, enter a filename for this budget file. Click inside the **File Name** text box and type in the name. QuickBooks will apply an `.iif` extension to this filename.

Finding a Folder

You may be asking yourself, which lucky folder gets my export file today? Actually, if you want to just leave well enough alone, as Mom used to say, QuickBooks will export your file into the default QuickBooks folder. You'll have to hunt around a bit for this folder when you're ready to pull the file into Excel. Whether you use the default folder or choose one of your own, just remember where the file is saved so you can find it again when you get over to Excel.

4. Click **Save** to perform the export ceremony, wait while QuickBooks provides you with some soothing churning sounds, and then a prompt box appears. Click **OK**, which is your way of congratulating QuickBooks on successfully completing its mission.

5. Open your Excel program and open the budget file. To do this, display the File menu and select **Open** in Excel.

6. In the Open dialog box, change the **Files of Type** field to All Files (click the drop-down arrow and locate All Files on the list).

7. Now locate the folder and file you saved back in steps 3 and 4. Select the file-name, and then click **Open**.

8. A Text Import Wizard appears, complete with magic wands and secret hand-shakes, of course. You can fool with the instructions in this window if you like, but really all you have to do is click **Finish**, and the budget file will open in an Excel worksheet.

9. There is a column in the budget (see the following figure) called StartDate, and this column contains a year for each budgeted amount. Select the column by clicking on the letter at the top of the column, and then open the Edit menu and choose **Replace**. This opens the Replace dialog box.

10. In the Replace dialog box, indicate the year *from* which you want to copy in the Find What field (for example, 1/1/98). Indicate the year *to* which you want the budgeted amounts to apply in the Replace With field (for example, 1/1/99). Then click the **Replace All** button.

11. Save the file, keeping the .iif extension intact. At this time you can close Excel if you like.

Change the start date on the spreadsheet version of your budget so that you can copy the budget to another year.

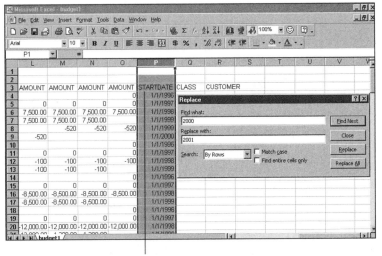

Select this column, and
then find and replace old
dates with new dates

12. Back in QuickBooks, open the File menu and choose **Import**. The Import win-dow will appear, from which you are to choose your newly revised budget.

13. Select the budget file that you saved in Excel, and then click **Open**. QuickBooks imports your file and displays a prompt box telling you the transfer was a suc-cess. Click **OK**. The file is now available for your use in QuickBooks.

Note that you can revise the numbers in the budget file, either in QuickBooks or while the file is in Excel.

Using Your Budget Effectively

You've created your budget in QuickBooks. Now what? Many people wait until the end of the year, take a look at their budget, and say, uh-oh—guess we'll have to do a better job next year.

Others look at the budget, see how close they came, congratulate themselves if they exceeded the income expectations of their budget, berate themselves if they didn't meet expectations, and then go out for pizza and talk about how they might improve their business next year.

Budget? What Budget?

Believe it or not, there really are people who prepare a budget at the beginning of the year and then never look at it again. How effective do you suppose that budget is? To make it useful, you have to take it out often and look at it!

Waiting until the end of the year to compare your actual performance to your budgeted performance does give you an interesting retrospective picture of your business' financial activity for the year. Comparing your actual financial progress with your estimates from a year ago may give you some insight into how good a fortuneteller you are. But waiting until the end of the year to do your analysis doesn't give you the opportunity to perform effective financial planning during the course of the year.

You don't have to use your budget simply as a fortune-telling device. You can refer to your budget during the year, and it will provide you with a reminder of what your expectations are as well as a guideline to help you stay on track.

For example, if you are considering purchasing some new equipment or making some other large cash outlay, you can look to your budget to see if your projected cash flow can accommodate an additional expense, or to see if you can handle a loan payment as an additional monthly expense. Analyze your budget to help determine where you might be able to cut back in one area or improve your income in another area in order to provide cash flow for the item you want to purchase.

And what if your budget analysis turns up an inconsistency? For example, perhaps you have had unexpected costs, or maybe your income is below budget. Waiting until the year is over to determine the reasons behind inconsistencies leaves you with plenty of time to ponder what happened, but no opportunity to address a problem when it arises.

Budget Reports Brought to You by QuickBooks

As soon as you finalize your budget, print out a hard copy so you have your budget in hand and can refer to it frequently.

Open the Reports menu and choose **Budget Reports**. (If you're using QuickBooks Navigator, click the **Company** tab, click the **Budget** report at the bottom of the window, and then select the budget you want to view.) You will see six budget reports from which you can choose:

➤ An Overview budget report provides you with a profit and loss statement, showing you all income and expense amounts that were budgeted, listed by account (see the figure below).

Print a copy of your budget so you will be able to refer to it easily.

Click here to print the report

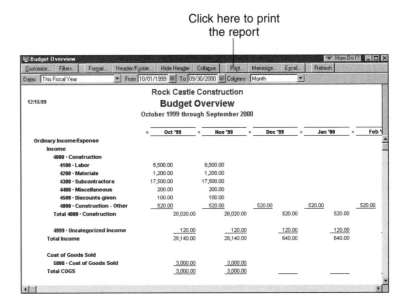

➤ The Budget versus Actual report shows not just the budget but how your budget compares to your actual company activity. You will see a dollar amount as well as a percentage amount, representing the difference between actual numbers and budgeted numbers (see the next figure).

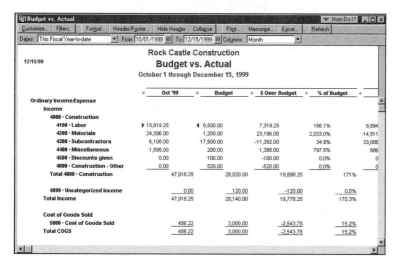

A comparison budget report such as the Budget versus Actual report compares actual performance to budgeted expectations.

➤ If you've created budget information on a job-by-job basis, the By Job Overview report gives you a budget report based on job information that you've entered. The Job budget is an income statement budget.

➤ The By Job Comparison report shows budget to actual job information, comparing actual performance to budgeted expectations.

➤ If you've budgeted for your balance sheet amounts, the Balance Sheet Overview report shows you a summary of the budgeted balance sheet.

➤ The Balance Sheet Comparison report displays a comparison between budgeted and actual balance sheet amounts.

You can print any budget report by clicking the **Print** button at the top of the report screen when a budget report is visible. You can also export these statements to Excel by clicking the **Excel** button at the top of the report and then clicking **OK**. QuickBooks will open Excel and pull the budget into Excel, where you can work with it, alter it, add information, or change the appearance, making the report more attractive. You can then print your budget from Excel.

Look What You've Done!

Budgets give you a sense of control over your business. Rather than operating in the dark, when you create and use a budget you will feel like you have a handle on where your business is heading. Here's what we covered in this chapter:

➤ You need a budget as a bellwether to help guide you through your year of business. See "Why You Need a Budget."

➤ You can create a budget for financial statement numbers as well as on a job-by-job basis. See "Creating a Basic Budget."

➤ Use last year's budget as the starting point for next year. See "Copying Last Year's Budget."

➤ Take advantage of your budget by using it for planning expenditures, analyzing performance, and forecasting future financial activity. See "Using Your Budget Effectively."

➤ QuickBooks provides several budget reports for your use. See "Budget Reports Brought to You by QuickBooks."

Chapter 19

Making Friends with Microsoft

In This Chapter

➤ Dressing up QuickBooks reports in Microsoft Excel

➤ Form letters are a breeze with Microsoft Word

Starting with QuickBooks 99, the folks at Intuit and the folks at Microsoft have formed a pact and made it easy to access features in Microsoft Excel and Word directly from QuickBooks. Does this mean animated paper clips are going to start laughing at us from the corner of our QuickBooks screens and we'll soon be able to draw crazy pictures all over our financial statements with the click of a mouse? Gosh, I hope so...

Obviously you have to own Microsoft Excel and Word and have them installed on your computer to take advantage of these features. Assuming you have your Microsoft programs, here's the scoop on how all these programs communicate with one another.

Exporting Reports to Excel

If you're familiar with Excel, then you're familiar with the incredible power behind the Excel spreadsheet program in terms of creating attractive and useful spreadsheets as well as incorporating complex mathematical formulas into your spreadsheets.

You know that you can create graphs and customize them to look any way you want, and you can add fancy titles, shading, and graphic features to further enhance the appearance of your spreadsheets. Excel goes way beyond QuickBooks in terms of enabling you to create really presentable and powerful spreadsheet information.

To work with the reporting capabilities in Excel, start with a report in QuickBooks. Choose a report that includes the basic information you want to display. Click the **Excel** button at the top of the report window (see the following figure) to go to the land of high-powered spreadsheets.

You can get to Excel from any typical QuickBooks report with a click of a button.

Click me!

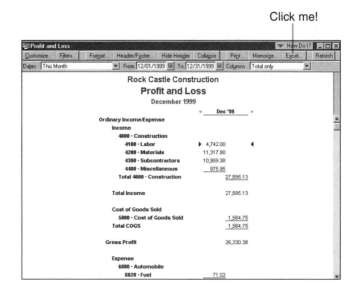

A box appears, as shown in the figure below, that lets you send the report to Excel as a new file or stuff it into an existing file. Most of the time you'll want to view the report as a new Excel file, so go with the default selection of **Send report to a new Excel Spreadsheet** and click **OK**. If you do decide to place the report in an existing spreadsheet, you'll have to specify which one (use the **Browse** button to locate the file).

Choose from the two file options, and then move on.

288

When Excel opens, you'll see all the numbers from your QuickBooks report on an Excel worksheet just waiting to be manipulated by you (see the next figure).

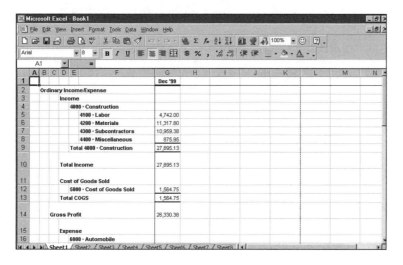

Voila! A QuickBooks report, Excel style.

You're now free of QuickBooks and can apply any Excel procedures to this report. A report that you dress up in Excel does not export back to QuickBooks, so don't feel you have any restrictions to keep in mind when working on your report in Excel. You can do anything you want to the report in Excel, and then you can print it or save it as an Excel file.

Here are some examples of what you can do to your report once Excel has gotten hold of it:

Once an Excel File, Always an Excel File

When you export a report to Excel, the report becomes associated exclusively with Excel. Any changes you make in the report, including changes to the numbers, will not have any effect on information in your QuickBooks file.

➤ Change the headings so that they include multiple lines of text

➤ Change the typeface of various areas of your report

➤ Change the display of numbers to include (or exclude) a specific number of decimal places

➤ Add or remove dollar signs and commas

➤ Include complex formulas and calculations

➤ Use Excel functions to determine averages

➤ Prepare "what if?" scenarios to examine how various changes might influence the numbers in your worksheet

➤ Incorporate additional columns of information

➤ Highlight certain areas with color, bold, italics, shading, or borders

➤ Change the spacing, or relocate chunks of the worksheet from one area to another

➤ Link the information in this worksheet to another worksheet for further manipulation

➤ Create various charts based on the information in the worksheet

Needless to say, you can do a lot with your numbers once you get them into Excel.

Okay, Excel, Show Us Your Stuff!

For Further Information...

If you are new to Excel (or even if you're not), you may be interested in some additional Excel resources. This author recommends Que Publishing's *Using Excel, Special Edition*, and *The Complete Idiot's Guide to Excel* as two places to start.

Let's use a sample QuickBooks report and see what might be beneficial about exporting this report to Excel. Let's say I open a standard profit and loss statement report for the current month. A click on the **Excel** button at the top of the QuickBooks report produces the Export Report to Excel box you saw earlier. Click **OK** and Excel will open, and the report will appear on an Excel worksheet (see the figure below).

You are free to change anything in this report, once it is in Excel.

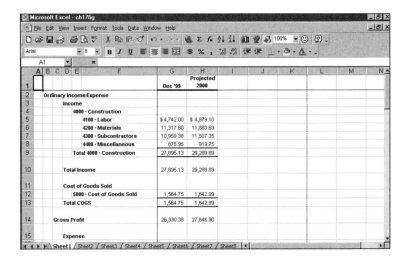

Account Numbers Getting in the Way?

The worksheet shown in this chapter contains account numbers along with the account names. You may want to use account numbers in QuickBooks but not in your reports. Consider turning off account numbers in QuickBooks before exporting a report to Excel, and then turning them on again. To turn account numbers on or off in QuickBooks, open the File menu and choose **Preference**. Next, click the **Accounting** icon, and display the Company Preferences tab, and check or uncheck the **Use account numbers** box (phew!). Click **OK** to exit and apply the change.

You can use Excel to create a chart that will show a graphical representation of certain areas of your worksheet (as shown in the next figure). Drag your mouse over the area containing the titles and numbers you want to include on your chart (in the example shown here, I highlighted cells F5 to H9). Then click the **Chart Wizard** button (pointed out in the figure below) on the Excel toolbar. In the series of wizard dialog boxes that appear, make appropriate choices about the type of chart you want to use, click the **Finish** button at the last dialog box, and the chart will appear onscreen.

Click here to
create a chart

Highlight an area of the worksheet that you want to use in a chart.

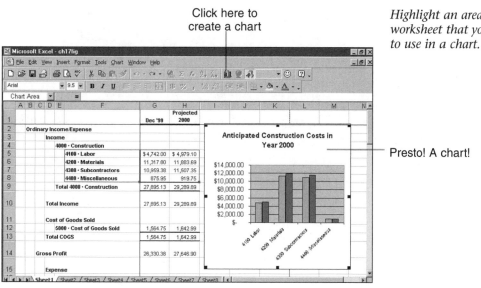

Presto! A chart!

Using Word for QuickBooks-Related Correspondence

There is a collection of business letters available in QuickBooks (starting with version 99) that you can use in conjunction with Microsoft Word (version 97 or higher). The way you use these letters is to select the type of form letter you want, and then click a few buttons to select which QuickBooks data you want to include in the form letters.

Don't worry if the wording on these letters doesn't suit you. You can customize them and save your customized version for future use.

Here's an example of a collection letter that you can create and send to customers who are overdue on their payments. Follow these steps:

1. Open the Activities menu and select **Write Letters**. If you prefer to do this from the QuickBooks Navigator window, click the **Company** tab and click **Write Letters** (the icon is also available on the Sales and Customers tab). The Write Letters window will appear (see the next figure), and you can choose from collection letters, announcements, thank you letters, and more.

QuickBooks provides an array of form letters from which you can choose.

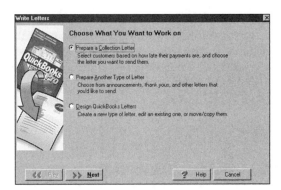

2. Choose **Prepare a Collection Letter** and click **Next**.

3. In the next window, choose which types of customers you want to receive the letter (see the figure below). Click **Next** to proceed.

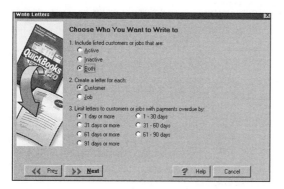

Choose from active or inactive customers, customers or jobs, and the length of time invoices are overdue.

4. Verify the names of the customers who will be included in the mailing. If you want to extend the list to include other customers, click **Prev** to return to the previous screen and adjust your criteria. Click **Next** to continue.

5. Do you want to be nice, or do you want to get ugly? Choose from a variety of styles of collection letters, and then click **Next**.

6. Enter the signature information that should appear on each letter (see the next figure).

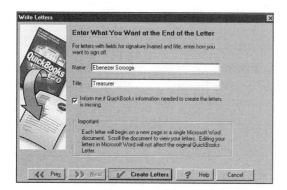

Enter the name and title that should appear in the signature area of each form letter.

7. Click the **Create Letters** button. Microsoft Word will open, and your letter will appear as a Word document (see the next figure), with a page break separating each letter. You can make any necessary revisions, and then print the letters by opening the File menu and choosing **Print**.

The finished product (complete with dancing paper clip).

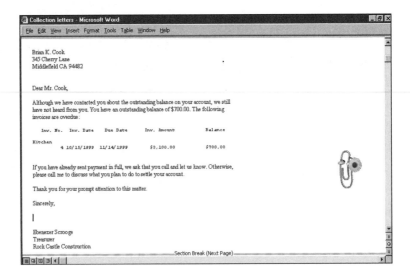

8. If you want to save these collection letters in Word, you can open the File menu, choose **Save**, and give the document a name.

If you're not satisfied with the form letters offered by QuickBooks, you can design your own letter. On the initial Write Letters screen, choose **Design QuickBooks Letters**, and then indicate if you want to design a letter from scratch.

You will give the letter a name, and then click **Create Letter**, and Word will open. Enter the information you want to include in the letter, and then save the letter. The letter will be saved to the directory that contains other QuickBooks form letters and will be available for future use.

Now You've Done It!

This new QuickBooks capability to work in tandem with Microsoft Excel and Word opens a new world of flexibility and power in your program.

➤ You are no longer limited to the standard report formats. See "Exporting Reports to Excel."

➤ Your Vendor and Customer Lists become instant mailing lists when combined with a form letter in Word. See "Using Word for QuickBooks-Related Correspondence."

QuickBooks and the Internet

If you are one of the few people who have not yet experienced the vast resources of the World Wide Web, let me be the first to tell you that you are in for a treat.

The adjective "vast" is an understatement that hardly does justice to the amount of information you will find at your fingertips when you "get online." Imagine, if you will, a sort of space-age library, huge beyond imagination, where all you need to do is mention a topic and you will be inundated with articles, book excerpts, personal commentary, illustrations, cross-references to related information, even names of people intimately familiar with your topic who are willing to answer personal questions you might ask. Experts and professionals from every field and discipline provide information and insight heretofore available only to the most dedicated researchers and professionals. And the amount of information available at this enormous library grows on a daily basis, so that you can return to the library tomorrow with the same question and get even more information.

This description gives you a mere sample of what a small part of the Internet is like. Embrace the Internet, reach for it, learn from it, and extend your own expertise so that others can learn, for this is the future, and it's on your desktop today.

Jumping Onto the Web from QuickBooks

Intuit, the maker of QuickBooks, has a slew of Web pages you'll find of interest. You can get right to the Intuit family of Web sites from within your QuickBooks program, if you have a modem and Internet service on your computer. Open the **Online** menu and select **Intuit Web Sites**, then click on any of the menu choices that are listed, including the **Intuit Home Page**, **QuickBooks.com Technical Support**, and others. The first time you use a QuickBooks online feature, the Launch Web Browser prompt box appears. Click **OK** and QuickBooks' embedded browser window opens and dials your Internet service. The following figure shows what the embedded browser looks like.

You can jump onto the Web directly from your QuickBooks window.

The embedded browser window works just like your Internet Explorer browser window; click on links to view other Web pages and use the **Back** and **Forward** buttons at the top of the window to navigate between pages you've viewed. To exit the embedded browser and return to your regular QuickBooks window, click the **Exit** button.

The embedded browser is handy for when you want to check out Intuit's site, but you might want to launch your full-scale browser to access other sites. If you select an Internet feature in QuickBooks, such as a link, the Internet Explorer window opens automatically. For the remainder of this chapter, I'll use Internet Explorer to show you my favorite sites.

New to the Net?

Are you new to the Internet and the World Wide Web? If so, don't think you have to feel your way in the dark. Take a look at *The Complete Idiot's Guide to the Internet, Fifth Edition*, available from Macmillan Publishing, for insights and advice on getting started in cyberspace.

Using Internet Explorer

Internet Explorer 4.0 is QuickBooks' browser of choice. (You can use Netscape Navigator, but QuickBooks warns you that some of its online features might not work with Navigator.) If you haven't set up QuickBooks to work with your Internet service and Web browser yet, you'll need to use the Internet Connection Setup Wizard to do so; select **Online, Internet Connection Setup** and follow the prompts.

QuickBooks comes with the latest version of Internet Explorer, and you'll find it on the QuickBooks CD-ROM. To install the program, display the **Start** menu on the Windows taskbar, select **Run**, then type `Autorun.exe` and click **OK**. Choose your installation options and start installing.

Paying a Visit to the QuickBooks Web Site

Begin your Internet tour with a stopover at `www.quickbooks.com`, where you will find useful information about your program, including links to FAQs (modern lingo for Frequently Asked Questions), as well as information resource links for small businesses, current payroll tables that you can download (for a fee), and information about how you can get technical support (see the following figure).

Start with www. quickbooks.com for your small business needs.

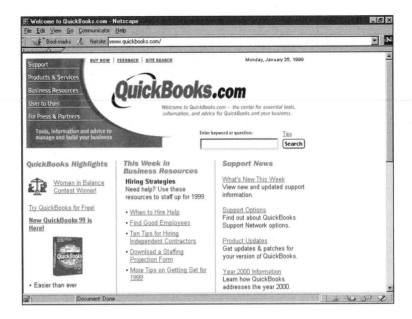

You can also slide over to QuickBooks' sister sites, www.Quicken.com and www.turbotax.com, where you will find additional information about Intuit's software programs and links to various financial and tax-related resources. You can place orders online for any of the Intuit software programs at their respective sites.

Looking for business forms? You'll note that Intuit offers business forms for sale at its Web sites. You can also perform a search for "business forms" and come up with hundreds of other locations that offer competitive prices and customization opportunities.

Beyond QuickBooks, Quicken, and TurboTax, you can search for other software online. You may need more comprehensive depreciation software or inventory control software than that offered in your QuickBooks program.

To search for a particular company or for a topic describing the type of software in which you are interested (for example, depreciation software or inventory software), you can use any of a number of search engines, programs that enable you to enter a keyword or string of words (contained in quotes), and search through the millions of Internet sites at the click of a mouse. Some common search engines include:

Excite	www.excite.com
AltaVista	www.altavista.com
Yahoo	www.yahoo.com

Lycos	www.lycos.com
LookSmart	www.looksmart.com
HotBot	www.hotbot.com

This is just a small sampling of some of the search engines available. You will find that a search from each one of these sites provides you with slightly different results. You can find hundreds of other Internet search engines by conducting a search for search engines.

Other Fun Stuff on the Internet

It won't take you long at all to discover that there is truly an unlimited amount of information available to you on the Internet. If you are overwhelmed (and who isn't?), you may find you want some ideas for places to start—Web sites from which you can launch your own discovery mission. Here's a sampling of some Internet locations that can get you started. From these locations you can follow links to the information that will be most useful for you.

Interesting and Useful Links for Small Businesses

Start with the U.S. Small Business Administration (www.sba.gov) for general information about starting and running a small business.

Check out information on various types of insurance, including what insurance is and what types of insurance you need, comparative rates for insurance, and a risk evaluator that will help you determine the areas in which you and your assets are at risk. The site, www.insuremarket.com, is sponsored by Intuit and includes links to insurance providers.

Extra money to invest? There are plenty of online brokerage houses that will gladly help you with your stock trades for a minimal fee (sometimes for no fee at all). Consider Charles Schwab at www.schwab.com, Datek at www.datek.com, and etrade at www.etrade.com, then search around for competitive services until you find the online trader that is right for you. All of the stock service sites offer online quotes and links to other business resources. Many offer research and news articles about selected publicly traded companies.

Need a loan? Several Web sites offer loan calculators with which you can calculate how much you can afford to borrow, as well as links to financial institutions that will gladly provide you with online loan applications. Take a look at www.financenter.com (see the next figure) for personal financial advice, loan calculators, and much more.

You can calculate loan payments, learn about budgeting, find links to insurance information, and much more at www.financenter.com.

A Taxing Situation

Leave it to the IRS to get in on the Internet craze. And we thought their computer was stuck in the last century. The IRS' Web site, shown in the figure that follows, offers humor (humor from the IRS? What is the world coming to?), downloadable tax forms and IRS publications, the latest tax news, and an opportunity for you to send email directly to the IRS Commissioner.

The very cool IRS Web site can be found at www.irs.ustreas.gov.

The IRS site is only the beginning of a wealth of tax information available for you in cyberspace. A few of my favorite sites are

Essential Links to Taxes at `http://www.EL.com/elinks/taxes/`

The Roth IRA Web Site Home Page at `www.rothira.com`

U.S. State Tax Resources at
`http://shell5.ba.best.com/~ftmexpat/html/taxsites/formstat.html`

The Research Institute of America at `www.riatax.com`

Tax and Accounting Sites Directory at `www.taxsites.com`

Fun With Taxes (a compilation of my own tax columns!) at
`http://home.sprintmail.com/~rjpranitis/FunwithTaxes.html`

Internet Sites You May Not Want to Live Without

We all have our favorite Internet sites, places that we drop in on regularly. My favorite sites aren't all tax and accounting related, as you might suspect. One area in which I can't seem to get enough information is current news. So here is a sampling of my favorite news sites, places where the presses never seem to close. Many of these sites offer a free subscription and will deliver an electronic version of their news to your email doorstep.

All the news that's fit to print, from the New York Times online at `www.nytimes.com.`

The pulse of the nation can be checked at the Washington Post online, www.washingtonpost.com.

The quick take on today's news can be found at www.usatoday.com.

Now You've Done It!

This chapter provides only a tiny sampling of available resources on the Internet. See for yourself. You'll be hooked in no time. Meanwhile, here's what you've learned so far:

➤ Intuit tries to keep its customers up to date with answers to frequently asked questions, links to business resources, and the latest versions of their various software programs.

➤ You can use search engines as a tool for poking around the Internet to your heart's content.

➤ There is a wealth of current tax information available online for the asking, including free downloadable tax forms.

➤ You can stay on top of the news by visiting nearly every major newspaper in the world in the online versions.

Installing QuickBooks and Network Considerations

Don't you hate it when you have to ask someone for help installing a program? It seems like this should be the easy part, but sometimes even the installation can be daunting. If you installed your program without problems, or if you aren't using QuickBooks on a network, you won't need this section (but you may want to peek at the hints here anyway). You can always read this part under your covers at night with a flashlight, and then show up at work the next day all ready to install your new program, just like a pro! (And don't think the pros don't do the same thing!)

What's Under the Hood?

Before you begin installing your QuickBooks program, check out this list to make sure your computer is up to the task. If your equipment is better than the requirements listed here, your program is bound to run better and more efficiently. Here are the minimum requirements that will make sure your program hums. (Check the manuals that came with your computer if any of these descriptions sounds Greek to you.)

> ➤ 486/66 PC or higher.
> ➤ 16MB of RAM.
> ➤ Hard disk with 35MB free space (45MB for QuickBooks Pro). Add an additional 40MB if you install the Microsoft Internet Explorer version 4.0. Add 9MB more if you want to install the QuickBooks Timer.
> ➤ CD-ROM drive (however, if you contact Intuit and say "Pretty please," they'll send you 3.5" disks).
> ➤ 8-bit sound card, unless you're not interested in sound effects.

➤ VGA monitor capable of displaying 256 colors and with resolution of 800×600.

➤ Windows 95, Windows NT 4.0 with Service Pack 3.

➤ You also need extra stuff like Microsoft Word and Excel 97 (or later) if you plan to share files with these programs, some form of backup system (unless you want to trust your precious data to the whims of modern technology) and, of course, you need the QuickBooks program so that you can install it on all this cool equipment.

I've Got the Hardware, What's Next?

The installation of QuickBooks is relatively quick and painless. There should be no other programs running on your computer when you install QuickBooks. Ideally, you should be able to insert the QuickBooks CD-ROM in your drive and Presto!, the QuickBooks Installation window should appear onscreen.

Whoa!

If you are installing multiple copies of QuickBooks, purchased together in the Five User Value Pack, there is only one Installation Key Code for the entire package. See the next section for information on installing QuickBooks on multiple machines.

Should the Installation window fail to appear, or if you are installing from disks, click the **Start** button and choose **Settings** and **Control Panel**. Select **Add/Remove Programs** from the Control Panel screen and click the **Install** button in the window that appears.

Click **Next** and your computer will seek out your disk or CD-ROM. Click **Finish** and the Installation window will appear. Follow the onscreen instructions (including entering the Installation Key Code number, which appears on your QuickBooks package) to install your program.

As you can see, the installation process is quick and easy. Once you've completed these steps, you're ready to use your program!

Hey, Everybody! Let's All Use QuickBooks at the Same Time!

You may have purchased multiple copies of QuickBooks Pro or the QuickBooks Pro 5-user pack, so now you are ready to install your QuickBooks program on as many as four additional computers. When you install QuickBooks Pro on multiple computers, you can save your data file on your network so that each user has access to the file simultaneously. (More than five computers in an office can use QuickBooks at the same time, but only five users can access the same data file.)

To install multiple copies of QuickBooks Pro (you'll need the Pro version to do this), you must have a separate QuickBooks Pro program for each computer. If you purchased the 5-user pack, each user will install from a separate CD-ROM, but will use the same Installation Key Code number, found on the outside of the main package. If you are installing separately purchased QuickBooks programs, each program will have a different Installation Key Code number.

Who's Been Messing with These Numbers?

When you aren't the only person using QuickBooks and accessing your company's file, you will want to make sure that the reports you produce include the most current figures. QuickBooks makes it easy for you to get the latest numbers with a Refresh button at the top-right corner of every report and graph. Click this button and you will know that your report includes the most up-to-date information.

You may notice a Refresh Needed button after the title on a report or graph. If this message appears, it is just a reminder that information has changed since you produced the report. Click the Refresh button; the report will be updated, and the message will disappear.

What Happens to QuickBooks when People Share a File?

Your QuickBooks program will do a good job of keeping up with you and your co-workers when you share your company file. You may notice some sluggishness in creating reports, depending on the number of users and the size of the reports. If this is a problem, it is recommended that you try to hold off producing reports until other users are finished with the program.

Something's Gone Wrong!

Chances are excellent that your installation will proceed seamlessly. This is a very easy program to install, and there are no known problems that occur frequently on installation. That doesn't mean there won't be a problem. I can't anticipate how your computer equipment will greet its new software, but I can tell you who can.

The technical support folks at Intuit have heard every story, and they are extremely gentle and patient with new users. Furthermore, they don't keep you on hold forever. Give tech support a call if you run into any questions while installing: 888-222-7276. There is no fee for help with installation.

Tax Agencies

No matter what type of business yours is, sooner or later you will have to answer to Uncle Sam and his state-level minions. Between income taxes, payroll taxes, sales taxes, property taxes, franchise taxes, and use taxes, it seems that giving lots of money to the government is part of the American way of doing business.

To make your tax life slightly easier, this section of the book is dedicated to providing names, addresses, telephone numbers, and Web sites that can assist you in communicating with and sending the right amount of money to all the proper taxing authorities.

Federal Tax Collection

Federal income tax is paid to the Internal Revenue Service (IRS) . When starting a business, you must register your existence with the IRS so that they know where you are and can pay friendly visits to you in case you neglect to pay your fair share (and then some) of taxes.

Start by contacting your local IRS office (address and phone number will be found in the government section of your telephone book). Read all about income taxes and download any forms you might need at the IRS's Web site: www.irs.ustreas.gov.

Ask questions on the telephone by calling the IRS at 800-829-1040. Get tax forms by fax from the IRS at 703-368-9694 (must dial from a fax machine). Tax assistance for the hearing impaired using TTY/TDD equipment may be obtained at 800-829-4059.

State Tax Collection

Every state has its own tax agency, the place that collects sales, property, payroll, and state income tax. Some states don't have income tax for corporations, and some states don't tax individuals (which would include sole proprietorships), but every state taxes payroll, property, and sales.

There are special rules for payroll taxes if your employees live in one state and work in another (this is of particular interest to companies located near a state border). In addition, there are special rules regarding collection and payment of sales taxes and use taxes if you do business in more than one state. Be sure to check with your own state taxing authority to make sure you know all the rules that apply to you.

State Tax Agencies:

Alabama—334-242-1000
Department of Revenue
P.O. Box 327410
Montgomery, AL 36132-7410
www.ador.state.al.us/

Alaska—907-465-2320
Department of Revenue
State Office Building
P.O. Box 110420
Juneau, AK 99811-0420
www.revenue.state.ak.us

Arizona—602-542-4260
Department of Revenue
1600 W. Monroe St.
Phoenix, AZ 85007-2650
www.revenue.state.az.us/

Arkansas—501-682-1100
Department of Finance & Administration—Revenue Division
P.O. Box 8055
Little Rock, AR 72203
www.state.ar.us/revenue/rev1.html

California—800-852-5711
Franchise Tax Board
P.O. Box 942840
Sacramento, CA 94140-0070
www.ftb.ca.gov

Colorado—303-232-2416
Department of Revenue
1375 Sherman St.
Denver, CO 80261
www.state.co.us

Connecticut—203-297-4753
Department of Revenue Services
State Tax Department
25 Sigourney St.
Hartford, CT 06106
www.state.ct.us/drs/

Delaware—302-577-3300
Department of Finance
Division of Revenue
Delaware State Building
820 N. French St.
Wilmington, DE 19801
www.state.de.us/govern/agencies/revenue/revenue.htm

District of Columbia—202-727-6170
Department of Finance & Revenue
Room 1046
300 Indiana Ave., N.W.
Washington, D.C. 20001
www.dccfo.com/taxpmain.html

Florida—904-922-9645
Department of Revenue
Supply Department
168-A Blounstown Highway
Tallahassee, FL 32304
http://sun6.dms.state.fl.us/dor/

Georgia—404-656-4293
Department of Revenue
P.O. Box 38007
Atlanta, GA 30334
www.state.ga.us/departments/dor

Hawaii—800-222-3229
First Taxation District
830 Punchbowl St.
P.O. Box 259
Honolulu, HI 96809
www.hawaii.gov/icsd/tax/tax.htm

Idaho—208-334-7789
State Tax ommission
P.O. Box 36
Boise, ID 83722
www.idwr.state.id.us/apa/idapa35/taxindex.htm

Illinois—800-356-6302
Department of Revenue
101 W. Jefferson
Springfield, IL 26794
www.revenue.state.il.us

Indiana—317-232-2240
Department of Revenue
100 North Senate Avenue
Indianapolis, IN 46204
www.ai.org/dor/

Iowa—515-281-3114
Department of Revenue & Finance
P.O. Box 10457
Des Moines, IA 50306
www.state.ia.us/government/drf/index.html

Kansas—913-296-4937
Department of Revenue
Division of Taxation
Taxpayer Assistance Bureau
P.O. Box 12001
Topeka, KS 66612-2001
www.ink.org/public/kdor

Kentucky—502-564-3658
Revenue Cabinet
200 Fair Oaks Lane, Bldg. 2
Frankfort, KY 40602
Revweb@mail.state.ky.us

Louisiana—504-925-7532
Department of Revenue
P.O. Box 201
Baton Rouge, LA 70821
www.rev.state.la.us

Maine—207-624-7894
Bureau of Taxation
State Office Bldg., Station 24
Augusta, ME 04332
www.state.me.us/taxation

Maryland—410-974-3951
Comptroller of the Treasury
Revenue Administration
110 Carroll St.
Annapolis, MD 21411
www.comp.state.md.us

Massachusetts—617-887-6367
Department of Revenue
Customer Service Bureau
P.O. Box 7010
Boston, MA 02204
www.magnet.state.ma.us/dor/dorpg.htm

Michigan—800-367-6263
Department of the Treasury
Revenue Administrative Services
The Treasury Building
430 W. Allegan St.
Lansing, MI 48922
www.treas.state.mi.us/

Minnesota—800-652-9094
Department of Revenue
Mail Station 4450
St. Paul, MN 55146-4450
www.taxes.state.mn.us

Mississippi—601-354-6247
State Tax Commission
750 South Galatin
Jackson, MS 39204
http://www.treasury.state.ms.us/

Missouri—800-877-6881
Department of Revenue
P.O. Box 3022
Jefferson City, MO 65105-3022
www.state.mo.us/dor/tax

Montana—406-444-2837
Department of Revenue
P.O. Box 5805
Helena, MT 59604
www.mt.gov/revenue/rev.htm

Nebraska—800-747-8177
Department of Revenue
P.O. Box 94818
Lincoln, NE 68509-4818
www.nol.org/revenue

Nevada—702-687-4892
Department of Taxation
Capitol Complex
Carson City, NV 89710-0003
www.state.nv.us/taxation/

New Hampshire—603-271-2191
Department of Revenue Administration
State of New Hampshire
61 S. Spring St.
Concord, NH 03301
www.state.nh.us/

New Jersey—609-292-7613
Division of Taxation
CN 269
Trenton, NJ 08646
www.state.nj.us/treasury/taxation/

New Mexico—505-827-0700
Taxation and Revenue Department
P.O. Box 630
Santa Fe, NM 87504-0630
www.state.nm.us/tax

New York—800-462-8100
Department of Taxation & Finance
Taxpayer Service Bureau
W. Averell Harriman Campus
Albany, NY 12227
www.tax.state.ny.us/

North Carolina—919-715-0397
Department of Revenue
P.O. Box 25000
Raleigh, NC 27640
www.dor.state.nc.us/DOR/

North Dakota—701-328-3017
Office of State Tax Commissioner
State Capitol
600 E. Boulevard Ave.
Bismarck, ND 58505-0599
www.state.nd.us/taxdpt/

Ohio—614-433-7750
Department of Taxation
P.O. Box 2476
Columbus, OH 43266-0076
www.state.oh.us/tax/

Oklahoma—405-521-3108
Tax Commission
2501 Lincoln Blvd.
Oklahoma City, OK 73194
www.oktax.state.ok.us/

Oregon—503-378-4988
Department of Revenue
955 Center St., N.E.
Salem, OR 97310
www.dor.state.or.us

Pennsylvania—717-787-8201
Department of Revenue
Strawberry Square
Harrisburg, PA 17128
www.revenue.state.pa.us

Rhode Island—401-277-3934
Division of Taxation
One Capitol Hill
Providence, RI 02908-5800
www.tax.state.ri.us

South Carolina—803-737-5000
Tax Commission
P.O. Box 125
Columbia, SC 29214
www.state.sc.us/dor/dor.html

South Dakota—605-773-3311
Department of Revenue
700 Governors Dr.
Pierre, SD 57501
www.state.sd.us/state/executive/revenue/revenue.html

Tennessee—615-741-4465
Department of Revenue
Andrew Jackson State Office Bldg.
500 Deaderick St., 4th Floor
Nashville, TN 37242
www.state.tn.us/revenue

Texas—512-463-4600
Comptroller of Public Accounts
State of Texas
111 West 6th
Starr Building
Austin, TX 78701
www.window.state.tx.us

Utah—801-297-2200
State Tax Commission
210 North 1950 West
Salt Lake City, UT 84134
www.tax.ex.state.ut.us

Vermont—802-828-2515
Department of Taxes
109 State St.
Montpelier, VT 05609
www.state.vt.us/tax/

Virginia—804-367-8031
Department of Taxation
Taxpayers Assistance
P.O. Box 1880
Richmond, VA 23282-1880
www.state.va.us/tax/tax.html

Washington—360-786-6100
Department of Revenue
General Administration Bldg.
P.O. Box 47478
Olympia, WA 98504-7478
www.ga.gov/dor/wador.htm

West Virginia—304-558-3333
State Tax Department
Taxpayer Service Division
P.O. Box 3784
Charleston, WV 25337-3784
www.state.wv.us/taxrev/

Wisconsin—608-266-1961
Department of Revenue
P.O. Box 8903
Madison, WI 53708-8903
www.dor.state.wi.us

Wyoming—307-777-7378
The State of Wyoming
Revenue Department
Herschler Building
122 W. 25th
Cheyenne, WY 82002
www.state.wy.us

TechnoTalk: The Language of Computer and Accounting Geeks

account   A record for maintaining financial information. A separate record, or account, is used for each type of information, such as cash, sales revenue, repairs expense, and so on.

accounts payable   An account that tracks the amounts you owe for items or services you purchase.

accounts receivable   An account that keeps a running balance of the amounts your customers owe you.

accrual basis   A system of accounting in which revenue is reported when it is earned and expenses are reported when they are incurred, regardless of the actual dates on which money is received or payments are made. Contrast to *cash basis*.

accumulated depreciation   An account comprised of the total of depreciation expense deducted.

aging   (a)Something your skin, cheese, and fine wine have in common. (b)The process of tracking due dates of unpaid bills.

amortization schedule   A report that shows the balance of a loan after each payment is made and a breakdown of the interest and principal portions of payments on the loan.

assets   Rights and resources that belong to your company and have future value.

balance sheet   A report showing the value of a business based on assets (items and resources owned), liabilities (amounts owed), and equity (the difference between assets and liabilities).

base pay rate   The rate for working standard hours, as distinct from a rate for overtime or holiday hours.

book value   The value of the company's assets (items that the company owns) minus what the company owes (amounts due to others). Also called *equity*.

capital   (a)THE OPPOSITE OF lowercase. (b)Amounts invested in a company by its owners.

cash basis   An accounting system under which revenue is reported as income only when it is received and expenses are reported only when the bills are actually paid. A retail store, where income is recorded as it is received in the cash register, is an example of a cash basis business. Compare to *accrual basis*.

chart of accounts   A group of categories into which you will separate your company's income, expenses, debts, and assets so that you can make sense of all your business transactions in the form of professional-looking financial statements.

contra asset   A type of asset account whose purpose is to offset the value of the assets by the amount of the accumulating depreciation. Also called an *accumulated depreciation account*.

cost of goods sold   The cost of goods held in inventory and then sold.

credit   Depending on the type of account, either an increase or a decrease in the balance of the account. Liability, equity, and income accounts are increased with credits. Asset and expense accounts are decreased with credits.

credit memo   A statement that reduces the balance due on a purchase, usually a result of returned merchandise or a defect in merchandise.

customer type   Categorizations of different kinds of customers, such as wholesale, commercial, (grumpy), (stingy), (friendly), and retail customers.

daily activities   QuickBooks activities that should be performed daily, such as entering bills, checks, deposits, sales, and employee time.

debit   Depending on the type of account, either an increase or a decrease in the balance of the account. Liability, equity, and income accounts are decreased with debits. Asset and expense accounts are increased with debits.

equity   The net worth of the company, or the total assets minus the total liabilities.

equity account   In describing different types of accounts, the term *net worth* is often applied to the sum of a company's *equity* accounts. If you add the value of the company's assets (items that the company owns) and subtract what the company owes (amounts due to others), the resulting amount is the *book value* of the company, or equity.

expenses   (a)Something of which there never seems to be an end. (b)Costs incurred in an attempt to obtain revenue.

FOB   Free On Board. Refers to the transfer of ownership of merchandise from seller to buyer and is based on where the merchandise is in the shipping process.

general journal entry   Adjustments that are made to the balances in your accounts without the use of forms, such as invoices, bills, and checks. A general journal entry must always have two sides—a debit and a credit.

income   Earnings or revenue. Something you hope to have a lot of.

inventory   The items you sell to earn money in your business. You may sell machine parts, books, or groceries that you purchase somewhere and offer for sale to others. Or you may produce your own inventory, such as clothing that you make, ships that you build, or pottery that you create.

job   A project that has a beginning and an end. You may have multiple jobs for the same customer. QuickBooks can track the income and expenses for each job separately.

job type   A categorization of the types of jobs you perform. For example, as a wedding photographer, you might offer a standard and a deluxe picture package.

liability   Obligations that you must satisfy by the disbursement of assets (such as payment of cash) or by the performance of services.

line of credit   A type of loan, usually a bank loan, from which you can draw money when needed and pay it back on a predetermined schedule.

maintenance releases   Downloadable updates to the QuickBooks software that fix small problems and offer the latest information.

net income   The result when total expenses are deducted from total income.

net worth   The term applied to the sum of a company's *equity accounts*. If you add the value of the company's assets (items that the company owns) and subtract what the company owes (amounts due to others), the resulting amount is the *book value* of the company, or equity.

parent account   (a)An account that children hope to be able to draw on when the going gets tough. (b)In QuickBooks, the major category of an account. You can provide more detail of the components of a parent account by creating subaccounts. The total value of all the subaccounts of one parent account equals the total value of the parent account.

principal   (a)The person you have to see when you get in trouble in school. (b)In QuickBooks, the face value of a loan.

profit and loss statement   A statement covering a specific time period and listing income earned and expenses incurred during the period.

progress billing   The act of billing for a job as the job progresses, rather than waiting to bill when the job is completed.

service item   A job you perform for which you charge a customer.

start date   The date on which you wish to begin tracking information in QuickBooks. When you set up a company in QuickBooks, you will need to enter all transactions that have occurred in the company from the start date to the present.

subaccount   (a)A line of credit at the local subway sandwich shop. (b)In QuickBooks, the subsidiary category of an account. You can provide more detail of the components of a parent account by creating subaccounts. The total value of the subaccounts of one parent make up the total amount in the parent account.

type lists   In a submenu of the Lists menu, you'll find Other Lists. Type lists allow you to further break down your lists into subgroups that make sense for your business.

vendor type   A categorization of the types of vendors with which you work. For example, as a restaurateur, perhaps you purchase consulting and marketing services to come up with plans to bring in more customers. You would not group these transactions in the same expense category as paper cups and food inventory. In this case, you'd set up two vendor types.

weighted average   A method of valuing your inventory on hand. As each new item is added to the total inventory, the cost of the new item is added to the cost of all pieces of the same item on hand to provide a total. When an item is sold, the total cost of all inventory items is divided by the number of pieces on hand to determine an average cost. This cost is reflected at the time of sale as the cost of sales for the item sold.

Index

Research Institute of America, 301
Rhode Island (state taxes), 315
Roth IRA, 301
Small Business Administration, 10
South Carolina (state taxes), 315
South Dakota (state taxes), 315
state tax agencies, 310-317
Tax and Accounting Sites Directory, 301
Tennessee (state taxes), 316
Texas (state taxes), 316
TurboTax, 298
U.S. Small Business Administration, 299
U.S. State Tax Resources, 301
USA Today, 302
Utah (state taxes), 316
Vermont (state taxes), 316
Virginia (state taxes), 316
Washington (state taxes), 316
Washington Post, 302
West Virginia (state taxes), 316
Wisconsin (state taxes, 317
Wyoming (state taxes), 317
Yahoo, 298
sizing windows, 29
Small Business Administration Web site, 10
software, inventory tracking software, 225

sole proprietorships, 8
South Carolina (state taxes) Web site, 315
South Dakota (state taxes) Web site, 315
Specific Identification inventory valuing method, 224
standard Chart of Accounts, 89
standard forms
customizing, 260-261
columns, 263
company information, 265-266
composition/layout, changing, 267-268
fields, 262-263
footers, 265
headers, 261
progress column, 264
text, 267
previewing, 267-268
Start button, 306
start dates
changing, 13
choosing, 12
starting QuickBooks, 24-25
state income taxes, 211, 310
state tax agencies, 203, 310-317
State Unemployment Tax Act (SUTA), 255
state unemployment taxes, 254
Subtotal items, 66-67
subtotals, items, 65
Summary payroll report, 250
SUTA (State Unemployment Tax Act), 255

T

Tax and Accounting Sites Directory Web site, 301
tax deductions, Section 179 deduction, 196-197
tax lines, assigning to accounts, 205
taxes
employee records, entering tax information, 244-245
federal
due dates, 208-209
IRS (Internal Revenue Service), 194, 300, 309
FUTA (Federal Unemployment Tax Act), 255
income taxes, 205-211
estimated payments, 207-210
federal income tax due dates, 208-209
Income Tax Detail Report, 206
Income Tax Summary Report, 206
state taxes, 211
tax lines, assigning, 205
IRS (Internal Revenue Service), 194, 300, 309
payroll taxes
Form 940, preparing, 255
Form 941, preparing, 251-254
tax return due dates, 254
sales tax, 202-204
items, creating, 202-203

337

Sales Tax Liability
Report, 204
state taxing agencies,
203
state, 310
state tax agencies
Web sites, 310-317
unemployment taxes,
254
SUTA (State
Unemployment Tax
Act), 255
technical support, 35, 45,
307
Template window, 123-124
Templates command (Lists
menu), 123
Templates window, 260
Tennessee (state taxes)
Web site, 316
Texas (state taxes) Web
site, 316
text (forms), customizing,
267
tiers (price layers), 224
time tracking (QuickBooks
Pro), 230
charging time to
customers, 236
entering time, 230-236
frequency of, 231
non-billable time,
235-236
single projects,
231-233
Weekly Timesheet
form, 233-235
paying employees based
on time entered,
237-238
Time/Enter Single Activity
window, 231
timer (QuickBooks Pro),
183-187
copying, 188

information files,
exporting, 186-187
installing, 184
personal timer files,
creating, 185
running, 185-186
setting up, 184-185
Title bar (program
window), 26
To Do Lists, 103
creating, 105
To Do Notes command
(Lists menu), 145
To Do Notes List, adding
notes, 105
tracking jobs (QuickBooks
Pro), 178-180
tracking time (QuickBooks
Pro), 230
charging time to
customers, 236
entering time, 230-236
frequency of, 231
non-billable time,
235-236
single projects,
231-233
Weekly Timesheet
form, 233-235
paying employees based
on time entered,
237-238
Transaction Detail payroll
report, 250
Transactions by Payee
payroll report, 250
Transfer Funds Between
Accounts window, 149
Transfer Money command
(Activities menu), 149
transferring funds between
accounts, 149-150
TurboTax, 207
Web site, 298
types of businesses, 8-10

U

U.S. Small Business
Administration Web site,
299
U.S. State Tax Resources
Web site, 301
unemployment taxes, 254
updating
Quickbooks, 26
reports, 307
USA Today Web site, 302
User List window, 40
users (security)
access rights, setting,
42-43
adding new users, 41-43
limits on access, 40-41
passwords, changing,
44-45
Utah (state taxes) Web site,
316

V

vacation time (employees),
setting up, 246-247
valuing inventory, 224
Vendor List, 102-103
new vendors, adding,
107-108
notes, adding, 105
Vermont (state taxes) Web
site, 316
Virginia (state taxes) Web
site, 316
voiding checks, 151-152

W

W-4 forms, 244-245
Washington (state taxes)
Web site, 316
Washington Post Web site,
302

Get **FREE** books and more...when you register this book online for our Personal Bookshelf Program

http://register.quecorp.com/

 Register online and you can sign up for our *FREE Personal Bookshelf Program*—immediate and unlimited access to the electronic version of more than 200 complete computer books! That means you'll have 100,000 pages of valuable information onscreen, at your fingertips!

 Plus, you can access product support, including complimentary downloads, technical support files, book-focused links, companion Web sites, author sites, and more!

 And, don't miss out on the opportunity to sign up for a *FREE subscription to a weekly email newsletter* to help you stay current with news, announcements, sample book chapters, and special events, including sweepstakes, contests, and various product giveaways.

 We value your comments! Best of all, the entire registration process takes only a few minutes to complete, so go online and get the greatest value going—absolutely FREE!

Don't Miss Out On This Great Opportunity!

QUE®is a brand of Macmillan Computer Publishing USA. For more information, visit *www.mcp.com*